CORE STATUTES ON
CRIMINAL LAW

CORE STATUTES ON CRIMINAL LAW

Kate Cook, Mark James and Richard Lee

Law Matters Publishing

Published by Law Matters Publishing

Law Matters Limited
33 Southernhay East
Exeter EX1 1NX
Tel: 01392 215577
www.lawmatterspublishing.co.uk

British Library Cataloguing-in-Publication Data

A catalogue record for this book is available from the British Library.

Crown copyright material is reproduced with the permission of the Controller of HMSO.

ISBN 10: 1 84641 034 7
ISBN 13: 978 1 84641 034 5

Typeset by Style Photosetting Ltd, Mayfield, East Sussex

Printed in Great Britain by Ashford Colour Press Ltd, Gosport, Hampshire

PREFACE

In designing this volume we have attempted to create a student friendly collection which focuses on the core offences covered by universities teaching criminal law courses. This book generally omits provisions on evidence and procedure, creating a value for money volume which is right up to date.

New entries in this edition include the character and hearsay provisions from the Criminal Justice Act 2003 and offences from the Serious Organised Crime and Police Act 2005 and the Terrorism Act 2006.

The cut-off date for inclusion of new provisions in this volume is 13 April 2006. Some Acts which have been given royal assent, but are not yet in force, are not incorporated here. The Religious and Racial Hatred Act 2006 will make amendments to the Public Order Act 1986 and the Drugs Act 2006 and the Identity Cards Act 2006 will create new offences.

Dr Mark James
Richard Lee
Dr Kate Cook
18 May 2006, Manchester.

CONTENTS

ABORTION ACT 1967

1. Medical termination of pregnancy

(1) Subject to the provisions of this section, a person shall not be guilty of any offence under the law relating to abortion when a pregnancy is terminated by a registered medical practitioner if two medical practitioners are of the opinion, formed in good faith—

    (a) that the pregnancy has not exceeded its twenty-fourth week and that the continuance of the pregnancy would involve risk, greater than if the pregnancy were terminated, of injury to the physical or mental health of the pregnant woman or any existing children of her family; or

    (b) that the termination is necessary to prevent grave permanent injury to the physical or mental health of the pregnant woman; or

    (c) that the continuance of the pregnancy would involve risk to the life of the pregnant woman, greater than if the pregnancy were terminated; or

    (d) that there is a substantial risk that if the child were born it would suffer from such physical or mental abnormalities as to be seriously handicapped.

(2) In determining whether the continuance of a pregnancy would involve such risk of injury to health as is mentioned in paragraph (a) or (b) of subsection (1) of this section, account may be taken of the pregnant woman's actual or reasonably foreseeable environment.

(3) Except as provided by subsection (4) of this section, any treatment for the termination of pregnancy must be carried out in a hospital vested in the Secretary of State for the purposes of his functions under the National Health Service Act 1977 or the National Health Service (Scotland) Act 1978 or in a hospital vested in a primary care trust or a National Health Service trust, or an NHS foundation trust, or in a place for the time being approved for the purposes of this section by the Secretary of State.

(4) Subsection (3) of this section, and so much of subsection (1) as relates to the opinion of two registered medical practitioners, shall not apply to the termination of a pregnancy by a registered practitioner in a case where he is of the opinion, formed in good faith, that the termination is immediately necessary to save the life or to prevent grave permanent injury to the physical or mental health of the pregnant woman.

2. Notification

(1) The Minister of Health in respect of England and Wales, and the Secretary of State in respect of Scotland, shall by statutory instrument make regulations to provide—

    (a) for requiring any such opinion as is referred to in section 1 of this Act to be certified by the practitioners or practitioner concerned in such form and at such time as may be prescribed by the regulations, and for requiring the preservation and disposal of certificates made for the purposes of the regulations;

    (b) for requiring any registered medical practitioner who terminates a pregnancy to give notice of the termination and such other information relating to the termination as may be so prescribed;

    (c) for prohibiting the disclosure, except to such persons or for such purposes as may be so prescribed, of notices given or information furnished pursuant to the regulations.

(3) Any person who wilfully contravenes or wilfully fails to comply with the requirements of regulations under subsection (1) of this section shall be liable on summary conviction to a fine not exceeding level 5 on the standard scale.

4. Conscientious objection to participation in treatment

(1) Subject to subsection (2) of this section, no person shall be under any duty, whether by contract or by any statutory or other legal requirement, to participate in any treatment authorised by this Act to which he has a conscientious objection:

    Provided that in any legal proceedings the burden of proof of conscientious objection shall rest on the person claiming to rely on it.

(2)   Nothing in subsection (1) of this section shall affect any duty to participate in treatment which is necessary to save the life or to prevent grave permanent injury to the physical or mental health of a pregnant woman.

5.   Supplementary provisions

(1)   No offence under the Infant Life (Preservation) Act 1929 shall be committed by a registered medical practitioner who terminates a pregnancy in accordance with the provisions of this Act.

(2)   For the purposes of the law relating to abortion, anything done with intent to procure a woman's miscarriage (or, in the case of a woman carrying more than one foetus, her miscarriage of any foetus) is unlawfully done unless authorised by section 1 of this Act and, in the case of a woman carrying more than one foetus, anything done with intent to procure her miscarriage of any foetus is authorised by that section if—

   (a)   the ground for termination of the pregnancy specified in subsection (1)(d) of that section applies in relation to any foetus and the thing is done for the purpose of procuring the miscarriage of that foetus, or

   (b)   any of the other grounds for termination of the pregnancy specified in that section applies.

6.   Interpretation

In this Act, the following expressions have meanings hereby assigned to them:—

   'the law relating to abortion' means sections 58 and 59 of the Offences against the Person Act 1861, and any rule of law relating to the procurement of abortion.

ACCESSORIES AND ABETTORS ACT 1861

8.   Abettors

Whosoever shall aid, abet, counsel, or procure the commission of any indictable offence, whether the same be an offence at common law or by virtue of any Act passed or to be passed, shall be liable to be tried, indicted, and punished as a principal offender.

ANTI-TERRORISM, CRIME AND SECURITY ACT 2001

113.   Use of noxious substances or things to cause harm and intimidate

(1)   A person who takes any action which—

   (a)   involves the use of a noxious substance or other noxious thing;

   (b)   has or is likely to have an effect falling within subsection (2); and

   (c)   is designed to influence the government or to intimidate the public or a section of the public,

is guilty of an offence.

(2)   Action has an effect falling within this subsection if it—

   (a)   causes serious violence against a person anywhere in the world;

   (b)   causes serious damage to real or personal property anywhere in the world;

   (c)   endangers human life or creates a serious risk to the health or safety of the public or a section of the public; or

   (d)   induces in members of the public the fear that the action is likely to endanger their lives or create a serious risk to their health or safety;

but any effect on the person taking the action is to be disregarded.

(3)   A person who—

   (a)   makes a threat that he or another will take any action which constitutes an offence under subsection (1); and

   (b)   intends thereby to induce in a person anywhere in the world the fear that the threat is likely to be carried out,

is guilty of an offence.

(5)   In this section—

'the government' means the government of the United Kingdom, of a part of the United Kingdom or of a country other than the United Kingdom; and

'the public' includes the public of a country other than the United Kingdom.

113A   Application of section 113

(1)   Section 113 applies to conduct done—

    (a)   in the United Kingdom; or

    (b)   outside the United Kingdom which satisfies the following two conditions.

(2)   The first condition is that the conduct is done for the purpose of advancing a political, religious or ideological cause.

(3)   The second condition is that the conduct is—

    (a)   by a United Kingdom national or a United Kingdom resident;

    (b)   by any person done to, or in relation to, a United Kingdom national, a United Kingdom resident or a protected person; or

    (c)   by any person done in circumstances which fall within section 63D(1)(b) and (c) or (3)(b) and (c) of the Terrorism Act 2000.

(4)   The following expressions have the same meaning as they have for the purposes of sections 63C and 63D of that Act—

    (a)   'United Kingdom national';

    (b)   'United Kingdom resident';

    (c)   'protected person'.

(5)   For the purposes of this section it is immaterial whether a person knows that another is a United Kingdom national, a United Kingdom resident or a protected person.

114.   Hoaxes involving noxious substances or things

(1)   A person is guilty of an offence if he—

    (a)   places any substance or other thing in any place; or

    (b)   sends any substance or other thing from one place to another (by post, rail or any other means whatever);

with the intention of inducing in a person anywhere in the world a belief that it is likely to be (or contain) a noxious substance or other noxious thing and thereby endanger human life or create a serious risk to human health.

(2)   A person is guilty of an offence if he communicates any information which he knows or believes to be false with the intention of inducing in a person anywhere in the world a belief that a noxious substance or other noxious thing is likely to be present (whether at the time the information is communicated or later) in any place and thereby endanger human life or create a serious risk to human health.

115.   Sections 113 and 114: supplementary

(1)   For the purposes of sections 113 and 114 'substance' includes any biological agent and any other natural or artificial substance (whatever its form, origin or method of production).

(2)   For a person to be guilty of an offence under section 113(3) or 114 it is not necessary for him to have any particular person in mind as the person in whom he intends to induce the belief in question.

AVIATION SECURITY ACT 1982

1.   Hijacking

(1)   A person on board an aircraft in flight who unlawfully, by the use of force or by threats of any kind, seizes the aircraft or exercises control of it commits the offence of hijacking, whatever his nationality, whatever the State in which the aircraft is registered and whether the aircraft is in the United Kingdom or elsewhere, but subject to subsection (2) below.

(2)   If—

    (a)   the aircraft is used in military, customs or police service, or

(b) both the place of take-off and the place of landing are in the territory of the State in which the aircraft is registered,

subsection (1) above shall not apply unless—

    (i) the person seizing or exercising control of the aircraft is a United Kingdom national; or

    (ii) his act is committed in the United Kingdom; or

    (iii) the aircraft is registered in the United Kingdom or is used in the military or customs service of the United Kingdom or in the service of any police force in the United Kingdom.

(3) A person who commits the offence of hijacking shall be liable, on conviction on indictment, to imprisonment for life.

(5) For the purposes of this section the territorial waters of any State shall be treated as part of its territory.

2. **Destroying, damaging or endangering safety of aircraft**

(1) It shall, subject to subsection (4) below, be an offence for any person unlawfully and intentionally—

    (a) to destroy an aircraft in service or so to damage such an aircraft as to render it incapable of flight or as to be likely to endanger its safety in flight; or

    (b) to commit on board an aircraft in flight any act of violence which is likely to endanger the safety of the aircraft.

(2) It shall also, subject to subsection (4) below, be an offence for any person unlawfully and intentionally to place, or cause to be placed, on an aircraft in service any device or substance which is likely to destroy the aircraft, or is likely so to damage it as to render it incapable of flight or as to be likely to endanger its safety in flight; but nothing in this subsection shall be construed as limiting the circumstances in which the commission of any act—

    (a) may constitute an offence under subsection (1) above, or

    (b) may constitute attempting or conspiring to commit, or aiding, abetting, counselling or procuring, or being art and part in, the commission of such an offence.

(3) Except as provided by subsection (4) below, subsections (1) and (2) above shall apply whether any such act as is therein mentioned is committed in the United Kingdom or elsewhere, whatever the nationality of the person committing the act and whatever the State in which the aircraft is registered.

(4) Subsections (1) and (2) above shall not apply to any act committed in relation to an aircraft used in military, customs or police service unless—

    (a) the act is committed in the United Kingdom, or

    (b) where the act is committed outside the United Kingdom, the person committing it is a United Kingdom national.

(5) A person who commits an offence under this section shall be liable, on conviction on indictment, to imprisonment for life.

(6) In this section 'unlawfully'—

    (a) in relation to the commission of an act in the United Kingdom, means so as (apart from this Act) to constitute an offence under the law of the part of the United Kingdom in which the act is committed, and

    (b) in relation to the commission of an act outside the United Kingdom, means so that the commission of the act would (apart from this Act) have been an offence under the law of England and Wales if it had been committed in England and Wales or of Scotland if it had been committed in Scotland.

(7) In this section 'act of violence' means—

    (a) any act done in the United Kingdom which constitutes the offence of murder, attempted murder, manslaughter, culpable homicide or assault or an offence under section 18, 20, 21, 22, 23, 24, 28 or 29 of the Offences against the Person Act 1861 or under section 2 of the Explosive Substances Act 1883, and

    (b) any act done outside the United Kingdom which, if done in the United Kingdom, would constitute such an offence as is mentioned in paragraph (a) above.

3.   Other acts endangering or likely to endanger safety of aircraft

(1)   It shall, subject to subsections (5) and (6) below, be an offence for any person unlawfully and intentionally to destroy or damage any property to which this subsection applies, or to interfere with the operation of any such property, where the destruction, damage or interference is likely to endanger the safety of aircraft in flight.

(2)   Subsection (1) above applies to any property used for the provision of air navigation facilities, including any land, building or ship so used, and including any apparatus or equipment so used, whether it is on board an aircraft or elsewhere.

(3)   It shall also, subject to subsections (4) and (5) below, be an offence for any person intentionally to communicate any information which is false, misleading or deceptive in a material particular, where the communication of the information endangers the safety of an aircraft in flight or is likely to endanger the safety of aircraft in flight.

(4)   It shall be a defence for a person charged with an offence under subsection (3) above to prove—

(a)   that he believed, and had reasonable grounds for believing, that the information was true; or

(b)   that, when he communicated the information, he was lawfully employed to perform duties which consisted of or included the communication of information and that he communicated the information in good faith in the performance of those duties.

(5)   Subsections (1) and (3) above shall not apply to the commission of any act unless either the act is committed in the United Kingdom, or, where it is committed outside the United Kingdom—

(a)   the person committing it is a United Kingdom national; or

(b)   the commission of the act endangers or is likely to endanger the safety in flight of a civil aircraft registered in the United Kingdom or chartered by demise to a lessee whose principal place of business, or (if he has no place of business) whose permanent residence, is in the United Kingdom; or

(c)   the act is committed on board a civil aircraft which is so registered or so chartered; or

(d)   the act is committed on board a civil aircraft which lands in the United Kingdom with the person who committed the act still on board.

(6)   Subsection (1) above shall also not apply to any act committed outside the United Kingdom and so committed in relation to property which is situated outside the United Kingdom and is not used for the provision of air navigation facilities in connection with international air navigation, unless the person committing the act is a United Kingdom national.

(7)   A person who commits an offence under this section shall be liable, on conviction on indictment, to imprisonment for life.

(8)   In this section 'civil aircraft' means any aircraft other than an aircraft used in military, customs or police service and 'unlawfully' has the same meaning as in section 2 of this Act.

4.   Offences in relation to certain dangerous articles

(1)   It shall be an offence for any person without lawful authority or reasonable excuse (the proof of which shall lie on him) to have with him—

(a)   in any aircraft registered in the United Kingdom, whether at a time when the aircraft is in the United Kingdom or not, or

(b)   in any other aircraft at a time when it is in, or in flight over, the United Kingdom, or

(c)   in any part of an aerodrome in the United Kingdom, or

(d)   in any air navigation installation in the United Kingdom which does not form part of an aerodrome,

any article to which this section applies.

(2)   This section applies to the following articles, that is to say—

(a)   any firearm, or any article having the appearance of being a firearm, whether capable of being discharged or not;

(b)   any explosive, any article manufactured or adapted (whether in the form of a bomb, grenade or otherwise) so as to have the appearance of being an explosive, whether it is capable of producing a practical effect by explosion or not, or any article marked or labelled so as to indicate that it is or contains an explosive; and

(c) any article (not falling within either of the preceding paragraphs) made or adapted for use for causing injury to or incapacitating a person or for destroying or damaging property, or intended by the person having it with him for such use, whether by him or by any other person.

(3) For the purposes of this section a person who is for the time being in an aircraft, or in part of an aerodrome, shall be treated as having with him in the aircraft, or in that part of the aerodrome, as the case may be, an article to which this section applies if—

(a) where he is in an aircraft, the article, or an article in which it is contained, is in the aircraft and has been caused (whether by him or by any other person) to be brought there as being, or as forming part of, his baggage on a flight in the aircraft or has been caused by him to be brought there as being, or as forming part of, any other property to be carried on such a flight, or

(b) where he is in part of an aerodrome (otherwise than in an aircraft), the article, or an article in which it is contained, is in that or any other part of the aerodrome and has been caused (whether by him or by any other person) to be brought into the aerodrome as being, or as forming part of, his baggage on a flight from that aerodrome or has been caused by him to be brought there as being, or as forming part of, any other property to be carried on such a flight on which he is also to be carried,

notwithstanding that the circumstances may be such that (apart from this subsection) he would not be regarded as having the article with him in the aircraft or in a part of the aerodrome, as the case may be.

(4) A person guilty of an offence under this section shall be liable—

(a) on summary conviction, to a fine not exceeding the statutory maximum or to imprisonment for a term not exceeding three months or to both;

(b) on conviction on indictment, to a fine or to imprisonment for a term not exceeding five years or to both.

(5) Nothing in subsection (3) above shall be construed as limiting the circumstances in which a person would, apart from that subsection, be regarded as having an article with him as mentioned in subsection (1) above.

38. Interpretation etc.

(1) In this Act, except in so far as the context otherwise requires—

'aerodrome' means the aggregate of the land, buildings and works comprised in an aerodrome within the meaning of the Civil Aviation Act 1982 and (if and so far as not comprised in an aerodrome as defined in that Act) any land, building or works situated within the boundaries of an area designated, by an order made by the Secretary of State which is for the time being in force, as constituting the area of an aerodrome for the purposes of this Act;

'air navigation installation' means any building, works, apparatus or equipment used wholly or mainly for the purpose of assisting air traffic control or as an aid to air navigation, together with any land contiguous or adjacent to any such building, works, apparatus or equipment and used wholly or mainly for purposes connected therewith;

'aircraft registered or operating in the United Kingdom' means any aircraft which is either—

(a) an aircraft registered in the United Kingdom, or

(b) an aircraft not so registered which is for the time being allocated for use on flights which (otherwise than in exceptional circumstances) include landing at or taking off from one or more aerodromes in the United Kingdom;

'article' includes any substance, whether in solid or liquid form or in the form of a gas or vapour;

'constable' includes any person having the powers and privileges of a constable;

'explosive' means any article manufactured for the purpose of producing a practical effect by explosion, or intended for that purpose by a person having the article with him;

'firearm' includes an airgun or air pistol;

'manager', in relation to an aerodrome, means the person (whether . . . the Civil Aviation Authority, a local authority or any other person) by whom the aerodrome is managed;

'military service' includes naval and air force service;

'measures' (without prejudice to the generality of that expression) includes the construction, execution, alteration, demolition or removal of buildings or other works and also includes the institution or modification, and the supervision and enforcement, of any practice or procedure;

'operator' has the same meaning as in the Civil Aviation Act 1982;

'property' includes any land, buildings or works, any aircraft or vehicle and any baggage, cargo or other article of any description;

'United Kingdom national' means an individual who is—

(a)　a British citizen, a British Overseas Territories citizen, a British National (Overseas) or a British Overseas citizen;

(b)　a person who under the British Nationality Act 1981 is a British subject; or

(c)　a British protected person (within the meaning of that Act).

(2)　For the purposes of this Act—

(a)　in the case of an air navigation installation provided by, or used wholly or mainly by, the Civil Aviation Authority, that Authority, and

(b)　in the case of any other air navigation installation, the manager of an aerodrome by whom it is provided, or by whom it is wholly or mainly used,

shall be taken to be the authority responsible for that air navigation installation.

(3)　For the purposes of this Act—

(a)　the period during which an aircraft is in flight shall be deemed to include any period from the moment when all its external doors are closed following embarkation until the moment when any such door is opened for disembarkation, and, in the case of a forced landing, any period until the competent authorities take over responsibility for the aircraft and for persons and property on board; and

(b)　an aircraft shall be taken to be in service during the whole of the period which begins with the pre-flight preparation of the aircraft for a flight and ends 24 hours after the aircraft lands having completed that flight, and also at any time (not falling within that period) while, in accordance with the preceding paragraph, the aircraft is in flight, and anything done on board an aircraft while in flight over any part of the United Kingdom shall be treated as done in that part of the United Kingdom.

(4)　For the purposes of this Act the territorial waters adjacent to any part of the United Kingdom shall be treated as included in that part of the United Kingdom.

CHILD ABDUCTION ACT 1984

1.　Offence of abduction of child by parent, etc.

(1)　Subject to subsections (5) and (8) below, a person connected with a child under the age of sixteen commits an offence if he takes or sends the child out of the United Kingdom without the appropriate consent.

(2)　A person is connected with a child for the purposes of this section if—

(a)　he is a parent of the child; or

(b)　in the case of a child whose parents were not married to each other at the time of his birth, there are reasonable grounds for believing that he is the father of the child; or

(c)　he is a guardian of the child; or

(ca)　he is a special guardian of the child; or

(d)　he is a person in whose favour a residence order is in force with respect to the child; or

(e)　he has custody of the child.

(3)　In this section 'the appropriate consent' in relation to a child, means—

(a)　the consent of each of the following—

(i)　the child's mother;

(ii)   the child's father, if he has parental responsibility for him;

(iii) any guardian of the child;

(iiia) any special guardian of the child;

(iv)   any person in whose favour a residence order is in force with respect to the child;

(v)   any person who has custody of the child; or

(b) the leave of the court granted under or by virtue of any provision of Part II of the Children Act 1989; or

(c) if any person has custody of the child, the leave of the court which awarded custody to him.

(4) A person does not commit an offence under this section by taking or sending a child out of the United Kingdom without obtaining the appropriate consent if—

(a) he is a person in whose favour there is a residence order in force with respect to the child, and he takes or sends him out of the United Kingdom for a period of less than one month; or

(b) he is a special guardian of the child, and he takes or sends the child out of the United Kingdom for a period of less than three months.

(4A) Subsection (4) above does not apply if the person taking or sending the child out of the United Kingdom does so in breach of an order under Part II of the Children Act 1989.

(5) A person does not commit an offence under this section by doing anything without the consent of another person whose consent is required under the foregoing provisions if—

(a) he does it in the belief that the other person—

(i)   has consented; or

(ia)   who is a special guardian of the child; or

(ii)   would consent if he was aware of all the relevant circumstances; or

(b) he has taken all reasonable steps to communicate with the other person but has been unable to communicate with him; or

(c) the other person has unreasonably refused to consent.

(5A) Subsection (5)(c) above does not apply if—

(a) the person who refused to consent is a person—

(i)   in whose favour there is a residence order in force with respect to the child; or

(ii)   who has custody of the child; or

(b) the person taking or sending the child out of the United Kingdom is, by so acting, in breach of an order made by a court in the United Kingdom.

(6) Where, in proceedings for an offence under this section, there is sufficient evidence to raise an issue as to the application of subsection (5) above, it shall be for the prosecution to prove that the subsection does not apply.

(7) For the purposes of this section—

(a) 'guardian of a child', 'special guardian' 'residence order' and 'parental responsibility' have the same meaning as in the Children Act 1989; and

(b) a person shall be treated as having custody of a child if there is in force an order of a court in the United Kingdom awarding him (whether solely or jointly with another person) custody, legal custody or care and control of the child.

(8) This section shall have effect subject to the provisions of the Schedule to this Act in relation to a child who is in the care of a local authority detained in a place of safety, remanded to a local authority accommodation or the subject of proceedings or an order relating to adoption.

2.   Offence of abduction of child by other persons

(1) Subject to subsection (3) below, a person, other than one mentioned in subsection (2) below, commits an offence if, without lawful authority or reasonable excuse, he takes or detains a child under the age of sixteen—

(a) so as to remove him from the lawful control of any person having lawful control of the child; or

(b) so as to keep him out of the lawful control of any person entitled to lawful control of the child.

(2)   The persons are—
    (a)   where the father and mother of the child in question were married to each other at the time of his birth, the child's father and mother;
    (b)   where the father and mother of the child in question were not married to each other at the time of his birth, the child's mother; and
    (c)   any other person mentioned in section 1(2)(c) to (e) above.

(3)   In proceedings against any person for an offence under this section, it shall be a defence for that person to prove—
    (a)   where the father and mother of the child in question were not married to each other at the time of his birth—
        (i)   that he is the child's father; or
        (ii)   that, at the time of the alleged offence, he believed, on reasonable grounds, that he was the child's father; or
    (b)   that, at the time of the alleged offence, he believed that the child had attained the age of sixteen.

3.   Construction of references to taking, sending and detaining

For the purposes of this Part of this Act—
(a)   a person shall be regarded as taking a child if he causes or induces the child to accompany him or any other person or causes the child to be taken;
(b)   a person shall be regarded as sending a child if he causes the child to be sent;
(c)   a person shall be regarded as detaining a child if he causes the child to be detained or induces the child to remain with him or any other person; and
(d)   references to a child's parents and to a child whose parents were (or were not) married to each other at the time of his birth shall be construed in accordance with section 1 of the Family Law Reform Act 1987 (which extends their meaning).

CHILDREN ACT 2004

58.   Reasonable punishment

(1)   In relation to any offence specified in subsection (2), battery of a child cannot be justified on the ground that it constituted reasonable punishment.
(2)   The offences referred to in subsection (1) are—
    (a)   an offence under section 18 or 20 of the Offences against the Person Act 1861 (wounding and causing grievous bodily harm);
    (b)   an offence under section 47 of that Act (assault occasioning actual bodily harm);
    (c)   an offence under section 1 of the Children and Young Persons Act 1933 (cruelty to persons under 16).
(3)   Battery of a child causing actual bodily harm to the child cannot be justified in any civil proceedings on the ground that it constituted reasonable punishment.
(4)   For the purposes of subsection (3) 'actual bodily harm' has the same meaning as it has for the purposes of section 47 of the Offences against the Person Act 1861.

CHILDREN AND YOUNG PERSONS ACT 1933

1.   Cruelty to persons under sixteen

(1)   If any person who has attained the age of sixteen years and has responsibility for any child or young person under that age, wilfully assaults, ill-treats, neglects, abandons, or exposes him, or causes or procures him to be assaulted, ill-treated, neglected, abandoned, or exposed, in a manner likely to cause him unnecessary suffering or injury to health (including injury to or loss of sight, or hearing, or limb, or organ of the body, and any mental derangement), that person shall be guilty of an offence . . .
(2)   For the purposes of this section—

        (a)   a parent or other person legally liable to maintain a child or young person, or the legal guardian of a child or young person, shall be deemed to have neglected him in a manner likely to cause injury to his health if he has failed to provide adequate food, clothing, medical aid or lodging for him, or if, having been unable otherwise to provide such food, clothing, medical aid or lodging, he has failed to take steps to procure it to be provided under the enactments applicable in that behalf;

        (b)   where it is proved that the death of an infant under three years of age was caused by suffocation (not being suffocation caused by disease or the presence of any foreign body in the throat or air passages of the infant) while the infant was in bed with some other person who has attained the age of sixteen years, that other person shall, if he was, when he went to bed, under the influence of drink, be deemed to have neglected the infant in a manner likely to cause injury to its health.

  (3)   A person may be convicted of an offence under this section—

        (a)   notwithstanding that actual suffering or injury to health, or the likelihood of actual suffering or injury to health, was obviated by the action of another person;

        (b)   notwithstanding the death of the child or young person in question.

3.   **Allowing persons under sixteen to be in brothels**

  (1)   If any person having responsibility for a child or young person who has attained the age of four years and is under the age of sixteen years, allows that child or young person to reside in or to frequent a brothel, he shall be liable on summary conviction, to a fine not exceeding level 2 on the standard scale, or alternatively . . . or in addition thereto, to imprisonment for any term not exceeding six months.

5.   **Giving intoxicating liquor to children under five**

If any person gives, or causes to be given, to any child under the age of five years any alcohol (within the meaning given by section 191 of the Licensing Act 2003, but disregarding subsection 1(f)–(i) of that section), except upon the order of a duly qualified medical practitioner, or in case of sickness, apprehended sickness, or other urgent cause, he shall, on summary conviction, be liable to a fine not exceeding level 1 on the standard scale.

7.   **Sale of tobacco, etc., to persons under sixteen**

  (1)   Any person who sells to a person under the age of sixteen years any tobacco or cigarette papers, whether for his own use or not, shall be liable on summary conviction to a fine not exceeding level 4 on the standard scale:

       . . .

  (1A) It shall be a defence for a person charged with an offence under subsection (1) above to prove that he took all reasonable precautions and exercised all due diligence to avoid the commission of the offence.

  (5)   For the purposes of this section the expression 'tobacco' includes cigarettes, any product containing tobacco and intended for oral or nasal use and smoking mixtures intended as a substitute for tobacco, and the expression 'cigarette' includes cut tobacco rolled up in papers, tobacco leaf, or other material in such form as to be capable of immediate use for smoking.

11.   **Exposing children under twelve to risk of burning**

If any person who has attained the age of sixteen years, having responsibility for any child under the age of twelve years, allows the child to be in any room containing an open fire grate or any heating appliance liable to cause injury to a person by contact therewith not sufficiently protected to guard against the risk of his being burnt or scalded without taking reasonable precautions against that risk, and by reason thereof the child is killed or suffers serious injury, he shall on summary conviction be liable to a fine not exceeding level 1 on the standard scale:

    Provided that neither this section, nor any proceedings taken thereunder shall affect any liability of any such person to be proceeded against by indictment for any indictable offence.

17. Interpretation of Part I

(1) For the purposes of this Part of this Act, the following shall be presumed to have responsibility for a child or young person—

(a) Any person who—

(i) has parental responsibility for him (within the meaning of the Children Act 1989); or

(ii) is otherwise legally liable to maintain him; and

(b) any person who has care of him.

(2) A person who is presumed to be responsible for a child or young person by virtue of subsection (1)(a) shall not be taken to have ceased to be responsible for him by reason only that he does not have care of him.

18. Restrictions on employment of children

(1) Subject to the provisions of this section and of any byelaws regulations made thereunder no child shall be employed—

(a) so long as he is under the age of fourteen years; or

(aa) to do any work other than light work; or

(b) before the close of school hours on any day on which he is required to attend school; or

(c) before seven o'clock in the morning or after seven o'clock in the evening on any day; or

(d) for more than two hours on any day on which he is required to attend school; or

(da) for more than twelve hours in any week in which he is required to attend school; or

(e) for more than two hours on any Sunday; or

(f) . . .

(g) for more than eight hours or, if he is under the age of fifteen years, for more than five hours in any day—

(i) on which he is not required to attend school, and

(ii) which is not a Sunday; or

(h) for more than thirty-five hours or, if he is under the age of fifteen years, for more than twenty-five hours in any week in which he is not required to attend school; or

(i) for more than four hours in any day without a rest break of one hour; or

(j) at any time in a year unless at that time he has had, or could still have, during a period in the year in which he is not required to attend school, at least two consecutive weeks without employment.

23. Prohibition against persons under sixteen taking part in performances endangering life or limb

No person under the age of sixteen years, and no child aged sixteen years, shall take part in any performance to which section 37(2) of the Children and Young Persons Act 1963 applies and in which his life or limbs are endangered and every person who causes or procures such a person or child, or being his parent or guardian allows him, to take part in such a performance, shall be liable on summary conviction to a fine not exceeding level 3 on the standard scale:

Provided that no proceedings shall be taken under this subsection except by or with the authority of a chief officer of police.

24. Restrictions on training for performances of a dangerous nature

(1) No child under the age of twelve years shall be trained to take part in performances of a dangerous nature, and no child who has attained that age shall be trained to take part in such performances except under and in accordance with the terms of a licence granted and in force under this section; and every person who causes or procures a person, or being his parent or guardian allows him, to be trained to take part in performances of a dangerous nature in contravention of this section, shall be liable on summary conviction to a fine not exceeding level 3 on the standard scale.

(2) A local authority may grant a licence for a child who has attained the age of twelve years but is under the age of sixteen years to be trained to take part in performances of a dangerous nature.

50. Age of criminal responsbility

It shall be conclusively presumed that no child under the age of ten years can be guilty of any offence.

COMPUTER MISUSE ACT 1990

1. Unauthorised access to computer material

(1) A person is guilty of an offence if—

    (a) he causes a computer to perform any function with intent to secure access to any program or data held in any computer;

    (b) the access he intends to secure is unauthorised; and

    (c) he knows at the time when he causes the computer to perform the function that that is the case.

(2) The intent a person has to have to commit an offence under this section need not be directed at—

    (a) any particular program or data;

    (b) a program or data of any particular kind; or

    (c) a program or data held in any particular computer.

2. Unauthorised access with intent to commit or facilitate commission of further offences

(1) A person is guilty of an offence under this section if he commits an offence under section 1 above ('the unauthorised access offence') with intent—

    (a) to commit an offence to which this section applies; or

    (b) to facilitate the commission of such an offence (whether by himself or by any other person);

and the offence he intends to commit or facilitate is referred to below in this section as the further offence.

(2) This section applies to offences—

    (a) for which the sentence is fixed by law; or

    (b) for which a person of twenty-one years of age or over (not previously convicted) may be sentenced to imprisonment for a term of five years (or, in England and Wales, might be so sentenced but for the restrictions imposed by section 33 of the Magistrates' Courts Act 1980).

(3) It is immaterial for the purposes of this section whether the further offence is to be committed on the same occasion as the unauthorised access offence or on any future occasion.

(4) A person may be guilty of an offence under this section even though the facts are such that the commission of the further offence is impossible.

3. Unauthorised modification of computer material

(1) A person is guilty of an offence if—

    (a) he does any act which causes an unauthorised modification of the contents of any computer; and

    (b) at the time when he does the act he has the requisite intent and the requisite knowledge.

(2) For the purposes of subsection (1)(b) above the requisite intent is an intent to cause a modification of the contents of any computer and by so doing—

    (a) to impair the operation of any computer;

    (b) to prevent or hinder access to any program or data held in any computer; or

    (c) to impair the operation of any such program or the reliability of any such data.

(3)   The intent need not be directed at—
- (a)   any particular computer;
- (b)   any particular program or data or a program or data of any particular kind; or
- (c)   any particular modification or a modification of any particular kind.

(4)   For the purposes of subsection (1)(b) above the requisite knowledge is knowledge that any modification he intends to cause is unauthorised.

(5)   It is immaterial for the purposes of this section whether an unauthorised modification or any intended effect of it of a kind mentioned in subsection (2) above is, or is intended to be, permanent or merely temporary.

(6)   For the purposes of the Criminal Damage Act 1971 a modification of the contents of a computer shall not be regarded as damaging any computer or computer storage medium unless its effect on that computer or computer storage medium impairs its physical condition.

4.   Territorial scope of offences under this Act

(1)   Except as provided below in this section, it is immaterial for the purposes of any offence under section 1 or 3 above—
- (a)   whether any act or other event proof of which is required for conviction of the offence occured in the home country concerned; or
- (b)   whether the accused was in the home country concerned at the time of any such act or event.

(2)   Subject to subsection (3) below, in the case of such an offence at least one significant link with domestic jurisdiction must exist in the circumstances of the case for the offence to be committed.

(3)   There is no need for any such link to exist for the commission of an offence under section 1 above to be established in proof of an allegation to that effect in proceedings for an offence under section 2 above.

(4)   Subject to section 8 below, where—
- (a)   any such link does in fact exist in the case of an offence under section 1 above; and
- (b)   commission of that offence is alleged in proceedings for an offence under section 2 above;

section 2 above shall apply as if anything the accused intended to do or facilitate in any place outside the home country concerned which would be an offence to which section 2 applies if it took place in the home country concerned were the offence in question.

(6)   References in this Act to the home country concerned are references—
- (a)   in application of this Act to England and Wales, to England and Wales;
- (b)   in the application of this Act to Scotland, to Scotland; and
- (c)   in the application of this Act to Northern Ireland, to Northern Ireland.

5.   Significant links with domestic jurisdiction

(1)   The following provisions of this section apply for the interpretation of section 4 above.

(2)   In relation to an offence under section 1, either of the following is a significant link with domestic jurisdiction—
- (a)   that the accused was in the home country concerned at the time when he did the act which caused the computer to perform the function; or
- (b)   that any computer containing any program or data to which the accused secured or intended to secure unauthorised access by doing that act was in the home country concerned at that time.

(3)   In relation to an offence under section 3, either of the following is a significant link with domestic jurisdiction—
- (a)   that the accused was in the home country concerned at the time when he did the act which caused the unauthorised modification; or
- (b)   that the unauthorised modification took place in the home country concerned.

6.   Territorial scope of inchoate offences related to offences under this Act

(1)   On a charge of conspiracy to commit an offence under this Act the following questions are immaterial to the accused's guilt—

   (a)   the question where any person became a party to the conspiracy; and

   (b)   the question whether any act, omission or other event occured in the home country concerned.

(2)   On a charge of attempting to commit an offence under section 3 above the following questions are immaterial to the accused's guilt—

   (a)   the question where the attempt was made; and

   (b)   the question whether it had an effect in the home country concerned.

(3)   On a charge of incitement to commit an offence under this Act the question where the incitement took place is immaterial to the accused's guilt.

7.   Territorial scope of inchoate offences related to offences under external law corresponding to offences under this Act

(4)   Subject to section 8 below, if any act done by a person in England and Wales would amount to the offence of incitement to commit an offence under this Act but for the fact that what he had in view would not be an offence triable in England and Wales—

   (a)   what he had in view shall be treated as an offence under this Act for the purposes of any charge of incitement brought in respect of that act; and

   (b)   any such charge shall accordingly be triable in England and Wales.

8.   Relevance of external law

(1)   A person is guilty of an offence triable by virtue of section 4(4) above only if what he intended to do or facilitate would involve the commission of an offence under the law in force where the whole or any part of it was intended to take place.

(3)   A person is guilty of an offence triable by virtue of section 1(1A) of the Criminal Attempts Act 1981 or by virtue of section 7(4) above only if what he had in view would involve the commission of an offence under the law in force where the whole or any part of it was intended to take place.

(4)   Conduct punishable under the law in force in any place is an offence under that law for the purposes of this section, however it is described in that law.

(5)   Subject to subsection (7) below, a condition specified in subsections (1) or (3) above shall be taken to be satisfied unless not later than rules of court may provide the defence serve on the prosecution a notice—

   (a)   stating that, on the facts as alleged with respect to the relevant conduct, the condition is not in their opinion satisfied;

   (b)   showing their grounds for that opinion; and

   (c)   requiring the prosecution to show that it is satisfied.

(6)   In subsection (5) above 'the relevant conduct' means—

   (a)   where the condition in subsection (1) above is in question, what the accused intended to do or facilitate; and

   (c)   where the condition in subsection (3) above is in question, what the accused had in view.

(7)   The court, if it thinks fit, may permit the defence to require the prosecution to show that the condition is satisfied without the prior service of a notice under subsection (5) above.

(9)   In the Crown Court the question whether the condition is satisfied shall be decided by the judge alone.

9.   British citizenship immaterial

(1)   In any proceedings brought in England and Wales in respect of any offence to which this section applies it is immaterial to guilt whether or not the accused was a British citizen at the time of any act, omission or other event proof of which is required for conviction of the offence.

(2)   This section applies to the following offences—

   (a)   any offence under this Act;

    (c)   any attempt to commit an offence under section 3 above; and

    (d)   incitement to commit an offence under this Act.

17.   Interpretation

(1)   The following provisions of this section apply for the interpretation of this Act.

(2)   A person secures access to any program or data held in a computer if by causing a computer to perform any function he—

    (a)   alters or erases the program or data;

    (b)   copies or moves it to any storage medium other than that in which it is held or to a different location in the storage medium in which it is held;

    (c)   uses it; or

    (d)   has it output from the computer in which it is held (whether by having it displayed or in any other manner);

and references to access to a program or data (and to an intent to secure such access) shall be read accordingly.

(3)   For the purposes of subsection (2)(c) above a person uses a program if the function he causes the computer to perform—

    (a)   causes the program to be executed; or

    (b)   is itself a function of the program.

(4)   For the purposes of subsection (2)(d) above—

    (a)   a program is output if the instructions of which it consists are output; and

    (b)   the form in which any such instructions or any other data is output (and in particular whether or not it represents a form in which, in the case of instructions, they are capable of being executed or, in the case of data, it is capable of being processed by a computer) is immaterial.

(5)   Access of any kind by any person to any program or data held in a computer is unauthorised if—

    (a)   he is not himself entitled to control access of the kind in question to the program or data; and

    (b)   he does not have consent to access by him of the kind in question to the program or data from any person who is so entitled.

(6)   References to any program or data held in a computer include references to any program or data held in any removable storage medium which is for the time being in the computer; and a computer is to be regarded as containing any program or data held in any such medium.

(7)   A modification of the contents of any computer takes place if, by the operation of any function of the computer concerned or any other computer—

    (a)   any program or data held in the computer concerned is altered or erased; or

    (b)   any program or data is added to its contents;

and any act which contributes towards causing such a modification shall be regarded as causing it.

(8)   Such a modification is unauthorised if—

    (a)   the person whose act causes it is not himself entitled to determine whether the modification should be made; and

    (b)   he does not have consent to the modification from any person who is so entitled.

(9)   References to the home country concerned shall be read in accordance with section 4(6) above.

(10)   References to a program include references to part of a program.

CRIME AND DISORDER ACT 1998

28.   Meaning of 'racially or religiously aggravated'

(1)   An offence is racially or religiously aggravated for the purposes of sections 29 to 32 below if—

(a)   at the time of committing the offence, or immediately before or after doing so, the offender demonstrates towards the victim of the offence hostility based on the victim's membership (or presumed membership) of a racial or religious group; or

(b)   the offence is motivated (wholly or partly) by hostility towards members of a racial or religious group based on their membership of that group.

(2)   In subsection (1)(a) above—

'membership', in relation to a racial or religious group, includes association with members of that group;

'presumed' means presumed by the offender.

(3)   It is immaterial for the purposes of paragraph (a) or (b) of subsection (1) above whether or not the offender's hostility is also based, to any extent, on any other factor not mentioned in that paragraph.

(4)   In this section 'racial group' means a group of persons defined by reference to race, colour, nationality (including citizenship) or ethnic or national origins.

(5)   In this section 'religious group' means a group of persons defined by reference to religious belief or lack of religious belief.

29.   Racially or religiously aggravated assaults

(1)   A person is guilty of an offence under this section if he commits—

(a)   an offence under section 20 of the Offences Against the Person Act 1861 (malicious wounding or grievous bodily harm);

(b)   an offence under section 47 of that Act (actual bodily harm); or

(c)   common assault,

which is racially or religiously aggravated for the purposes of this section.

30.   Racially or religiously aggravated criminal damage

(1)   A person is guilty of an offence under this section if he commits an offence under section 1(1) of the Criminal Damage Act 1971 (destroying or damaging property belonging to another) which is racially or religiously aggravated for the purposes of this section.

(3)   For the purposes of this section, section 28(1)(a) above shall have effect as if the person to whom the property belongs or is treated as belonging for the purposes of that Act were the victim of the offence.

31.   Racially or religiously aggravated public order offences

(1)   A person is guilty of an offence under this section if he commits—

(a)   an offence under section 4 of the Public Order Act 1986 (fear or provocation of violence);

(b)   an offence under section 4A of that Act (intentional harassment, alarm or distress); or

(c)   an offence under section 5 of that Act (harassment, alarm or distress),

which is racially or religiously aggravated for the purposes of this section.

(6)   If, on the trial on indictment of a person charged with an offence falling within subsection (1)(a) or (b) above, the jury find him not guilty of the offence charged, they may find him guilty of the basic offence mentioned in that provision.

(7)   For the purposes of subsection (1)(c) above, section 28(1)(a) above shall have effect as if the person likely to be caused harassment, alarm or distress were the victim of the offence.

32.   Racially or religiously aggravated harassment etc.

(1)   A person is guilty of an offence under this section if he commits—

(a)   an offence under section 2 of the Protection from Harassment Act 1997 (offence of harassment); or

(b)   an offence under section 4 of that Act (putting people in fear of violence),

which is racially or religiously aggravated for the purposes of this section.

(5)   If, on the trial on indictment of a person charged with an offence falling within subsection (1)(a) above, the jury find him not guilty of the offence charged, they may find him guilty of the basic offence mentioned in that provision.

(6) If, on the trial on indictment of a person charged with an offence falling within subsection (1)(b) above, the jury find him not guilty of the offence charged, they may find him guilty of an offence falling within subsection (1)(a) above.

34. Abolition of rebuttable presumption that a child is doli incapax

The rebuttable presumption of criminal law that a child aged 10 or over is incapable of committing an offence is hereby abolished.

CRIMINAL APPEAL ACT 1968

1. Right of appeal

(1) Subject to subsection (3) below a person convicted of an offence on indictment may appeal to the Court of Appeal against his conviction.

(2) An appeal under this section lies only—

    (a) with the leave of the Court of Appeal; or

    (b) if the judge of the court of trial grants a certificate that the case if fit for appeal.

2. Grounds for allowing an appeal under s 1

(1) Subject to the provisions of this Act, the Court of Appeal—

    (a) shall allow an appeal against conviction if they think that the conviction is unsafe; and

    (b) shall dismiss such an appeal in any other case.

(2) In the case of an appeal against conviction the Court shall, if they allow the appeal, quash the conviction.

(3) An order of the Court of Appeal quashing a conviction shall, except when under section 7 below the appellant is ordered to be retried, operate as a direction to the court of trial to enter, instead of the record of conviction, a judgment and verdict of acquittal.

3. Power to substitute conviction of alternative offence

(1) This section applies on an appeal against conviction, where the appellant has been convicted of an offence to which he did not plead guilty and the jury could on the indictment have found him guilty of some other offence, and on the finding of the jury it appears to the Court of Appeal that the jury must have been satisfied of facts which proved him guilty of the other offence.

(2) The Court may, instead of allowing or dismissing the appeal, substitute for the verdict found by the jury a verdict of guilty of the other offence, and pass such sentence in substitution for the sentence passed at the trial as may be authorised by law for the other offence, not being a sentence of greater severity.

3A. Power to substitute conviction of alternative offence after guilty plea

(1) This section applies on an appeal against conviction where—

    (a) an appellant has been convicted of an offence to which he pleaded guilty,

    (b) if he had not so pleaded, he could on the indictment have pleaded, or been found, guilty of some other offence, and

    (c) it appears to the Court of Appeal that the plea of guilty indicates an admission by the appellant of facts which prove him guilty of the other offence.

(2) The Court of Appeal may, instead of allowing or dismissing the appeal, substitute for the appellant's plea of guilty a plea of guilty of the other offence and pass such sentence in substitution for the sentence passed at the trial as may be authorised by law for the other offence, not being a sentence of greater severity.

12. Appeal against verdict of not guilty by reason of insanity

A person in whose case there is returned a verdict of not guilty by reason of insanity may appeal to the Court of Appeal against the verdict—

(a) with the leave of the Court of Appeal; or

(b) if the judge of the court of trial grants a certificate that the case if fit for appeal.

13.   Disposal of appeal under s 12

(1)   Subject to the provisions of this section, the Court of Appeal—

(a)   shall allow an appeal under section 12 of this Act if they think that the verdict is unsafe; and

(b)   shall dismiss such an appeal in any other case.

(3)   Where apart from this subsection—

(a)   an appeal under section 12 of this Act would fall to be allowed; and

(b)   none of the grounds for allowing it relates to the question of the insanity of the accused,

the Court of Appeal may dismiss the appeal if they are of opinion that, but for the insanity of the accused, the proper verdict would have been that he was guilty of an offence other than the offence charged.

(4)   Where an appeal under section 12 of this Act is allowed, the following provisions apply—

(a)   if the ground, or one of the grounds, for allowing the appeal is that the finding of the jury as to the insanity of the accused ought not to stand and the Court of Appeal are of opinion that the proper verdict would have been that he was guilty of an offence (whether the offence charged or any other offence of which the jury could have found him guilty), the Court—

(i)   shall substitute for the verdict of not guilty by reason of insanity a verdict of guilty of that offence; and

(ii)   shall, subject to subsection (5) below, have the like powers of punishing or otherwise dealing with the appellant, and other powers, as the court of trial would have had if the jury had come to the substituted verdict; and

(b)   in any other case, the Court of Appeal shall substitute for the verdict of the jury a verdict of acquittal.

CRIMINAL ATTEMPTS ACT 1981

1.   Attempting to commit an offence

(1)   If, with intent to commit an offence to which this section applies, a person does an act which is more than merely preparatory to the commission of the offence, he is guilty of attempting to commit the offence.

(1A)   Subject to section 8 of the Computer Misuse Act 1990 (relevance of external law), if this subsection applies to an act, what the person doing it had in view shall be treated as an offence to which this section applies.

(1B)   Subsection (1A) above applies to an act if—

(a)   it is done in England and Wales; and

(b)   it would fall within subsection (1) above as more than merely preparatory to the commission of an offence under section 3 of the Computer Misuse Act 1990 but for the fact that the offence, if completed, would not be an offence triable in England and Wales.

(2)   A person may be guilty of attempting to commit an offence to which this section applies even though the facts are such that the commission of the offence is impossible.

(3)   In any case where —

(a)   apart from this subsection a person's intention would not be regarded as having amounted to an intent to commit an offence: but

(b)   if the facts of the case had been as he believed them to be, his intention would be so regarded, then, for the purposes of subsection (1) above, he shall be regarded as having had an intent to commit that offence.

(4)   This section applies to any offence which, if it were completed, would be triable in England and Wales as an indictable offence, other than —

(a)   conspiracy (at common law or under section 1 of the Criminal Law Act 1977 or any other enactment);

(b)   aiding, abetting, counselling, procuring or suborning the commission of an offence;

(c) offences under section 4 (1) (assisting offenders) or 5 (1) (accepting or agreeing to accept consideration for not disclosing information about an arrestable offence) of the Criminal Law Act 1967.

1A. Extended jurisdiction in relation to certain attempts

(1) If this section applies to an act, what the person doing the act had in view shall be treated as an offence to which section 1(1) above applies.

(2) This section applies to an act if—

    (a) it is done in England and Wales, and

    (b) it would fall within section 1(1) above as more than merely preparatory to the commission of a Group A offence but for the fact that that offence, if completed, would not be an offence triable in England and Wales.

(3) In this section 'Group A offence' has the same meaning as in Part 1 of the Criminal Justice Act 1993.

(4) Subsection (1) above is subject to the provisions of section 6 of the Act of 1993 (relevance of external law).

(5) Where a person does any act to which this section applies, the offence which he commits shall for all purposes be treated as the offence of attempting to commit the relevant Group A offence.

4. Trial and penalties

(1) A person guilty by virtue of section 1 above of attempting to commit an offence shall —

    (a) if the offence attempted is murder or any other offence the sentence for which is fixed by law, be liable on conviction on indictment to imprisonment for life; and

    (b) if the offence attempted is indictable but does not fall within paragraph (a) above, be liable on conviction on indictment to any penalty to which he would have been liable on conviction on indictment of that offence; and

    (c) if the offence attempted is triable either way, be liable on summary conviction to any penalty to which he would have been liable on summary conviction of that offence.

(2) In any case in which a court may proceed to summary trial of an information charging a person with an offence and an information charging him with an offence under section 1 above of attempting to commit it or an attempt under a special statutory provision, the court may, without his consent, try the informations together.

(3) Where, in proceedings against a person for an offence under section 1 above, there is evidence sufficient in law to support a finding that he did an act falling within subsection (1) of that section, the question whether or not his act fell within that subsection is a question of fact.

6. Effect on common law

(1) The offence of attempt at common law and any offence at common law of procuring materials for crime are hereby abolished for all purposes not relating to acts done before the commencement of this Act.

(2) Except as regards offences committed before the commencement of this Act, references in any enactment passed before this Act which fall to be construed as references to the offence of attempt at common law shall be construed as references to the offence under section 1 above.

9. Interference with vehicles

(1) A person is guilty of the offence of vehicle interference if he interferes with a motor vehicle or trailer or with anything carried in or on a motor vehicle or trailer with the intention that any offence specified in subsection (2) below shall be committed by himself or some other person.

(2) The offences mentioned in subsection (1) above are—

    (a) theft of the motor vehicle or trailer or part of it;

    (b) theft of anything carried in or on the motor vehicle or trailer; and

(c)   an offence under section 12(1) of the Theft Act 1968 (taking and driving away without consent);

and, if it is shown that a person accused of an offence under this section intended that one of those offences should be committed, it is immaterial that it cannot be shown which it was.

(5)   In this section 'motor vehicle' and 'trailer' have the meanings assigned to them by section 190(1) of the Road Traffic Act 1972.

CRIMINAL DAMAGE ACT 1971

1.   **Destroying or damaging property**

(1)   A person who without lawful excuse destroys or damages any property belonging to another intending to destroy or damage any such property or being reckless as to whether any such property would be destroyed or damaged shall be guilty of an offence.

(2)   A person who without lawful excuse destroys or damages any property, whether belonging to himself or another—

     (a)   intending to destroy or damage any property or being reckless as to whether any property would be destroyed or damaged; and

     (b)   intending by the destruction or damage to endanger the life of another or being reckless as to whether the life of another would be thereby endangered;

   shall be guilty of an offence.

(3)   An offence committed under this section by destroying or damaging property by fire shall be charged as arson.

2.   **Threats to destroy or damage property**

A person who without lawful excuse makes to another a threat, intending that that other would fear it would be carried out,—

(a)   to destroy or damage any property belonging to that other or a third person; or

(b)   to destroy or damage his own property in a way which he knows is likely to endanger the life of that other or a third person;

shall be guilty of an offence.

3.   **Possessing anything with intent to destroy or damage property**

A person who has anything in his custody or under his control intending without lawful excuse to use it or cause or permit another to use it—

(a)   to destroy or damage any property belonging to some other person; or

(b)   to destroy or damage his own or the user's property in a way which he knows is likely to endanger the life of some other person;

shall be guilty of an offence.

4.   **Punishment of offences**

(1)   A person guilty of arson under section 1 above or of an offence under section 1 (2) above (whether arson or not) shall on conviction on indictment be liable to imprisonment for life.

(2)   A person guilty of any other offence under this Act shall on conviction on indictment be liable to imprisonment for a term not exceeding ten years.

5.   **'Without lawful excuse'**

(1)   This section applies to any offence under section 1(1) above and any offence under section 2 or 3 above other than one involving a threat by the person charged to destroy or damage property in a way which he knows is likely to endanger the life of another or involving an intent by the person charged to use or cause or permit the use of something in his custody or under his control so to destroy or damage property.

(2)   A person charged with an offence to which this section applies shall whether or not he would be treated for the purposes of this Act as having a lawful excuse apart from this subsection, be treated for those purposes as having a lawful excuse—

     (a)   if at the time of the act or acts alleged to constitute the offence he believed that the person or persons whom he believed to be entitled to consent to the destruction of or damage to the property in question had so consented, or would have so consented to it if he or they had known of the destruction or damage and its circumstances; or

(b)   if he destroyed or damaged or threatened to destroy or damage the property in question or, in the case of a charge of an offence under section 3 above, intended to use or cause or permit the use of something to destroy or damage it, in order to protect property belonging to himself or another or a right or interest in property which was or which he believed to be vested in himself or another, and at the time of the act or acts alleged to constitute the offence he believed—

    (i)   that the property, right or interest was in immediate need of protection; and

    (ii)   that the means of protection adopted or proposed to be adopted were or would be reasonable having regard to all the circumstances.

(3)   For the purposes of this section it is immaterial whether a belief is justified or not if it is honestly held.

(4)   For the purposes of subsection (2) above a right or interest in property includes any right or privilege in or over land, whether created by grant, licence or otherwise.

(5)   This section shall not be construed as casting doubt on any defence recognised by law as a defence to criminal charges.

10.   Interpretation

(1)   In this Act 'property' means property of a tangible nature, whether real or personal, including money and—

(a)   including wild creatures which have been tamed or are ordinarily kept in captivity, and any other wild creatures or their carcasses if, but only if, they have been reduced into possession which has not been lost or abandoned or are in the course of being reduced into possession; but

(b)   not including mushrooms growing wild on any land or flowers, fruit or foliage of a plant growing wild on any land.

For the purposes of this subsection 'mushroom' includes any fungus and 'plant' includes any shrub or tree.

(2)   Property shall be treated for the purposes of this Act as belonging to any person—

(a)   having the custody or control of it;

(b)   having in it any proprietary right or interest (not being an equitable interest arising only from an agreement to transfer or grant an interest); or

(c)   having a charge on it.

(3)   Where property is subject to a trust, the persons to whom it belongs shall be so treated as including any person having a right to enforce the trust.

(4)   Property of a corporation sole shall be so treated as belonging to the corporation notwithstanding a vacancy in the corporation.

CRIMINAL JUSTICE ACT 1925

47.   Abolition of presumption of coercion of married woman by husband

Any presumption of law that an offence committed by a wife in the presence of her husband is committed under the coercion of the husband is hereby abolished, but on a charge against a wife for any offence other than treason or murder it shall be a good defence to prove that the offence was committed in the presence of, and under the coercion of, the husband.

CRIMINAL JUSTICE ACT 1967

8.   Proof of criminal intent

A court or jury, in determining whether a person has committed an offence,—

(a)   shall not be bound in law to infer that he intended or foresaw a result of his actions by reason only of its being a natural and probable consequence of those actions; but

(b) shall decide whether he did intend or foresee that result by reference to all the evidence, drawing such inferences from the evidence as appear proper in the circumstances.

CRIMINAL JUSTICE ACT 1987

12.   Charges of and penalty for conspiracy to defraud

(1) If—

    (a) a person agrees with any other person or persons that a course of conduct shall be pursued; and

    (b) that course of conduct will necessarily amount to or involve the commission of any offence or offences by one or more of the parties to the agreement if the agreement is carried out in accordance with their intentions,

the fact that it will do so shall not preclude a charge of conspiracy to defraud being brought against any of them in respect of the agreement.

CRIMINAL JUSTICE ACT 1988

39.   Common assault and battery to be summary offences

Common assault and battery shall be summary offences and a person guilty of either of them shall be liable to a fine not exceeding level 5 on the standard scale, to imprisonment for a term not exceeding six months, or to both.

134.   Torture

(1) A public official or person acting in an official capacity, whatever his nationality, commits the offence of torture if in the United Kingdom or elsewhere he intentionally inflicts severe pain or suffering on another in the performance or purported performance of his official duties.

(2) A person not falling within subsection (1) above commits the offence of torture, whatever his nationality, if—

    (a) in the United Kingdom or elsewhere he intentionally inflicts severe pain or suffering on another at the instigation or with the consent or acquiescence—

        (i) of a public official; or

        (ii) of a person acting in an official capacity; and

    (b) the official or other person is performing or purporting to perform his official duties when he instigates the commission of the offence or consents to or acquiesces in it.

(3) It is immaterial whether the pain or suffering is physical or mental and whether it is caused by an act or an omission.

(4) It shall be a defence for a person charged with an offence under this section in respect of any conduct of his to prove that he had lawful authority, justification or excuse for that conduct.

(5) For the purposes of this section 'lawful authority, justification or excuse' means—

    (a) in relation to pain or suffering inflicted in the United Kingdom, lawful authority, justification or excuse under the law of the part of the United Kingdom where it was inflicted;

    (b) in relation to pain or suffering inflicted outside the United Kingdom—

        (i) if it was inflicted by a United Kingdom official acting under the law of the United Kingdom or by a person acting in an official capacity under that law, lawful authority, justification or excuse under that law;

        (ii) if it was inflicted by a United Kingdom official acting under the law of any part of the United Kingdom or by a person acting in an official capacity under such law, lawful authority, justification or excuse under the law of the part of the United Kingdom under whose law he was acting; and

        (iii) in any other case, lawful authority, justification or excuse under the law of the place where it was inflicted.

    (6)   A person who commits the offence of torture shall be liable on conviction on indictment to imprisonment for life.

139. Having article with blade or point in public place

    (1)   Subject to subsections (4) and (5) below, any person who has an article to which this section applies with him in a public place shall be guilty of an offence.

    (2)   Subject to subsection (3) below, this section applies to any article which has a blade or is sharply pointed except a folding pocketknife.

    (3)   This section applies to a folding pocketknife if the cutting edge of its blade exceeds 3 inches.

    (4)   It shall be a defence for a person charged with an offence under this section to prove that he had good reason or lawful authority for having the article with him in a public place.

    (5)   Without prejudice to the generality of subsection (4) above, it shall be a defence for a person charged with an offence under this section to prove that he had the article with him—

        (a)   for use at work;

        (b)   for religious reasons; or

        (c)   as part of any national costume.

    (6)   A person guilty of an offence under subsection (1) above shall be liable—

        (a)   on summary conviction, to imprisonment for a term not exceeding six months, or a fine not exceeding the statutory maximum, or both;

        (b)   on conviction on indictment, to imprisonment for a term not exceeding two years, or a fine, or both.

    (7)   In this section 'public place' includes any place to which at the material time the public have or are permitted access, whether on payment or otherwise.

139A. Offence of having article with blade or point (or offensive weapon) on school premises

    (1)   Any person who has an article to which section 139 of this Act applies with him on school premises shall be guilty of an offence.

    (2)   Any person who has an offensive weapon within the meaning of section 1 of the Prevention of Crime Act 1953 with him on school premises shall be guilty of an offence.

    (3)   It shall be a defence for a person charged with an offence under subsection (1) or (2) above to prove that he had good reason or lawful authority for having the article or weapon with him on the premises in question.

    (4)   Without prejudice to the generality of subsection (3) above, it shall be a defence for a person charged with an offence under subsection (1) or (2) above to prove that he had the article or weapon in question with him—

        (a)   for use at work,

        (b)   for educational purposes,

        (c)   for religious reasons, or

        (d)   as part of any national costume.

    (6)   In this section and section 139B, 'school premises' means land used for the purposes of a school excluding any land occupied solely as a dwelling by a person employed at the school; and 'school' has the meaning given by section 4 of the Education Act 1996.

141. Offensive weapons

    (1)   Any person who manufactures, sells or hires or offers for sale or hire, exposes or has in his possession for the purpose of sale or hire, or lends or gives to any other person, a weapon to which this section applies shall be guilty of an offence and liable on summary conviction to imprisonment for a term not exceeding six months or to a fine not exceeding level 5 on the standard scale or both.

    (2)   The Secretary of State may by order made by statutory instrument direct that this section shall apply to any description of weapon specified in the order except—

        (a)   any weapon subject to the Firearms Act 1968; and

        (b)   crossbows.

(3)   A statutory instrument containing an order under this section shall not be made unless a draft of the instrument has been laid before Parliament and has been approved by a resolution of each House of Parliament.

(4)   The importation of a weapon to which this section applies is hereby prohibited.

(5)   It shall be a defence for any person charged in respect of any conduct of his relating to a weapon to which this section applies—

(a)   with an offence under subsection (1) above; or

(b)   with an offence under section 50(2) or (3) of the Customs and Excise Management Act 1979 (improper importation),

to prove that his conduct was only for the purposes of functions carried out on behalf of the Crown or of a visiting force.

(8)   It shall be a defence for any person charged in respect of any conduct of his relating to a weapon to which this section applies—

(a)   with an offence under subsection (1) above; or

(b)   with an offence under section 50(2) or (3) of the Customs and Excise Management Act 1979,

to prove that the conduct in question was only for the purposes of making the weapon available to a museum or gallery to which this subsection applies.

(9)   If a person acting on behalf of a museum or gallery to which subsection (8) above applies is charged with hiring or lending a weapon to which this section applies, it shall be a defence for him to prove that he had reasonable grounds for believing that the person to whom he lent or hired it would use it only for cultural, artistic or educational purposes.

(10) Subsection (8) above applies to a museum or gallery only if it does not distribute profits.

141A. Sale of knives and certain articles with blade or point to persons under sixteen

(1)   Any person who sells to a person under the age of sixteen years an article to which this section applies shall be guilty of an offence and liable on summary conviction to imprisonment for a term not exceeding six months, or a fine not exceeding level 5 on the standard scale, or both.

(2)   Subject to subsection (3) below, this section applies to—

(a)   any knife, knife blade or razor blade,

(b)   any axe, and

(c)   any other article which has a blade or which is sharply pointed and which is made or adapted for use for causing injury to the person.

(3)   This section does not apply to any article described in—

(a)   section 1 of the Restriction of Offensive Weapons Act 1959,

(b)   an order made under section 141(2) of this Act, or

(c)   an order made by the Secretary of State under this section.

(4)   It shall be a defence for a person charged with an offence under subsection (1) above to prove that he took all reasonable precautions and exercised all due diligence to avoid the commission of the offence.

160. Possession of indecent photograph of child

(1)   Subject to subsection (1A) it is an offence for a person to have any indecent photograph or pseudo-photograph of a child . . . in his possession.

(2)   Where a person is charged with an offence under subsection (1) above, it shall be a defence for him to prove—

(a)   that he had a legitimate reason for having the photograph or pseudo-photograph in his possession; or

(b)   that he had not himself seen the photograph or pseudo-photograph and did not know, nor had any cause to suspect, it to be indecent; or

(c)   that the photograph or pseudo-photograph was sent to him without any prior request made by him or on his behalf and that he did not keep it for an unreasonable time.

(2A) A person shall be liable on conviction on indictment of an offence under this section to imprisonment for a term not exceeding five years or a fine, or both.

(4)   Sections 1(3), 2(3), 3 and 7 of the Protection of Children Act 1978 shall have effect as if any reference in them to that Act included a reference to this section.

160A. Marriage and other relationships

(1)   This section applies where, in proceedings for an offence under section 160 relating to an indecent photograph of a child, the defendant proves that the photograph was of the child aged 16 or over, and that at the time of the offence charged the child and he—
    (a)   were married or civil partners of each other, or
    (b)   lived together as partners in an enduring family relationship.

(2)   This section also applies where, in proceedings for an offence under section 160 relating to an indecent photograph of a child, the defendant proves that the photograph was of the child aged 16 or over, and that at the time when he obtained it the child and he—
    (a)   were married or civil partners of each other, or
    (b)   lived together as partners in an enduring family relationship.

(3)   This section applies whether the photograph showed the child alone or with the defendant, but not if it showed any other person.

(4)   If sufficient evidence is adduced to raise an issue as to whether the child consented to the photograph being in the defendant's possession, or as to whether the defendant reasonably believed that the child so consented, the defendant is not guilty of the offence unless it is proved that the child did not so consent and that the defendant did not reasonably believe that the child so consented.

CRIMINAL JUSTICE ACT 1993

1.   Offences to which this Part applies

(1)   This Part applies to two groups of offences–
    (a)   any offence mentioned in subsection (2) (a 'Group A offence') and
    (b)   any offence mentioned in subsection (3) (a 'Group B offence').

(2)   The Group A offences are—
    (a)   an offence under any of the following provisions of the Theft Act 1968—
        section 1 (theft);
        section 15 (obtaining property by deception));
        section 15A (obtaining a money transfer by deception);
        section 16 (obtaining pecuniary advantage by deception);
        section 17 (false accounting);
        section 19 (false statements by company directors, etc);
        section 20(2) (procuring execution of valuable security by deception);
        section 21 (blackmail);
        section 22 (handling stolen goods);
        section 24A (retaining credits from dishonest sources, etc);
    (b)   an offence under either of the following provisions of the Theft Act 1978—
        section 1 (obtaining services by deception);
        section 2 (avoiding liability by deception);
    (c)   an offence under any of the following provisions of the Forgery and Counterfeiting Act 1981—
        section 1 (forgery);
        section 2 (copying a false instrument);
        section 3 (using a false instrument);
        section 4 (using a copy of a false instrument);
        section 5 (offences which relate to money orders, share certificates, passports, etc);
        section 14 (offences of counterfeiting notes and coins);
        section 15 (offences of passing etc counterfeit notes and coins);
        section 16 (offences involving the custody or control of counterfeit notes and coins);

section 17 (offences involving the making or custody or control of counterfeiting materials and implements);

section 20 (prohibition of importation of counterfeit notes and coins);

section 21 (prohibition of exportation of counterfeit notes and coins);

(d) the common law offence of cheating in relation to the public revenue.

(3) The Group B offences are—

(a) conspiracy to commit a Group A offence;

(b) conspiracy to defraud;

(c) attempting to commit a Group A offence;

(d) incitement to commit a Group A offence.

(4) The Secretary of State may by order amend subsection (2) or (3) by adding or removing any offence.

(5) The power to make such an order shall be exercisable by statutory instrument.

(6) No order shall be made under subsection (4) unless a draft of it has been laid before and approved by a resolution of each House of Parliament.

2.   Jurisdiction in respect of Group A offences

(1) For the purposes of this Part, 'relevant event', in relation to any Group A offence, means any act or omission or other event (including any result of one or more acts or omissions) proof of which is required for conviction of the offence.

(2) For the purpose of determining whether or not a particular event is a relevant event in relation to a Group A offence, any question as to where it occurred is to be disregarded.

(3) A person may be guilty of a Group A offence if any of the events which are relevant events in relation to the offence occurred in England and Wales.

3.   Questions immaterial to jurisdiction in the case of certain offences.

(1) A person may be guilty of a Group A or Group B offence whether or not—

(a) he was a British citizen at any material time;

(b) he was in England and Wales at any such time.

(2) On a charge of conspiracy to commit a Group A offence, or on a charge of conspiracy to defraud in England and Wales, the defendant may be guilty of the offence whether or not—

(a) he became a party to the conspiracy in England and Wales;

(b) any act or omission or other event in relation to the conspiracy occurred in England and Wales.

(3) On a charge of attempting to commit a Group A offence, the defendant may be guilty of the offence whether or not—

(a) the attempt was made in England and Wales;

(b) it had an effect in England and Wales.

(4) Subsection (1)(a) does not apply where jurisdiction is given to try the offence in question by an enactment which makes provision by reference to the nationality of the person charged.

(5) Subsection (2) does not apply in relation to any charge under the Criminal Law Act 1977 brought by virtue of section 1A of that Act.

(6) Subsection (3) does not apply in relation to any charge under the Criminal Attempts Act 1981 brought by virtue of section 1A of that Act.

4.   Rules for determining certain jurisdictional questions relating to the location of events

In relation to a Group A or Group B offence—

(a) there is an obtaining of property in England and Wales if the property is either despatched from or received at a place in England and Wales; and

(b) there is a communication in England and Wales of any information, instruction, request, demand or other matter if it is sent by any means—

(i) from a place in England and Wales to a place elsewhere; or

(ii) from a place elsewhere to a place in England and Wales.

5.   Conspiracy, attempt and incitement

(3)   A person may be guilty of conspiracy to defraud if—

(a)   a party to the agreement constituting the conspiracy, or a party's agent, did anything in England and Wales in relation to the agreement before its formation, or

(b)   a party to it became a party in England and Wales (by joining it either in person or through an agent), or

(c)   a party to it, or a party's agent, did or omitted anything in England and Wales in pursuance of it,

and the conspiracy would be triable in England and Wales but for the fraud which the parties to it had in view not being intended to take place in England and Wales.

6.   Relevance of external law

(1)   A person is guilty of an offence triable by virtue of section 5(3), only if the pursuit of the agreed course of conduct would at some stage involve—

(a)   an act or omission by one or more of the parties, or

(b)   the happening of some other event,

constituting an offence under the law in force where the act, omission or other event was intended to take place.

(2)   A person is guilty of an offence triable by virtue of section 1A of the Criminal Attempts Act 1981, or by virtue of section 5(4), only if what he had in view would involve the commission of an offence under the law in force where the whole or any part of it was intended to take place.

(3)   Conduct punishable under the law in force in any place is an offence under that law for the purposes of this section, however it is described in that law.

CRIMINAL JUSTICE ACT 2003

98.   Bad character

References in this Chapter to evidence of a person's 'bad character' are to evidence of, or of a disposition towards, misconduct on his part, other than evidence which—

(a)   has to do with the alleged facts of the offence with which the defendant is charged, or

(b)   is evidence of misconduct in connection with the investigation or prosecution of that offence.

99   Abolition of common law rules

(1)   The common law rules governing the admissibility of evidence of bad character in criminal proceedings are abolished.

(2)   Subsection (1) is subject to section 118(1) in so far as it preserves the rule under which in criminal proceedings a person's reputation is admissible for the purposes of proving his bad character.

100   Non-defendant's bad character

(1)   In criminal proceedings evidence of the bad character of a person other than the defendant is admissible if and only if—

(a)   it is important explanatory evidence,

(b)   it has substantial probative value in relation to a matter which—

(i)   is a matter in issue in the proceedings, and

(ii)   is of substantial importance in the context of the case as a whole, or

(c) all parties to the proceedings agree to the evidence being admissible.

(2)   For the purposes of subsection (1)(a) evidence is important explanatory evidence if—

(a)   without it, the court or jury would find it impossible or difficult properly to understand other evidence in the case, and

(b)   its value for understanding the case as a whole is substantial.

(3)   In assessing the probative value of evidence for the purposes of subsection (1)(b) the court must have regard to the following factors (and to any others it considers relevant)—

    (a)   the nature and number of the events, or other things, to which the evidence relates;

    (b)   when those events or things are alleged to have happened or existed;

    (c)   where—

        (i)   the evidence is evidence of a person's misconduct, and

        (ii) it is suggested that the evidence has probative value by reason of similarity between that misconduct and other alleged misconduct,

        the nature and extent of the similarities and the dissimilarities between each of the alleged instances of misconduct;

    (d)   where—

        (i)   the evidence is evidence of a person's misconduct,

        (ii) it is suggested that that person is also responsible for the misconduct charged, and

        (iii) the identity of the person responsible for the misconduct charged is disputed,

        the extent to which the evidence shows or tends to show that the same person was responsible each time.

  (4)   Except where subsection (1)(c) applies, evidence of the bad character of a person other than the defendant must not be given without leave of the court.

101   Defendant's bad character

  (1)   In criminal proceedings evidence of the defendant's bad character is admissible if, but only if—

    (a)   all parties to the proceedings agree to the evidence being admissible,

    (b)   the evidence is adduced by the defendant himself or is given in answer to a question asked by him in cross-examination and intended to elicit it,

    (c)   it is important explanatory evidence,

    (d)   it is relevant to an important matter in issue between the defendant and the prosecution,

    (e)   it has substantial probative value in relation to an important matter in issue between the defendant and a co-defendant,

    (f)   it is evidence to correct a false impression given by the defendant, or

    (g)   the defendant has made an attack on another person's character.

  (2)   Sections 102 to 106 contain provision supplementing subsection (1).

  (3)   The court must not admit evidence under subsection (1)(d) or (g) if, on an application by the defendant to exclude it, it appears to the court that the admission of the evidence would have such an adverse effect on the fairness of the proceedings that the court ought not to admit it.

  (4)   On an application to exclude evidence under subsection (3) the court must have regard, in particular, to the length of time between the matters to which that evidence relates and the matters which form the subject of the offence charged.

102   Important explanatory evidence

For the purposes of section 101(1)(c) evidence is important explanatory evidence if—

  (a)   without it, the court or jury would find it impossible or difficult properly to understand other evidence in the case, and

  (b)   its value for understanding the case as a whole is substantial.

103   Matter in issue between the defendant and the prosecution

  (1)   For the purposes of section 101(1)(d) the matters in issue between the defendant and the prosecution include—

    (a)   the question whether the defendant has a propensity to commit offences of the kind with which he is charged, except where his having such a propensity makes it no more likely that he is guilty of the offence;

    (b)   the question whether the defendant has a propensity to be untruthful, except where it is not suggested that the defendant's case is untruthful in any respect.

  (2)   Where subsection (1)(a) applies, a defendant's propensity to commit offences of the kind with which he is charged may (without prejudice to any other way of doing so) be established by evidence that he has been convicted of—

      (a)   an offence of the same description as the one with which he is charged, or

      (b)   an offence of the same category as the one with which he is charged.

(3)   Subsection (2) does not apply in the case of a particular defendant if the court is satisfied, by reason of the length of time since the conviction or for any other reason, that it would be unjust for it to apply in his case.

(4)   For the purposes of subsection (2)—

      (a)   two offences are of the same description as each other if the statement of the offence in a written charge or indictment would, in each case, be in the same terms;

      (b)   two offences are of the same category as each other if they belong to the same category of offences prescribed for the purposes of this section by an order made by the Secretary of State.

(5)   A category prescribed by an order under subsection (4)(b) must consist of offences of the same type.

(6)   Only prosecution evidence is admissible under section 101(1)(d).

104   Matter in issue between the defendant and a co-defendant

(1)   Evidence which is relevant to the question whether the defendant has a propensity to be untruthful is admissible on that basis under section 101(1)(e) only if the nature or conduct of his defence is such as to undermine the co-defendant's defence.

(2)   Only evidence—

      (a)   which is to be (or has been) adduced by the co-defendant, or

      (b)   which a witness is to be invited to give (or has given) in cross-examination by the co-defendant,

    is admissible under section 101(1)(e).

105   Evidence to correct a false impression

(1)   For the purposes of section 101(1)(f)—

      (a)   the defendant gives a false impression if he is responsible for the making of an express or implied assertion which is apt to give the court or jury a false or misleading impression about the defendant;

      (b)   evidence to correct such an impression is evidence which has probative value in correcting it.

(2)   A defendant is treated as being responsible for the making of an assertion if—

      (a)   the assertion is made by the defendant in the proceedings (whether or not in evidence given by him),

      (b)   the assertion was made by the defendant—

          (i)   on being questioned under caution, before charge, about the offence with which he is charged, or

          (ii)   on being charged with the offence or officially informed that he might be prosecuted for it, and evidence of the assertion is given in the proceedings,

      (c)   the assertion is made by a witness called by the defendant,

      (d)   the assertion is made by any witness in cross-examination in response to a question asked by the defendant that is intended to elicit it, or is likely to do so, or

      (e)   the assertion was made by any person out of court, and the defendant adduces evidence of it in the proceedings.

(3)   A defendant who would otherwise be treated as responsible for the making of an assertion shall not be so treated if, or to the extent that, he withdraws it or disassociates himself from it.

(4)   Where it appears to the court that a defendant, by means of his conduct (other than the giving of evidence) in the proceedings, is seeking to give the court or jury an impression about himself that is false or misleading, the court may if it appears just to do so treat the defendant as being responsible for the making of an assertion which is apt to give that impression.

(5)   In subsection (4) 'conduct' includes appearance or dress.

(6)   Evidence is admissible under section 101(1)(f) only if it goes no further than is necessary to correct the false impression.

(7)   Only prosecution evidence is admissible under section 101(1)(f).

106   Attack on another person's character

(1)   For the purposes of section 101(1)(g) a defendant makes an attack on another person's character if—

    (a)   he adduces evidence attacking the other person's character,

    (b)   he (or any legal representative appointed under section 38(4) of the Youth Justice and Criminal Evidence Act 1999 to cross-examine a witness in his interests) asks questions in cross-examination that are intended to elicit such evidence, or are likely to do so, or

    (c)   evidence is given of an imputation about the other person made by the defendant—

        (i)   on being questioned under caution, before charge, about the offence with which he is charged, or

        (ii)   on being charged with the offence or officially informed that he might be prosecuted for it.

(2)   In subsection (1) 'evidence attacking the other person's character' means evidence to the effect that the other person—

    (a)   has committed an offence (whether a different offence from the one with which the defendant is charged or the same one), or

    (b)   has behaved, or is disposed to behave, in a reprehensible way;

and 'imputation about the other person' means an assertion to that effect.

(3)   Only prosecution evidence is admissible under section 101(1)(g).

107   Stopping the case where evidence contaminated

(1)   If on a defendant's trial before a judge and jury for an offence—

    (a)   evidence of his bad character has been admitted under any of paragraphs (c) to (g) of section 101(1), and

    (b)   the court is satisfied at any time after the close of the case for the prosecution that—

        (i)   the evidence is contaminated, and

        (ii)   the contamination is such that, considering the importance of the evidence to the case against the defendant, his conviction of the offence would be unsafe, the court must either direct the jury to acquit the defendant of the offence or, if it considers that there ought to be a retrial, discharge the jury.

(2)   Where—

    (a)   a jury is directed under subsection (1) to acquit a defendant of an offence, and

    (b)   the circumstances are such that, apart from this subsection, the defendant could if acquitted of that offence be found guilty of another offence, the defendant may not be found guilty of that other offence if the court is satisfied as mentioned in subsection (1)(b) in respect of it.

(3)   If—

    (a)   a jury is required to determine under section 4A(2) of the Criminal Procedure (Insanity) Act 1964 whether a person charged on an indictment with an offence did the act or made the omission charged,

    (b)   evidence of the person's bad character has been admitted under any of paragraphs (c) to (g) of section 101(1), and

    (c)   the court is satisfied at any time after the close of the case for the prosecution that—

        (i)   the evidence is contaminated, and

        (ii)   the contamination is such that, considering the importance of the evidence to the case against the person, a finding that he did the act or made the omission would be unsafe,

the court must either direct the jury to acquit the defendant of the offence or, if it considers that there ought to be a rehearing, discharge the jury.

(4)   This section does not prejudice any other power a court may have to direct a jury to acquit a person of an offence or to discharge a jury.

(5)   For the purposes of this section a person's evidence is contaminated where—

    (a)   as a result of an agreement or understanding between the person and one or more others, or

    (b)   as a result of the person being aware of anything alleged by one or more others whose evidence may be, or has been, given in the proceedings, the evidence is false or misleading in any respect, or is different from what it would otherwise have been.

108   Offences committed by defendant when a child

(1)   Section 16(2) and (3) of the Children and Young Persons Act 1963 (offences committed by person under 14 disregarded for purposes of evidence relating to previous convictions) shall cease to have effect.

(2)   In proceedings for an offence committed or alleged to have been committed by the defendant when aged 21 or over, evidence of his conviction for an offence when under the age of 14 is not admissible unless—

    (a)   both of the offences are triable only on indictment, and

    (b)   the court is satisfied that the interests of justice require the evidence to be admissible.

(3)   Subsection (2) applies in addition to section 101.

109   Assumption of truth in assessment of relevance or probative value

(1)   Subject to subsection (2), a reference in this Chapter to the relevance or probative value of evidence is a reference to its relevance or probative value on the assumption that it is true.

(2)   In assessing the relevance or probative value of an item of evidence for any purpose of this Chapter, a court need not assume that the evidence is true if it appears, on the basis of any material before the court (including any evidence it decides to hear on the matter), that no court or jury could reasonably find it to be true.

110   Court's duty to give reasons for rulings

(1)   Where the court makes a relevant ruling—

    (a)   it must state in open court (but in the absence of the jury, if there is one) its reasons for the ruling;

    (b)   if it is a magistrates' court, it must cause the ruling and the reasons for it to be entered in the register of the court's proceedings.

(2)   In this section 'relevant ruling' means—

    (a)   a ruling on whether an item of evidence is evidence of a person's bad character;

    (b)   a ruling on whether an item of such evidence is admissible under section 100 or 101 (including a ruling on an application under section 101(3));

    (c)   a ruling under section 107.

112   Interpretation of Chapter 1

(1)   In this Chapter—

'bad character' is to be read in accordance with section 98;

'criminal proceedings' means criminal proceedings in relation to which the strict rules of evidence apply;

'defendant', in relation to criminal proceedings, means a person charged with an offence in those proceedings; and 'co-defendant', in relation to a defendant, means a person charged with an offence in the same proceedings;

'important matter' means a matter of substantial importance in the context of the case as a whole;

'misconduct' means the commission of an offence or other reprehensible behaviour;

'offence' includes a service offence;

'probative value', and 'relevant' (in relation to an item of evidence), are to be read in accordance with section 109;

'prosecution evidence' means evidence which is to be (or has been) adduced by the prosecution, or which a witness is to be invited to give (or has given) in cross-examination by the prosecution;

'service offence' means an offence under the Army Act 1955, the Air Force Act 1955 or the Naval Discipline Act 1957;

'written charge' has the same meaning as in section 29 and also includes an information.

(2) Where a defendant is charged with two or more offences in the same criminal proceedings, this Chapter (except section 101(3)) has effect as if each offence were charged in separate proceedings; and references to the offence with which the defendant is charged are to be read accordingly.

(3) Nothing in this Chapter affects the exclusion of evidence—

    (a) under the rule in section 3 of the Criminal Procedure Act 1865 against a party impeaching the credit of his own witness by general evidence of bad character,

    (b) under section 41 of the Youth Justice and Criminal Evidence Act 1999 (restriction on evidence or questions about complainant's sexual history), or

    (c) on grounds other than the fact that it is evidence of a person's bad character.

114 Admissibility of hearsay evidence

(1) In criminal proceedings a statement not made in oral evidence in the proceedings is admissible as evidence of any matter stated if, but only if—

    (a) any provision of this Chapter or any other statutory provision makes it admissible,

    (b) any rule of law preserved by section 118 makes it admissible,

    (c) all parties to the proceedings agree to it being admissible, or (d) the court is satisfied that it is in the interests of justice for it to be admissible.

(2) In deciding whether a statement not made in oral evidence should be admitted under subsection (1)(d), the court must have regard to the following factors (and to any others it considers relevant)—

    (a) how much probative value the statement has (assuming it to be true) in relation to a matter in issue in the proceedings, or how valuable it is for the understanding of other evidence in the case;

    (b) what other evidence has been, or can be, given on the matter or evidence mentioned in paragraph (a);

    (c) how important the matter or evidence mentioned in paragraph (a) is in the context of the case as a whole;

    (d) the circumstances in which the statement was made;

    (e) how reliable the maker of the statement appears to be;

    (f) how reliable the evidence of the making of the statement appears to be;

    (g) whether oral evidence of the matter stated can be given and, if not, why it cannot;

    (h) the amount of difficulty involved in challenging the statement;

    (i) the extent to which that difficulty would be likely to prejudice the party facing it.

(3) Nothing in this Chapter affects the exclusion of evidence of a statement on grounds other than the fact that it is a statement not made in oral evidence in the proceedings.

115 Statements and matters stated

(1) In this Chapter references to a statement or to a matter stated are to be read as follows.

(2) A statement is any representation of fact or opinion made by a person by whatever means; and it includes a representation made in a sketch, photofit or other pictorial form.

(3) A matter stated is one to which this Chapter applies if (and only if) the purpose, or one of the purposes, of the person making the statement appears to the court to have been—

    (a) to cause another person to believe the matter, or

    (b) to cause another person to act or a machine to operate on the basis that the matter is as stated.

Principal categories of admissibility

116 Cases where a witness is unavailable

(1) In criminal proceedings a statement not made in oral evidence in the proceedings is admissible as evidence of any matter stated if—

      (a)   oral evidence given in the proceedings by the person who made the statement would be admissible as evidence of that matter,

      (b)   the person who made the statement (the relevant person) is identified to the court's satisfaction, and

      (c)   any of the five conditions mentioned in subsection (2) is satisfied.

(2)   The conditions are—

      (a)   that the relevant person is dead;

      (b)   that the relevant person is unfit to be a witness because of his bodily or mental condition;

      (c)   that the relevant person is outside the United Kingdom and it is not reasonably practicable to secure his attendance;

      (d)   that the relevant person cannot be found although such steps as it is reasonably practicable to take to find him have been taken;

      (e)   that through fear the relevant person does not give (or does not continue to give) oral evidence in the proceedings, either at all or in connection with the subject matter of the statement, and the court gives leave for the statement to be given in evidence.

(3)   For the purposes of subsection (2)(e) 'fear' is to be widely construed and (for example) includes fear of the death or injury of another person or of financial loss.

(4)   Leave may be given under subsection (2)(e) only if the court considers that the statement ought to be admitted in the interests of justice, having regard—

      (a)   to the statement's contents,

      (b)   to any risk that its admission or exclusion will result in unfairness to any party to the proceedings (and in particular to how difficult it will be to challenge the statement if the relevant person does not give oral evidence),

      (c)   in appropriate cases, to the fact that a direction under section 19 of the Youth Justice and Criminal Evidence Act 1999 (special measures for the giving of evidence by fearful witnesses etc) could be made in relation to the relevant person, and

      (d)   to any other relevant circumstances.

(5)   A condition set out in any paragraph of subsection (2) which is in fact satisfied is to be treated as not satisfied if it is shown that the circumstances described in that paragraph are caused—

      (a)   by the person in support of whose case it is sought to give the statement in evidence, or

      (b)   by a person acting on his behalf,

in order to prevent the relevant person giving oral evidence in the proceedings (whether at all or in connection with the subject matter of the statement).

117 Business and other documents

(1)   In criminal proceedings a statement contained in a document is admissible as evidence of any matter stated if—

      (a)   oral evidence given in the proceedings would be admissible as evidence of that matter,

      (b)   the requirements of subsection (2) are satisfied, and

      (c)   the requirements of subsection (5) are satisfied, in a case where subsection (4) requires them to be.

(2)   The requirements of this subsection are satisfied if—

      (a)   the document or the part containing the statement was created or received by a person in the course of a trade, business, profession or other occupation, or as the holder of a paid or unpaid office,

      (b)   the person who supplied the information contained in the statement (the relevant person) had or may reasonably be supposed to have had personal knowledge of the matters dealt with, and

      (c)   each person (if any) through whom the information was supplied from the relevant person to the person mentioned in paragraph (a) received the information in the course of a trade, business, profession or other occupation, or as the holder of a paid or unpaid office.

(3)   The persons mentioned in paragraphs (a) and (b) of subsection (2) may be the same person.

(4)   The additional requirements of subsection (5) must be satisfied if the statement—
    (a)   was prepared for the purposes of pending or contemplated criminal proceedings, or for a criminal investigation, but
    (b)   was not obtained pursuant to a request under section 7 of the Crime (International Co-operation) Act 2003 or an order under paragraph 6 of Schedule 13 to the Criminal Justice Act 1988 (which relate to overseas evidence).

(5)   The requirements of this subsection are satisfied if—
    (a)   any of the five conditions mentioned in section 116(2) is satisfied (absence of relevant person etc), or
    (b)   the relevant person cannot reasonably be expected to have any recollection of the matters dealt with in the statement (having regard to the length of time since he supplied the information and all other circumstances).

(6)   A statement is not admissible under this section if the court makes a direction to that effect under subsection (7).

(7)   The court may make a direction under this subsection if satisfied that the statement's reliability as evidence for the purpose for which it is tendered is doubtful in view of—
    (a)   its contents,
    (b)   the source of the information contained in it,
    (c)   the way in which or the circumstances in which the information was supplied or received, or
    (d)   the way in which or the circumstances in which the document concerned was created or received.

118   Preservation of certain common law categories of admissibility

(1)   The following rules of law are preserved.

Public information etc

1   Any rule of law under which in criminal proceedings—
    (a)   published works dealing with matters of a public nature (such as histories, scientific works, dictionaries and maps) are admissible as evidence of facts of a public nature stated in them,
    (b)   public documents (such as public registers, and returns made under public authority with respect to matters of public interest) are admissible as evidence of facts stated in them,
    (c)   records (such as the records of certain courts, treaties, Crown grants, pardons and commissions) are admissible as evidence of facts stated in them, or
    (d)   evidence relating to a person's age or date or place of birth may be given by a person without personal knowledge of the matter.

Reputation as to character

2   Any rule of law under which in criminal proceedings evidence of a person's reputation is admissible for the purpose of proving his good or bad character.

Note

The rule is preserved only so far as it allows the court to treat such evidence as proving the matter concerned.

Reputation or family tradition

3   Any rule of law under which in criminal proceedings evidence of reputation or family tradition is admissible for the purpose of proving or disproving—
    (a)   pedigree or the existence of a marriage,
    (b)   the existence of any public or general right, or
    (c)   the identity of any person or thing.

Note

The rule is preserved only so far as it allows the court to treat such evidence as proving or disproving the matter concerned.

Res gestae

4   Any rule of law under which in criminal proceedings a statement is admissible as evidence of any matter stated if—

(a)   the statement was made by a person so emotionally overpowered by an event that the possibility of concoction or distortion can be disregarded,

(b)   the statement accompanied an act which can be properly evaluated as evidence only if considered in conjunction with the statement, or

(c)   the statement relates to a physical sensation or a mental state (such as intention or emotion).

Confessions etc

5   Any rule of law relating to the admissibility of confessions or mixed statements in criminal proceedings.

Admissions by agents etc

6   Any rule of law under which in criminal proceedings—

(a) an admission made by an agent of a defendant is admissible against the defendant as evidence of any matter stated, or

(b)   a statement made by a person to whom a defendant refers a person for information is admissible against the defendant as evidence of any matter stated.

Common enterprise

7   Any rule of law under which in criminal proceedings a statement made by a party to a common enterprise is admissible against another party to the enterprise as evidence of any matter stated.

Expert evidence

8   Any rule of law under which in criminal proceedings an expert witness may draw on the body of expertise relevant to his field.

(2)   With the exception of the rules preserved by this section, the common law rules governing the admissibility of hearsay evidence in criminal proceedings are abolished.

119   Inconsistent statements

(1)   If in criminal proceedings a person gives oral evidence and—

(a)   he admits making a previous inconsistent statement, or

(b)   a previous inconsistent statement made by him is proved by virtue of section 3, 4 or 5 of the Criminal Procedure Act 1865,

the statement is admissible as evidence of any matter stated of which oral evidence by him would be admissible.

(2)   If in criminal proceedings evidence of an inconsistent statement by any person is given under section 1 24(2)(c), the statement is admissible as evidence of any matter stated in it of which oral evidence by that person would be admissible.

120   Other previous statements of witnesses

(1)   This section applies where a person (the witness) is called to give evidence in criminal proceedings.

(2)   If a previous statement by the witness is admitted as evidence to rebut a suggestion that his oral evidence has been fabricated, that statement is admissible as evidence of any matter stated of which oral evidence by the witness would be admissible.

(3)   A statement made by the witness in a document—

(a)   which is used by him to refresh his memory while giving evidence,

(b)   on which he is cross-examined, and

(c)   which as a consequence is received in evidence in the proceedings,

is admissible as evidence of any matter stated of which oral evidence by him would be admissible.

(4)   A previous statement by the witness is admissible as evidence of any matter stated of which oral evidence by him would be admissible, if—

(a)   any of the following three conditions is satisfied, and

(b)   while giving evidence the witness indicates that to the best of his belief he made the statement, and that to the best of his belief it states the truth.

(5)   The first condition is that the statement identifies or describes a person, object or place.

(6)   The second condition is that the statement was made by the witness when the matters stated were fresh in his memory but he does not remember them, and cannot reasonably be expected to remember them, well enough to give oral evidence of them in the proceedings.

(7)   The third condition is that—
   (a)   the witness claims to be a person against whom an offence has been committed,
   (b)   the offence is one to which the proceedings relate,
   (c)   the statement consists of a complaint made by the witness (whether to a person in authority or not) about conduct which would, if proved, constitute the offence or part of the offence,
   (d)   the complaint was made as soon as could reasonably be expected after the alleged conduct,
   (e)   the complaint was not made as a result of a threat or a promise, and
   (f)   before the statement is adduced the witness gives oral evidence in connection with its subject matter.

(8)   For the purposes of subsection (7) the fact that the complaint was elicited (for example, by a leading question) is irrelevant unless a threat or a promise was involved.

Supplementary

121   Additional requirement for admissibility of multiple hearsay

(1)   A hearsay statement is not admissible to prove the fact that an earlier hearsay statement was made unless—
   (a)   either of the statements is admissible under section 117, 119 or 120,
   (b)   all parties to the proceedings so agree, or
   (c)   the court is satisfied that the value of the evidence in question, taking into account how reliable the statements appear to be, is so high that the interests of justice require the later statement to be admissible for that purpose.

(2)   In this section 'hearsay statement' means a statement, not made in oral evidence, that is relied on as evidence of a matter stated in it.

122   Documents produced as exhibits

(1)   This section applies if on a trial before a judge and jury for an offence—
   (a)   a statement made in a document is admitted in evidence under section 119 or 120, and
   (b)   the document or a copy of it is produced as an exhibit.

(2)   The exhibit must not accompany the jury when they retire to consider their verdict unless—
   (a)   the court considers it appropriate, or
   (b)   all the parties to the proceedings agree that it should accompany the jury.

123   Capability to make statement

(1)   Nothing in section 116, 119 or 120 makes a statement admissible as evidence if it was made by a person who did not have the required capability at the time when he made the statement.

(2)   Nothing in section 117 makes a statement admissible as evidence if any person who, in order for the requirements of section 117(2) to be satisfied, must at any time have supplied or received the information concerned or created or received the document or part concerned
   (a)   did not have the required capability at that time, or
   (b)   cannot be identified but cannot reasonably be assumed to have had the required capability at that time.

(3)   For the purposes of this section a person has the required capability if he is capable of—
   (a)   understanding questions put to him about the matters stated, and
   (b)   giving answers to such questions which can be understood.

(4)   Where by reason of this section there is an issue as to whether a person had the required capability when he made a statement—
   (a)   proceedings held for the determination of the issue must take place in the absence of the jury (if there is one);

(b)   in determining the issue the court may receive expert evidence and evidence from any person to whom the statement in question was made;

(c)   the burden of proof on the issue lies on the party seeking to adduce the statement, and the standard of proof is the balance of probabilities.

124   Credibility

(1)   This section applies if in criminal proceedings—

    (a)   a statement not made in oral evidence in the proceedings is admitted as evidence of a matter stated, and

    (b)   the maker of the statement does not give oral evidence in connection with the subject matter of the statement.

(2)   In such a case—

    (a)   any evidence which (if he had given such evidence) would have been admissible as relevant to his credibility as a witness is so admissible in the proceedings;

    (b)   evidence may with the court's leave be given of any matter which (if he had given such evidence) could have been put to him in cross-examination as relevant to his credibility as a witness but of which evidence could not have been adduced by the cross-examining party;

    (c)   evidence tending to prove that he made (at whatever time) any other statement inconsistent with the statement admitted as evidence is admissible for the purpose of showing that he contradicted himself.

(3)   If as a result of evidence admitted under this section an allegation is made against the maker of a statement, the court may permit a party to lead additional evidence of such description as the court may specify for the purposes of denying or answering the allegation.

(4)   In the case of a statement in a document which is admitted as evidence under section 117 each person who, in order for the statement to be admissible, must have supplied or received the information concerned or created or received the document or part concerned is to be treated as the maker of the statement for the purposes of subsections (1) to (3) above.

125   Stopping the case where evidence is unconvincing

(1)   If on a defendant's trial before a judge and jury for an offence the court is satisfied at any time after the close of the case for the prosecution that—

    (a)   the case against the defendant is based wholly or partly on a statement not made in oral evidence in the proceedings, and

    (b)   the evidence provided by the statement is so unconvincing that, considering its importance to the case against the defendant, his conviction of the offence would be unsafe,

the court must either direct the jury to acquit the defendant of the offence or, if it considers that there ought to be a retrial, discharge the jury.

(2)   Where—

    (a)   a jury is directed under subsection (1) to acquit a defendant of an offence, and

    (b)   the circumstances are such that, apart from this subsection, the defendant could if acquitted of that offence be found guilty of another offence,

the defendant may not be found guilty of that other offence if the court is satisfied as mentioned in subsection (1) in respect of it.

(3)   If—

    (a)   a jury is required to determine under section 4A(2) of the Criminal Procedure (Insanity) Act 1964 whether a person charged on an indictment with an offence did the act or made the omission charged, and

    (b)   the court is satisfied as mentioned in subsection (1) above at any time after the close of the case for the prosecution that

        (i)   the case against the defendant is based wholly or partly on a statement not made in oral evidence in the proceedings, and

   (ii)   the evidence provided by the statement is so unconvincing that, considering its importance to the case against the person, a finding that he did the act or made the omission would be unsafe,

the court must either direct the jury to acquit the defendant of the offence or, if it considers that there ought to be a rehearing, discharge the jury.

(4)   This section does not prejudice any other power a court may have to direct a jury to acquit a person of an offence or to discharge a jury.

126   Court's general discretion to exclude evidence

(1)   In criminal proceedings the court may refuse to admit a statement as evidence of a matter stated if—

   (a)   the statement was made otherwise than in oral evidence in the proceedings, and

   (b)   the court is satisfied that the case for excluding the statement, taking account of the danger that to admit it would result in undue waste of time, substantially outweighs the case for admitting it, taking account of the value of the evidence.

(2)   Nothing in this Chapter prejudices—

   (a)   any power of a court to exclude evidence under section 78 of the Police and Criminal Evidence Act 1984 (exclusion of unfair evidence), or

   (b)   any other power of a court to exclude evidence at its discretion (whether by preventing questions from being put or otherwise).

Miscellaneous

127   Expert evidence: preparatory work

(1)   This section applies if—

   (a)   a statement has been prepared for the purposes of criminal proceedings,

   (b)   the person who prepared the statement had or may reasonably be supposed to have had personal knowledge of the matters stated,

   (c)   notice is given under the appropriate rules that another person (the expert) will in evidence given in the proceedings orally or under section 9 of the Criminal Justice Act 1967 base an opinion or inference on the statement, and

   (d)   the notice gives the name of the person who prepared the statement and the nature of the matters stated.

(2)   In evidence given in the proceedings the expert may base an opinion or inference on the statement.

(3)   If evidence based on the statement is given under subsection (2) the statement is to be treated as evidence of what it states.

(4)   This section does not apply if the court, on an application by a party to the proceedings, orders that it is not in the interests of justice that it should apply.

(5)   The matters to be considered by the court in deciding whether to make an order under subsection (4) include—

   (a)   the expense of calling as a witness the person who prepared the statement;

   (b)   whether relevant evidence could be given by that person which could not be given by the expert;

   (c)   whether that person can reasonably be expected to remember the matters stated well enough to give oral evidence of them.

(6)   Subsections (1) to (5) apply to a statement prepared for the purposes of a criminal investigation as they apply to a statement prepared for the purposes of criminal proceedings, and in such a case references to the proceedings are to criminal proceedings arising from the investigation.

(7)   The appropriate rules are rules Criminal Procedure Rules made by virtue of—

   (a)   section 81 of the Police and Criminal Evidence Act 1984 (advance notice of expert evidence in Crown Court), or

   (b)   section 20(3) of the Criminal Procedure and Investigations Act 1996 (advance notice of expert evidence in magistrates' courts).

129   Representations other than by a person

(1)   Where a representation of any fact—

(a)   is made otherwise than by a person, but

(b)   depends for its accuracy on information supplied (directly or indirectly) by a person,

the representation is not admissible in criminal proceedings as evidence of the fact unless it is proved that the information was accurate.

(2)   Subsection (1) does not affect the operation of the presumption that a mechanical device has been properly set or calibrated.

133   Proof of statements in documents

Where a statement in a document is admissible as evidence in criminal proceedings, the statement may be proved by producing either—

(a)   the document, or

(b)   (whether or not the document exists) a copy of the document or of the material part of it, authenticated in whatever way the court may approve.

134   Interpretation of Chapter 2

(1)   In this Chapter—

'copy', in relation to a document, means anything on to which information recorded in the document has been copied, by whatever means and whether directly or indirectly;

'criminal proceedings' means criminal proceedings in relation to which the strict rules of evidence apply;

'defendant', in relation to criminal proceedings, means a person charged with an offence in those proceedings;

'document' means anything in which information of any description is recorded;

'oral evidence' includes evidence which, by reason of any disability, disorder or other impairment, a person called as a witness gives in writing or by signs or by way of any device;

'statutory provision' means any provision contained in, or in an instrument made under, this or any other Act, including any Act passed after this Act.

(2)   Section 115 (statements and matters stated) contains other general interpretative provisions.

(3)   Where a defendant is charged with two or more offences in the same criminal proceedings, this Chapter has effect as if each offence were charged in separate proceedings.

CRIMINAL JUSTICE AND PUBLIC ORDER ACT 1994

63.   Powers to remove persons attending or preparing for a rave

(1)   This section applies to a gathering on land in the open air of 100 or more persons (whether or not trespassers) at which amplified music is played during the night (with or without intermissions) and is such as, by reason of its loudness and duration and the time at which it is played, is likely to cause serious distress to the inhabitants of the locality; and for this purpose—

(a)   such a gathering continues during intermissions in the music and, where the gathering extends over several days, throughout the period during which amplified music is played at night (with or without intermissions); and

(b)   'music' includes sounds wholly or predominantly characterised by the emission of a succession of repetitive beats.

(1A)   This section also applies to a gathering if—

(a)   it is a gathering on land of 20 or more persons who are trespassing on the land; and

(b)   it would be a gathering of a kind mentioned in subsection (1) above if it took place on land in the open air.

(2)   If, as respects any land in the open air, a police officer of at least the rank of superintendent reasonably believes that—

(a)   two or more persons are making preparations for the holding there of a gathering to which this section applies,

     (b)   ten or more persons are waiting for such a gathering to begin there, or

     (c)   ten or more persons are attending such a gathering which is in progress,

he may give a direction that those persons and any other persons who come to prepare or wait for or to attend the gathering are to leave the land and remove any vehicles or other property which they have with them on the land.

(3)   A direction under subsection (2) above, if not communicated to the persons referred to in subsection (2) by the police officer giving the direction, may be communicated to them by any constable at the scene.

(4)   Persons shall be treated as having had a direction under subsection (2) above communicated to them if reasonable steps have been taken to bring it to their attention.

(5)   A direction under subsection (2) above does not apply to an exempt person.

(6)   If a person knowing that a direction has been given which applies to him—

     (a)   fails to leave the land as soon as reasonably practicable, or

     (b)   having left again enters the land within the period of 7 days beginning with the day on which the direction was given,

he commits an offence . . .

(7)   In proceedings for an offence under this section it is a defence for the accused to show that he had a reasonable excuse for failing to leave the land as soon as reasonably practicable or, as the case may be, for again entering the land.

(7A) A person commits an offence if—

     (a)   he knows that a direction under subsection (2) above has been given which applies to him, and

     (b)   he makes preparations for or attends a gathering to which this section applies within the period of 24 hours starting when the direction was given.

(10) In this section—

'exempt peson', in relation to land (or any gathering on land), means the occupier, any member of his family and any employee or agent of his and any person whose home is situated on the land;

'land in the open air' includes a place partly open to the air;

'occupier', 'trespasser' and 'vehicle' have the same meaning as in section 61.

68.   Offence of aggravated trespass

(1)   A person commits the offence of aggravated trespass if he trespasses on land . . . and, in relation to any lawful activity which persons are engaging in or are about to engage in on that or adjoining land . . . does there anything which is intended by him to have the effect—

     (a)   of intimidating those persons or any of them so as to deter them or any of them from engaging in that activity,

     (b)   of obstructing that activity, or

     (c)   of disrupting that activity.

(2)   Activity on any occasion on the part of a person or persons on land is 'lawful' for the purposes of this section if he or they may engage in the activity on the land on that occasion without committing an offence or trespassing on the land.

(5)   In this section 'land' does not include—

     (a)   the highways and roads excluded from the application of section 61 by paragraph (b) of the definition of 'land' in subsection (9) of that section;

     . . .

69.   Powers to remove persons committing or participating in aggravated trespass

(1)   If the senior police officer present at the scene reasonably believes—

     (a)   that a person is committing, has committed or intends to commit the offence of aggravated trespass on land . . .; or

     (b)   that two or more persons are trespassing on land in the open air and are present there with the common purpose of intimidating persons so as to deter them from engaging in a lawful activity or of obstructing or disrupting a lawful activity, he may direct that person or (as the case may be) those persons (or any of them) to leave the land.

(2) A direction under subsection (1) above, if not communicated to the persons referred to in subsection (1) by the police officer giving the direction, may be communicated to them by any constable at the scene.

(3) If a person knowing that a direction under subsection (1) above has been given which applies to him—
    (a) fails to leave the land as soon as practicable, or
    (b) having left again enters the land as a trespasser within the period of three months beginning with the day on which the direction was given,
    he commits an offence . . .

(4) In proceedings for an offence under subsection (3) it is a defence for the accused to show—
    (a) that he was not trespassing on the land, or
    (b) that he had a reasonable excuse for failing to leave the land as soon as practicable or, as the case may be, for again entering the land as a trespasser.

166. Sale of tickets by unauthorised persons

(1) It is an offence for an unauthorised person to sell, or offer or expose for sale, a ticket for a designated football match in any public place or place to which the public has access or, in the course of a trade or business, in any other place.

(2) For this purpose—
    (a) a person is 'unauthorised' unless he is authorised in writing to sell tickets for the match by the home club or by the organisers of the match;
    (b) a 'ticket' means anything which purports to be a ticket; and
    (c) a 'designated football match' means a football match . . . of a description or a particular football match, for the time being designated for the purposes of Part I of the Football Spectators Act 1989 or which is a regulated football match for the purposes of Part II of that Act.

CRIMINAL LAW ACT 1967

1. Abolition of distinction between felony and misdemeanour

(1) All distinctions between felony and misdemeanour are hereby abolished.

(2) Subject to the provisions of this Act, on all matters on which a distinction has previously been made between felony and misdemeanour, including mode of trial, the law and practice in relation to all offences cognisable under the law of England and Wales (including piracy) shall be the law and practice applicable at the commencement of this Act in relation to misdemeanour.

3. Use of force in making arrest, etc.

(1) A person may use such force as is reasonable in the circumstances in the prevention of crime, or in effecting or assisting in the lawful arrest of offenders or suspected offenders or of persons unlawfully at large.

(2) Subsection (1) above shall replace the rules of the common law on the question when force used for a purpose mentioned in the subsection is justified by that purpose.

4. Penalties for assisting offenders

(1) Where a person has committed a relevant offence, any other person who, knowing or believing him to be guilty of the offence or of some other relevant offence, does without lawful authority or reasonable excuse any act with intent to impede his apprehension or prosecution shall be guilty of an offence.

(1A) In this section and section 5 below, 'relevant offence' means—
    (a) an offence for which the sentence is fixed by law;

(b)   an offence for which a person of 18 years or over (not previously convicted) may be sentenced to imprisonment for a term of five years (or might so be sentenced but for the restrictions imposed by section 33 of the Magistrates' Court Act 1980).

(2)   If on the trial of an indictment for a relevant offence the jury are satisfied that the offence charged (or some other offence of which the accused might on that charge be found guilty) was committed, but find the accused not guilty of it, they may find him guilty of any offence under subsection (1) above of which they are satisfied that he is guilty in relation to the offence charged (or that other offence).

(3)   A person committing an offence under subsection (1) above with intent to impede another person's apprehension or prosecution shall on conviction on indictment be liable to imprisonment according to the gravity of the other person's offence, as follows:—

(a)   if that offence is one for which the sentence is fixed by law, he shall be liable to imprisonment for not more than ten years;

(b)   if it is one for which a person (not previously convicted) may be sentenced to imprisonment for a term of fourteen years, he shall be liable to imprisonment for not more than seven years;

(c)   if it is not one included above but is one for which a person (not previously convicted) may be sentenced to imprisonment for a term of ten years, he shall be liable to imprisonment for not more than five years;

(d)   in any other case, he shall be liable to imprisonment for not more than three years.

(4)   No proceedings shall be instituted for an offence under subsection (1) above except by or with the consent of the Director of Public Prosecutions.

5.   Penalties for concealing offences or giving false information

(1)   Where a person has committed a relevant offence, any other person who, knowing or believing that the offence or some other relevant offence has been committed, and that he has information which might be of material assistance in securing the prosecution or conviction of an offender for it, accepts or agrees to accept for not disclosing that information any consideration other than the making good of loss or injury caused by the offence, or the making of reasonable compensation for that loss or injury, shall be liable on conviction on indictment to imprisonment for not more than two years.

(2)   Where a person causes any wasteful employment of the police by knowingly making to any person a false report tending to show that an offence has been committed, or to give rise to apprehension for the safety of any persons or property, or tending to show that he has information material to any police inquiry, he shall be liable on summary conviction to imprisonment for not more than six months or to a fine of not more than level 4 on the standard scale or to both.

(3)   No proceedings shall be instituted for an offence under this section except by or with the consent of the Director of Public Prosecutions.

(5)   The compounding of an offence other than treason shall not be an offence otherwise than under this section.

6.   Trial of offences

(1)   Where a person is arraigned on an indictment—

(a)   he shall in all cases be entitled to make a plea of not guilty in addition to any demurrer or special plea;

(b)   he may plead not guilty of the offence specifically charged in the indictment but guilty of another offence of which he might be found guilty on that indictment;

(c)   if he stands mute of malice or will not answer directly to the indictment, the court may order a plea of not guilty to be entered on his behalf, and he shall then be treated as having pleaded not guilty.

(2)   On an indictment for murder a person found not guilty of murder may be found guilty—

(a)   of manslaughter, or of causing grievous bodily harm with intent to do so; or

(b)   of any offence of which he may be found guilty under an enactment specifically so providing, or under section 4(2) of this Act; or

(c)   of any attempt to commit murder, or an attempt to commit any other offence of which he might be found guilty;

but may not be found guilty of any offence not included above.

(3)   Where, on a person's trial on indictment for any offence except treason or murder, the jury find him not guilty of the offence specifically charged in the indictment, but the allegations in the indictment amount to or include (expressly or by implication) an allegation of another offence falling within the jurisdiction of the court of trial, the jury may find him guilty of that other offence or of an offence of which he could be found guilty on an indictment specifically charging that other offence.

(4)   For purposes of subsection (3) above any allegation of an offence shall be taken as including an allegation of attempting to commit that offence; and where a person is charged on an indictment with attempting to commit an offence or with any assault or other act preliminary to an offence, but not with the completed offence, then (subject to the discretion of the court to discharge the jury with a view to the preferment of an indictment for the completed offence) he may be convicted of the offence charged notwithstanding that he is shown to be guilty of the completed offence.

(5)   Where a person arraigned on an indictment pleads not guilty of an offence charged in the indictment but guilty of some other offence of which he might be found guilty on that charge, and he is convicted on that plea of guilty without trial for the offence of which he has pleaded not guilty, then (whether or not the two offences are separately charged in distinct counts) his conviction of the one offence shall be an acquittal of the other.

CRIMINAL LAW ACT 1977

1.   The offence of conspiracy

(1)   Subject to the following provisions of this Part of this Act, if a person agrees with any other person or persons that a course of conduct shall be pursued which, if the agreement is carried out in accordance with their intentions, either—

(a)   will necessarily amount to or involve the commission of any offence or offences by one or more parties to the agreement, or

(b)   would do so but for the existence of facts which render the commission of the offence or any offences impossible,

he is guilty of conspiracy to commit the offence or offences in question.

(2)   Where liability for any offence may be incurred without knowledge on the part of the person committing it of any particular fact or circumstance necessary for the commission of the offence, a person shall nevertheless not be guilty of conspiracy to commit that offence by virtue of subsection (1) above unless he and at least one other party to the agreement intend or know that that fact or circumstance shall or will exist at the time when the conduct constituting the offence is to take place.

(4)   In this Part of this Act 'offence' means an offence triable in England and Wales.

1A.   Conspiracy to commit offences outside the United Kingdom

(1)   Where each of the following conditions is satisfied in the case of an agreement, this Part of this Act has effect in relation to the agreement as it has effect in relation to an agreement falling within section 1(1) above.

(2)   The first condition is that the pursuit of the agreed course of conduct would at some stage involve—

(a)   an act by one or more of the parties, or

(b)   the happening of some other event, intended to take place in a country or territory outside the United Kingdom.

(3)   The second condition is that that act or other event constitutes an offence under the law in force in that country or territory.

(4)   The third condition is that the agreement would fall within section 1(1) above as an agreement relating to the commission of an offence but for the fact that the offence would

not be an offence triable in England and Wales if committed in accordance with the parties' intentions.

(5) The fourth condition is that—

    (a) a party to the agreement, or a party's agent, did anything in England and Wales in relation to the agreement before its formation, or

    (b) a party to the agreement became a party in England and Wales (by joining it either in person or through an agent), or

    (c) a party to the agreement, or a party's agent, did or omitted anything in England and Wales in pursuance of the agreement.

(6) In the application of this Part of this Act to an agreement in the case of which each of the above conditions is satisfied, a reference to an offence is to be read as a reference to what would be the offence in question but for the fact that it is not an offence triable in England and Wales.

(7) Conduct punishable under the law in force in any country or territory is an offence under that law for the purposes of this section, however it is described in that law.

(8) Subject to subsection (9) below, the second condition is to be taken to be satisfied unless, not later than rules of court may provide, the defence serve on the prosecution a notice—

    (a) stating that, on the facts as alleged with respect to the agreed course of conduct, the condition is not in their opinion satisfied.

    (b) showing their grounds for that opinion, and

    (c) requiring the prosecution to show that it is satisfied.

(9) The court may permit the defence to require the prosecution to show that the second condition is satisfied without the prior service of a notice under subsection (8) above.

(10) In the Crown Court the question whether the second condition is satisfied shall be decided by the judge alone, and shall be treated as a question of law for the purposes of—

    (a) section 9(3) of the Criminal Justice Act 1987 (preparatory hearing in fraud cases), and

    (b) section 31(3) of the Criminal Procedure and Investigations Act 1996 (preparatory hearing in other cases).

(11) Any act done by means of a message (however communicated) is to be treated for the purposes of the fourth condition as done in England and Wales if the message is sent or received in England and Wales.

(12) In any proceedings in respect of an offence triable by virtue of this section, it is immaterial to guilt whether or not the accused was a British citizen at the time of any act or other event proof of which is required for conviction of the offence.

(13) References in any enactment, instrument or document (except those in this Part of this Act) to an offence of conspiracy to commit an offence include an offence triable in England and Wales as such a conspiracy by virtue of this section (without prejudice to subsection (6)

(14) Nothing in this section—

    (a) applies to an agreement entered into before the day on which the Criminal Justice (Terrorism and Conspiracy) Act 1998 was passed, or

    (b) imposes criminal liability on any person acting on behalf of, or holding office under, the Crown.

2. Exemptions from liability for conspiracy

(1) A person shall not by virtue of section 1 above be guilty of conspiracy to commit any offence if he is an intended victim of that offence.

(2) A person shall not by virtue of section 1 above be guilty of conspiracy to commit any offence or offences if the only other person or persons with whom he agrees are (both initially and at all times during the currency of the agreement) persons of any one or more of the following descriptions, that is to say —

    (a) his spouse or civil partner;

    (b) a person under the age of criminal responsibility; and

    (c) an intended victim of that offence or of each of those offences.

(3) A person is under the age of criminal responsibility for the purposes of subsection (2) (b) above so long as it is conclusively presumed, by virtue of section 50 of the Children and Young Persons Act 1933, that he cannot be guilty of any offence.

3. Penalties for conspiracy

(1) A person guilty by virtue of section 1 above of conspiracy to commit any offence or offences shall be liable on conviction on indictment—

    (a) in a case falling within subsection (2) or (3) below, to imprisonment for a term related in accordance with that subsection to the gravity of the offence or offences in question (referred to below in this section as the relevant offence or offences); and

    (b) in any other case, to a fine.

Paragraph (b) above shall not be taken as prejudicing the application of section 163 of the Criminal Justice Act 2003 (general power of court to fine offender convicted on indictment) in a case falling within subsection (2) or (3) below.

(2) Where the relevant offence or any of the relevant offences is an offence of any of the following descriptions, that is to say —

    (a) murder, or any other offence the sentence for which is fixed by law;

    (b) an offence for which a sentence extending to imprisonment for life is provided; or

    (c) an indictable offence punishable with imprisonment for which no maximum term of imprisonment is provided,

the person convicted shall be liable to imprisonment for life.

(3) Where in a case other than one to which subsection (2) above applies the relevant offence or any of the relevant offences is punishable with imprisonment, the person convicted shall be liable to imprisonment for a term not exceeding the maximum term provided for that offence or (where more than one such offence is in question) for any one of those offences (taking the longer or the longest term as the limit for the purposes of this section where the terms provided differ).

In the case of an offence triable either way the references above in this subsection to the maximum term provided for that offence are references to the maximum term so provided on conviction on indictment.

4. Restrictions on the institution of proceedings for conspiracy

(1) Subject to subsection (2) below proceedings under section 1 above for conspiracy to commit any offence shall not be instituted against any person except by or with the consent of the Director of Public Prosecutions if the offence or (as the case may be) each of the offences in question is a summary offence.

(2) In relation to the institution of proceedings under section 1 above for conspiracy to commit—

    (a) an offence which is subject to a prohibition by or under any enactment on the institution of proceedings otherwise than by, or on behalf or with the consent of, the Attorney-General, or

    (b) two or more offences of which at least one is subject to such a prohibition,

subsection (1) above shall have effect with the substitution of a reference to the Attorney-General for the reference to the Director of Public Prosecutions.

(3) Any prohibition by or under any enactment on the institution of proceedings for any offence which is not a summary offence otherwise than by, or on behalf or with the consent of, the Director of Public Prosecutions or any other person shall apply also in relation to proceedings under section 1 above for conspiracy to commit that offence.

(4) Where—

    (a) an offence has been committed in pursuance of any agreement; and

    (b) proceedings may not be instituted for that offence because any time limit applicable to the institution of any such proceedings has expired,

proceedings under section 1 above for conspiracy to commit that offence shall not be instituted against any person on the basis of that agreement.

(5)   Subject to subsection (6) below, no proceedings for an offence triable by virtue of section 1A above may be instituted except by or with the consent of the Attorney General.

(6)   The Secretary of State may by order provide that subsection (5) above shall not apply, or shall not apply to any case of a description specified in the order.

(7)   An order under subsection (6) above—
    (a)   shall be made by statutory instrument, and
    (b)   shall not be made unless a draft has been laid before, and approved by resolution of, each House of Parliament.

5.   Abolitions, savings, transitional provisions, consequential amendment and repeals

(1)   Subject to the following provisions of this section, the offence of conspiracy at common law is hereby abolished.

(2)   Subsection (1) above shall not affect the offence of conspiracy at common law so far as relates to conspiracy to defraud.

(3)   Subsection (1) above shall not affect the offence of conspiracy at common law if and in so far as it may be committed by entering into an agreement to engage in conduct which—
    (a)   tends to corrupt public morals or outrages public decency; but
    (b)   would not amount to or involve the commission of an offence if carried out by a single person otherwise than in pursuance of an agreement.

(6)   The rules laid down by sections 1 and 2 above shall apply for determining whether a person is guilty of an offence of conspiracy under any enactment other than section 1 above, but conduct which is an offence under any such other enactment shall not also be an offence under section 1 above.

(7)   Incitement to commit the offence of conspiracy (whether the conspiracy incited would be an offence at common law or under section 1 above or any other enactment) shall cease to be an offence.

(8)   The fact that the person or persons who, so far as appears from the indictment on which any person has been convicted of conspiracy, were the only other parties to the agreement on which his conviction was based have been acquitted of conspiracy by reference to that agreement (whether after being tried with the person convicted or separately) shall not be a ground for quashing his conviction unless under all the circumstances of the case his conviction is inconsistent with the acquittal of the other person or persons in question.

(9)   Any rule of law or practice inconsistent with the provisions of subsection (8) above is hereby abolished.

6.   Violence for securing entry

(1)   Subject to the following provisions of this section, any person who, without lawful authority, uses or threatens violence for the purpose of securing entry into any premises for himself or for any other person is guilty of an offence, provided that—
    (a)   there is someone present on those premises at the time who is opposed to the entry which the violence is intended to secure; and
    (b)   the person using or threatening the violence knows that that is the case.

(1A) Subsection (1) above does not apply to a person who is a displaced residential occupier or a protected intending occupier of the premises in question or who is acting on behalf of such an occupier; and if the accused adduces sufficient evidence that he was, or was acting on behalf of, such an occupier he shall be presumed to be, or to be acting on behalf of, such an occupier unless the contrary is proved by the prosecution.

(2)   Subject to subsection (1A) above, the fact that a person has any interest in or right to possession or occupation of any premises shall not for the purposes of subsection (1) above constitute lawful authority for the use or threat of violence by him or anyone else for the purpose of securing his entry into those premises.

(4)   It is immaterial for the purposes of this section—
    (a)   whether the violence in question is directed against the person or against the property; and

(b)   whether the entry which the violence is intended to secure is for the purpose of acquiring possession of the premises in question or for any other purpose.

7.   Adverse occupation of residential premises

(1)   Subject to the following provisions of this section and to section 12A(9) below, any person who is on any premises as a trespasser after having entered as such is guilty of an offence if he fails to leave those premises on being required to do so by or on behalf of—

(a)   a displaced residential occupier of the premises; or

(b)   an individual who is a protected intending occupier of the premises.

(2)   In any proceedings for an offence under this section it shall be a defence for the accused to prove that he believed that the person requiring him to leave the premises was not a displaced residential occupier or protected intending occupier of the premises or a person acting on behalf of a displaced residential occupier or protected intending occupier.

(3)   In any proceedings for an offence under this section it shall be a defence for the accused to prove—

(a)   that the premises in question are or form part of premises used mainly for non-residential purposes; and

(b)   that he was not on any part of the premises used wholly or mainly for residential purposes.

(4)   Any reference in the preceding provisions of this section to any premises includes a reference to any access to them, whether or not any such access itself constitutes premises, within the meaning of this Part of this Act.

(7)   Section 12 below contains provisions which apply for determining when any person is to be regarded for the purposes of this Part of this Act as a displaced residential occupier of any premises or of any access to any premises and section 12A below contains provisions which apply for determining when any person is to be regarded for the purposes of this Part of this Act as a protected intending occupier of any premises or of any access to any premises.

8.   Trespassing with a weapon of offence

(1)   A person who is on any premises as a trespasser, after having entered as such, is guilty of an offence if, without lawful authority or reasonable excuse, he has with him on the premises any weapon of offence.

(2)   In subsection (1) above 'weapon of offence' means any article made or adapted for use for causing injury to or incapacitating a person, or intended by the person having it with him for such use.

9.   Trespassing on premises of foreign missions, etc.

(1)   Subject to subsection (3) below, a person who enters or is on any premises to which this section applies as a trespasser is guilty of an offence.

(2)   This section applies to any premises which are or form part of—

(a)   the premises of a diplomatic mission within the meaning of the definition in Article 1(i) of the Vienna Convention on Diplomatic Relations signed in 1961 as that Article has effect in the United Kingdom by virtue of section 2 of and Schedule 1 to the Diplomatic Privileges Act 1964;

(aa) the premises of a closed diplomatic mission;

(b)   consular premises within the meaning of the definition in paragraph 1(j) of Article 1 of the Vienna Convention on Consular Relations signed in 1963 as that Article has effect in the United Kingdom by virtue of section 1 of and Schedule 1 to the Consular Relations Act 1968;

(bb) the premises of a closed consular post;

(c)   any other premises in respect of which any organisation or body is entitled to inviolability by or under any enactment; and

(d)   any premises which are the private residence of a diplomatic agent (within the meaning of Article 1(e) of the Convention mentioned in paragraph (a) above) or of any other person who is entitled to inviolability of residence by or under any enactment.

(3)   In any proceedings for an offence under this section it shall be a defence for the accused to prove that he believed that the premises in question were not premises to which this section applies.

12.   Supplementary provisions

(1)   In this Part of this Act—

(a)   'premises' means any building, any part of a building under separate occupation, any land ancillary to a building, the site comprising any building or buildings together with any land ancillary thereto, and (for the purposes only of sections 10 and 11 above) any other place; and

(b)   'access' means, in relation to any premises, any part of any site or building within which those premises are situated which constitutes an ordinary means of access to those premises (whether or not that is its sole or primary use).

(2)   References in this section to a building shall apply also to any structure other than a movable one, and to any movable structure, vehicle or vessel designed or adapted for use for residential purposes; and for the purposes of subsection (1) above—

(a)   part of a building is under separate occupation if anyone is in occupation or entitled to occupation of that part as distinct from the whole; and

(b)   land is ancillary to a building if it is adjacent to it and used (or intended for use) in connection with the occupation of that building or any part of it.

(3)   Subject to subsection (4) below, any person who was occupying any premises as a residence immdiately before being excluded from occupation by anyone who entered those premises, or any access to those premises, as a trespasser is a displaced residential occupier of the premises for the purposes of this Part of this Act so long as he continues to be excluded from occupation of the premises by the original trespasser or by any subsequent trespasser.

(4)   A person who was himself occupying the premises in question as a trespasser immediately before being excluded from occupation shall not by virtue of subsection (3) above be a displaced residential occupier of the premises for the purposes of this Part of this Act.

(5)   A person who by virtue of subsection (3) above is a displaced residential occupier of any premises shall be regarded for the purposes of this Part of this Act as a displaced residential occupier also of any access to those premises.

12A.   Protected intending occupiers: supplementary provisions

(1)   For the purposes of this Part of this Act an individual is a protected intending occupier of any premises at any time if at that time he falls within subsections (2), (4) or (6) below.

(2)   An individual is a protected occupier of any premises if—

(a)   he has in those premises a freehold interest or a leasehold interest with not less than two years still to run;

(b)   he requires the premises for his own occupation as a residence;

(c)   he is excluded from occupation of the premises by a person who entered them, or any access to them, as a trespasser; and

(d)   he or a person acting on his behalf holds a written statement—

(i)   which specifies his interest in the premises;

(ii)   which states that he requires the premises for occupation as a residence for himself; and

(iii) with respect to which the requirements in subsection (3) below are fulfilled.

(3)   The requirements referred to in subsection (2)(d)(iii) above are—

(a)   that the statement is signed by the person whose interest is specified in it in the presence of a justice of the peace or commissioner for oaths; and

(b)   that the justice of the peace or commissioner for oaths has subscribed his name as a witness to the signature.

(4)   An individual is also a protected intending occupier of any premises if —

(a)   he has a tenancy of those premises (other than a tenancy falling within subsection (2)(a) above or (6)(a) below) or a licence to occupy those premises granted by a person with a freehold interest or a leasehold interest with not less than two years still to run in the premises;

(b)   he requires the premises for his own occupation as a residence;

(c)   he is excluded from occupation of the premises by a person who entered them, or any access to them, as a trespasser; and

(d)   he or a person acting on his behalf holds a written statement—

     (i)   which states that he has been granted a tenancy of those premises or a licence to occupy those premises;

     (ii)   which specifies the interest in the premises of the person who granted that tenancy or licence to occupy ('the landlord');

     (iii)   which states that he requires the premises for occupation as a residence for himself; and

     (iv)   with respect to which the requirements in subsection (5) below are fulfilled.

(5)   The requirements referred to in subsection (4)(d)(iv) above are—

    (a)   that the statement is signed by the landlord and by the tenant or licensee in the presence of a justice of the peace or commissioner for oaths;

    (b)   that the justice of the peace or commissioner for oaths has subscribed his name as a witness to the signatures.

(6)   An individual is also a protected intending occupier of any premises if —

    (a)   he has a tenancy of those premises (other than a tenancy falling within subsection (2)(a) or (4)(a) above) or a licence to occupy those premises granted by an authority to which this subsection applies;

    (b)   he requires the premises for his own occupation as a residence;

    (c)   he is excluded from occupation of the premises by a person who entered the premises, or any access to them, as a trespasser; and

    (d)   there has been issued to him by or on behalf of the authority referred to in paragraph (a) above a certificate stating that—

     (i)   he has been granted a tenancy of those premises or a licence to occupy those premises as a residence by the authority; and

     (ii)   the authority which granted that tenancy or licence to occupy is one to which this subsection applies, being of a description specified in the certificate.

(7)   Subsection (6) above applies to the following authorities—

    (a)   any body mentioned in section 14 of the Rent Act 1977 (landlord's interest belonging to local authority etc);

    (b)   the Housing Corporation;

    (c)   . . . and

    (d)   a registered social landlord within the meaning of the Housing Act 1985 (see section 5(4) and (5) of that Act).

(8)   A person is guilty of an offence if he makes a statement for the purposes of subsection (2)(d) or (4)(d) above which he knows to be false in a material particular or if he recklessly makes such a statement which is false in a material particular.

(9)   In any proceedings for an offence under section 7 of this Act where the accused was requested to leave the premises by a person claiming to be or to act on behalf of a protected intending occupier of the premises—

    (a)   it shall be a defence for the accused to prove that, although asked to do so by the accused at the time the accused was requested to leave, that person failed at that time to produce to the accused such a statement as is referred to in subsection (2)(d) or (4)(d) above or such a certificate as is referred to in subsection (6)(d) above; and

    (b)   any document purporting to be a certificate under subsection (6)(d) above shall be received in evidence and, unless the contrary is proved, shall be deemed to have been issued by or on behalf of the authority stated in the certificate.

(11)   A person who is protected intending occupier of any premises shall be regarded for the purposes of this Part of this Act as a protected intending occupier also of any access to those premises.

CRIMINAL PROCEDURE (INSANITY) ACT 1964

5.   **Powers to deal with persons not guilty by reason of insanity or unfit to plead etc.**
      (1)   This section applies where—
            (a)   a special verdict is returned that the accused is not guilty by reason of insanity; or
            (b)   findings have been made that the accused is under a disability and that he did the act or made the omission charged against him.
      (2)   The court shall make in respect of the accused—
            (a)   a hospital order (with or without a restriction order);
            (b)   a supervision order; or
            (c)   an order for his absolute discharge.
      (3)   Where—
            (a)   the offence to which the special verdict or the findings relate is an offence the sentence for which is fixed by law, and
            (b)   the court have power to make a hospital order,
            the court shall make a hospital order with a restriction order (whether or not they would have power to make a restriction order apart from this subsection).
      (4)   In this section—
            'hospital order' has the meaning given in section 37 of the Mental Health Act 1983;
            'restriction order' has the meaning given to it by section 41 of that Act;
            'supervision order' has the meaning given in Part 1 of Schedule 1A to this Act.

6.   **Evidence by prosecution of insanity or diminished responsibility**
      Where on a trial for murder the accused contends—
      (a)   that at the time of the alleged offence he was insane so as not to be responsible according to law for his actions; or
      (b)   that at that time he was suffering from such abnormality of mind as is specified in subsection (1) of section 2 of the Homicide Act 1957 (diminished responsibility),
      the court shall allow the prosecution to adduce or elicit evidence tending to prove the other of those contentions, and may give directions as to the stage of the proceedings at which the prosecution may adduce such evidence.

CRIMINAL PROCEDURE (INSANITY AND UNFITNESS TO PLEAD) ACT 1991

1.   **Acquittals on grounds of insanity**
      (1)   A jury shall not return a special verdict under section 2 of the Trial of Lunatics Act 1883 (acquittal on ground of insanity) except on the written or oral evidence of two or more registered medical practitioners at least one of whom is duly approved.

6.   **Interpretation etc.**
      (1)   In this Act—
            'duly approved', in relation to a registered medical practitioner, means approved for the purposes of section 12 of the 1983 Act by the Secretary of State as having special experience in the diagnosis or treatment of mental disorder.

DEALING IN CULTURAL OBJECTS (OFFENCES) ACT 2003

1.   **Offence of dealing in tainted cultural objects**
      (1)   A person is guilty of an offence if he dishonestly deals in a cultural object that is tainted, knowing or believing that the object is tainted.
      (2)   It is immaterial whether he knows or believes that the object is a cultural object.

2.   **Meaning of 'tainted cultural object'**

(1)   'Cultural object' means an object of historical, architectural or archaeological interest.

(2)   A cultural object is tainted if, after the commencement of this Act—

    (a)   a person removes the object in a case falling within subsection (4) or he excavates the object, and

    (b)   the removal or excavation constitutes an offence.

(3)   It is immaterial whether—

    (a)   the removal or excavation was done in the United Kingdom or elsewhere,

    (b)   the offence is committed under the law of a part of the United Kingdom or under the law of any other country or territory.

(4)   An object is removed in a case falling within this subsection if—

    (a)   it is removed from a building or structure of historical, architectural or archaeological interest where the object has at any time formed part of the building or structure, or

    (b)   it is removed from a monument of such interest.

(5)   'Monument' means—

    (a)   any work, cave or excavation,

    (b)   any site comprising the remains of any building or structure or of any work, cave or excavation,

    (c)   any site comprising, or comprising the remains of, any vehicle, vessel, aircraft or other movable structure, or part of any such thing.

(6)   'Remains' includes any trace or sign of the previous existence of the thing in question.

(7)   It is immaterial whether—

    (a)   a building, structure or work is above or below the surface of the land,

    (b)   a site is above or below water.

(8)   This section has effect for the purposes of section 1.

3.   **Meaning of 'deals in'**

(1)   A person deals in an object if (and only if) he—

    (a)   acquires, disposes of, imports or exports it,

    (b)   agrees with another to do an act mentioned in paragraph (a), or

    (c)   makes arrangements under which another person does such an act or under which another person agrees with a third person to do such an act.

(2)   'Acquires' means buys, hires, borrows or accepts.

(3)   'Disposes of' means sells, lets on hire, lends or gives.

(4)   In relation to agreeing or arranging to do an act, it is immaterial whether the act is agreed or arranged to take place in the United Kingdom or elsewhere.

(5)   This section has effect for the purposes of section 1.

5.   **Offences by bodies corporate**

(1)   If an offence under section 1 committed by a body corporate is proved—

    (a)   to have been committed with the consent or connivance of an officer, or

    (b)   to be attributable to any neglect on his part,

    he (as well as the body corporate) is guilty of the offence and liable to be proceeded against and punished accordingly.

(2)   'Officer', in relation to a body corporate, means—

    (a)   a director, manager, secretary or other similar officer of the body,

    (b)   a person purporting to act in any such capacity.

(3)   If the affairs of a body corporate are managed by its members, subsection (1) applies in relation to the acts and defaults of a member in connection with his functions of management as if he were a director of the body.

DOMESTIC VIOLENCE, CRIME AND VICTIMS ACT 2004

PART 1
DOMESTIC VIOLENCE ETC.

5.   **Causing or allowing the death of a child or vulnerable adult**

(1)   A person ('D') is guilty of an offence if—

    (a)   a child or vulnerable adult ('V') dies as a result of the unlawful act of a person who—

        (i)   was a member of the same household as V, and

        (ii)   had frequent contact with him,

    (b)   D was such a person at the time of that act,

    (c)   at that time there was a significant risk of serious physical harm being caused to V by the unlawful act of such a person, and

    (d)   either D was the person whose act caused V's death or—

        (i)   D was, or ought to have been, aware of the risk mentioned in paragraph (c),

        (ii)   D failed to take such steps as he could reasonably have been expected to take to protect V from the risk, and

        (iii) the act occurred in circumstances of the kind that D foresaw or ought to have foreseen.

(2)   The prosecution does not have to prove whether it is the first alternative in subsection (1)(d) or the second (sub-paragraphs (i) to (iii)) that applies.

(3)   If D was not the mother or father of V—

    (a)   D may not be charged with an offence under this section if he was under the age of 16 at the time of the act that caused V's death;

    (b)   for the purposes of subsection (1)(d)(ii) D could not have been expected to take any such step as is referred to there before attaining that age.

(4)   For the purposes of this section—

    (a)   a person is to be regarded as a 'member' of a particular household, even if he does not live in that household, if he visits it so often and for such periods of time that it is reasonable to regard him as a member of it;

    (b)   where V lived in different households at different times, 'the same household as V' refers to the household in which V was living at the time of the act that caused V's death.

(5)   For the purposes of this section an 'unlawful' act is one that—

    (a)   constitutes an offence, or

    (b)   would constitute an offence but for being the act of—

        (i)   a person under the age of ten, or

        (ii)   a person entitled to rely on a defence of insanity.

Paragraph (b) does not apply to an act of D.

(6)   In this section—

'act' includes a course of conduct and also includes omission;

'child' means a person under the age of 16;

'serious' harm means harm that amounts to grievous bodily harm for the purposes of the Offences against the Person Act 1861;

'vulnerable adult' means a person aged 16 or over whose ability to protect himself from violence, abuse or neglect is significantly impaired through physical or mental disability or illness, through old age or otherwise.

(7)   A person guilty of an offence under this section is liable on conviction on indictment to imprisonment for a term not exceeding 14 years or to a fine, or to both.

EXPLOSIVE SUBSTANCES ACT 1883

2.   Causing explosion likely to endanger life or property
A person who in the United Kingdom or (being a citizen of the United Kingdom and Colonies) in the Republic of Ireland unlawfully and maliciously causes by any explosive substance an explosion of a nature likely to endanger life or to cause serious injury to person or property shall, whether any injury to person or property has been actually caused or not, be guilty of an offence and on conviction on indictment shall be liable to imprisonment for life.

3.   Attempt to cause explosion, or making or keeping explosive with intent to endanger life or property
A person who in the United Kingdom or a dependency or (being a citizen of the United Kingdom and Colonies) elsewhere unlawfully and maliciously—
(a)   does any act with intent to cause, or conspires to cause by an explosive substance, an explosion of a nature likely to endanger life or to cause serious injury to property, whether in the United Kingdom or the Republic of Ireland, or
(b)   makes or has in his possession or under his control an explosive substance with intent by means thereof to endanger life, or cause serious injury to property whether in the United Kingdom or the Republic of Ireland, or to enable any other person so to do,
shall, whether any explosion does or not take place, and whether any injury to person or property has been actually caused or not, be guilty of an offence and on conviction on indictment shall be liable to imprisonment for life, and the explosive substance shall be forfeited.

4.   Punishment for making or possession of explosive under suspicious circumstances
(1)   Any person who makes or knowingly has in his possession or under his control any explosive substance, under such circumstances as to give rise to a reasonable suspicion that he is not making it or does not have it in his possession or under his control for a lawful object, shall, unless he can show that he made it or had it in his possession or under his control for a lawful object, be guilty of an offence, and, on conviction, shall be liable to imprisonment for a term not exceeding fourteen years . . .

5.   Punishment of accessories
Any person who within or (being a subject of Her Majesty) without Her Majesty's dominions by the supply of or solicitation for money, the providing of premises, the supply of materials, or in any manner whatsoever, procures, counsels, aids, abets, or is accessory to, the commission of any crime under this Act, shall be guilty of an offence, and shall be liable to be tried and punished for that crime, as if he had been guilty as a principal.

9.   Definitions
(1)   In this Act, unless the context otherwise requires—
The expression 'explosive substance' shall be deemed to include any materials for making any explosive substance; also any apparatus, machine, implement, or materials used, or intended to be used, or adapted for causing, or aiding in causing, any explosion in or with any explosive substance; also any part of any such apparatus, machine, or implement.

FEMALE GENITAL MUTILATION ACT 2003

1.   Offence of female genital mutilation
(1)   A person is guilty of an offence if he excises, infibulates or otherwise mutilates the whole or any part of a girl's labia majora, labia minora or clitoris.
(2)   But no offence is committed by an approved person who performs—
(a)   a surgical operation on a girl which is necessary for her physical or mental health, or
(b)   a surgical operation on a girl who is in any stage of labour, or has just given birth, for purposes connected with the labour or birth.
(3)   The following are approved persons—

(a)   in relation to an operation falling within subsection (2)(a), a registered medical practitioner,

(b)   in relation to an operation falling within subsection (2)(b), a registered medical practitioner, a registered midwife or a person undergoing a course of training with a view to becoming such a practitioner or midwife.

(4)   There is also no offence committed by a person who—

    (a)   performs a surgical operation falling within subsection (2)(a) or (b) outside the United Kingdom, and

    (b)   in relation to such an operation exercises functions corresponding to those of an approved person.

(5)   For the purpose of determining whether an operation is necessary for the mental health of a girl it is immaterial whether she or any other person believes that the operation is required as a matter of custom or ritual.

2.   Offence of assisting a girl to mutilate her own genitalia

A person is guilty of an offence if he aids, abets, counsels or procures a girl to excise, infibulate or otherwise mutilate the whole or any part of her own labia majora, labia minora or clitoris.

3.   Offence of assisting a non-UK person to mutilate overseas a girl's genitalia

(1)   A person is guilty of an offence if he aids, abets, counsels or procures a person who is not a United Kingdom national or permanent United Kingdom resident to do a relevant act of female genital mutilation outside the United Kingdom.

(2)   An act is a relevant act of female genital mutilation if—

    (a)   it is done in relation to a United Kingdom national or permanent United Kingdom resident, and

    (b)   it would, if done by such a person, constitute an offence under section 1.

(3)   But no offence is committed if the relevant act of female genital mutilation—

    (a)   is a surgical operation falling within section 1(2)(a) or (b), and

    (b)   is performed by a person who, in relation to such an operation, is an approved person or exercises functions corresponding to those of an approved person.

4.   Extension of sections 1 to 3 to extra-territorial acts

(1)   Sections 1 to 3 extend to any act done outside the United Kingdom by a United Kingdom national or permanent United Kingdom resident.

(2)   If an offence under this Act is committed outside the United Kingdom—

    (a)   proceedings may be taken, and

    (b)   the offence may for incidental purposes be treated as having been committed,

in any place in England and Wales or Northern Ireland.

6.   Definitions

(1)   Girl includes woman.

(2)   A United Kingdom national is an individual who is—

    (a)   a British citizen, a British overseas territories citizen, a British National (Overseas) or a British Overseas citizen,

    (b)   a person who under the British Nationality Act 1981 is a British subject, or

    (c)   a British protected person within the meaning of that Act.

(3)   A permanent United Kingdom resident is an individual who is settled in the United Kingdom (within the meaning of the Immigration Act 1971.

(4)   This section has effect for the purposes of this Act.

FIREARMS ACT 1968

1.   Requirement of firearm certificate

(1)   Subject to any exemption under this Act, it is an offence for a person—

    (a)   to have in his possession, or to purchase or acquire, a firearm to which this section applies without holding a firearm certificate in force at the time, or otherwise than as authorised by such a certificate;

    (b)   to have in his possession, or to purchase or acquire, any ammunition to which this section applies without holding a firearm certificate in force at the time, or otherwise than as authorised by such a certificate, or in quantities in excess of those so authorised.

(2)   It is an offence for a person to fail to comply with a condition subject to which a firearm certificate is held by him.

(3)   This section applies to every firearm except—

    (a)   a shot gun within the meaning of this Act, that is to say a smooth-bore gun (not being an air gun) which—

        (i)   has a barrel not less than 24 inches in length and does not have any barrel with a bore exceeding 2 inches in diameter;

        (ii)   either has no magazine or has a non-detachable magazine incapable of holding more than two cartridges; and

        (iii)   is not a revolver gun; and

    (b)   an air weapon (that is to say, an air rifle, air gun or air pistol which does not fall within section 5(1) and which is not of a type declared by rules made by the Secretary of State under section 53 of this Act to be specially dangerous).

(3A) A gun which has been adapted to have such a magazine as is mentioned in subsection (3)(a)(ii) above shall not be regarded as falling within that provision unless the magazine bears a mark approved by the Secretary of State for denoting that fact and that mark has been made, and the adaptation has been certified in writing as having been carried out in a manner approved by him, either by one of the two companies mentioned in section 58(1) of this Act or by such other person as may be approved by him for that purpose.

(4)   This section applies to any ammunition for a firearm, except the following articles, namely:—

    (a)   cartridges containing five or more shot, none of which exceeds 0.36 inch in diameter;

    (b)   ammunition for an air gun, air rifle or air pistol; and

    (c)   blank cartridges not more than one inch in diameter measured immediately in front of the rim or cannelure of the base of the cartridge.

2.   Requirement of certificate for possession of shot guns

(1)   Subject to any exemption under this Act, it is an offence for a person to have in his possession, or to purchase or acquire, a shot gun without holding a certificate under this Act authorising him to possess shot guns.

(2)   It is an offence for a person to fail to comply with a condition subject to which a shot gun certificate is held by him.

3.   Business and other transactions with firearms and ammunition

(1)   A person commits an offence if, by way of trade or business, he—

    (a)   manufactures, sells, transfers, repairs, tests or proves any firearm or ammunition to which section 1 of this Act applies, or a shot gun; or

    (b)   exposes for sale or transfer, or has in his possession for sale, transfer, repair, test or proof any such firearm or ammunition, or a shot gun,

without being registered under this Act as a firearms dealer.

(2)   It is an offence for a person to sell or transfer to any other person in the United Kingdom, other than a registered firearms dealer, any firearm or ammunition to which section 1 of this Act applies, or a shot gun, unless that other produces a firearm certificate authorising him to purchase or acquire it or as the case may be, his shot gun certificate, or shows that he is by virtue of this Act entitled to purchase or acquire it without holding a certificate.

(3)   It is an offence for a person to undertake the repair, tests or proof of a firearm or ammunition to which section 1 of this Act applies, or of a shot gun, for any other person in the United Kingdom other than a registered firearms dealer as such, unless that other produces or

causes to be produced a firearm certificate authorising him to have possession of the firearm or ammunition or, as the case may be, his shot gun certificate, or shows that he is by virtue of this Act entitled to have possession of it without holding a certificate.

(4) Subsections (1) and (3) above have effect subject to any exemption under subsequent provisions of this Part of this Act.

(5) A person commits an offence if, with a view to purchasing or acquiring, or procuring the repair, test or proof of, any firearm or ammunition to which section 1 of this Act applies, or a shot gun, he produces a false certificate or a certificate in which any false entry has been made, or personates a person to whom a certificate has been granted, or knowingly or recklessly makes a statement false in any material particular.

(6) It is an offence for a pawnbroker to take in pawn any firearm or ammunition to which section 1 of this Act applies, or a shot gun.

4. Conversion of weapons

(1) Subject to this section, it is an offence to shorten the barrel of a shot gun to a length less than 24 inches.

(2) It is not an offence under subsection (1) above for a registered firearms dealer to shorten the barrel of a shot gun for the sole purpose of replacing a defective part of the barrel so as to produce a barrel not less than 24 inches in length.

(3) It is an offence for a person other than a registered firearms dealer to convert into a firearm anything which, though having the appearance of being a firearm, is so constructed as to be incapable of discharging any missile through its barrel.

(4) A person who commits an offence under section 1 of this Act by having in his possession, or purchasing or acquiring, a shotgun which has been shortened contrary to subsection (1) above or a firearm which has been converted contrary to subsection (3) above (whether by a registered firearms dealer or not), without holding a firearm certificate authorising him to have it in his possession, or to purchase or acquire it, shall be treated for the purposes of provisions of this Act relating to the punishment of offences as committing that offence in an aggravated form.

5. Weapons subject to general prohibition

(1) A person commits an offence if, without the authority of the Defence Council, he has in his possession, or purchases or acquires, or manufactures, sells or transfers—

    (a) any firearm which is so designed or adapted that two or more missiles can be successively discharged without repeated pressure on the trigger;

    (ab) any self-loading or pump-action rifled gun other than one which is chambered for .22 rim-fire cartridges;

    (aba) any firearm which either has a barrel less than 30 centimetres in length or is less than 60 centimetres in length overall, other than an air weapon, a muzzle-loading gun or a firearm designed as signalling apparatus;

    (ac) any self-loading or pump-action smooth-bore gun which is not an air weapon or chambered for .22 rim-fire cartridges and either has a barrel less than 24 inches in length or (excluding any detachable folding, retractable or other movable butt-stock) is less than 40 inches in length overall;

    (ad) any smooth-bore revolver gun other than one which is chambered for 9mm rim-fire cartridges or a muzzle-loading gun;

    (ae) any rocket launcher, or any mortar, for projecting a stabilised missile, other than a launcher or mortar designed for line-throwing or pyrotechnic purposes or as signalling apparatus;

    (af) any air rifle, air gun or air pistol which uses, or is designed or adapted for use with, a self-contained gas cartridge system;

    (b) any weapon of whatever description designed or adapted for the discharge of any noxious liquid, gas or other thing; and

    (c) any cartridge with a bullet designed to explode on or immediately before impact, any ammunition containing or designed or adapted to contain any such noxious thing as is mentioned in paragraph (b) above and, if capable of being used with a firearm of any description, any grenade, bomb (or other like missile), or rocket or shell designed to explode as aforesaid.

(1A) Subject to section 5A of this Act, a person commits an offence if, without the authority of the Secretary of State, he has in his possession, or purchases or acquires, or sells or transfers—

(a)   any firearm which is disguised as another object;

(b)   any rocket or ammunition not falling within paragraph (c) of subsection (1) of this section which consists in or incorporates a missile designed to explode on or immediately before impact and is for military use;

(c)   any launcher or other projecting apparatus not falling within paragraph (ae) of that subsection which is designed to be used with any rocket or ammunition falling within paragraph (b) above or with ammunition which would fall within that paragraph but for its being ammunition falling within paragraph (c) of this subsection;

(d)   any ammunition for military use which consists in or incorporates a missile designed so that a substance contained in the missile will ignite on or immediately before impact;

(e)   any ammunition for military use which consists in or incorporates a missile designed, on account of its having a jacket and hard-core, to penetrate armour plating, armour screening or body armour;

(f)   any ammunition which incorporates a missile designed or adapted to expand on impact;

(g)   anything which is designed to be projected as a missile from any weapon and is designed to be, or has been, incorporated in—

    (i)   any ammunition falling within any of the preceding paragraphs; or

    (ii)   any ammunition which would fall within any of those paragraphs but for its being specified in subsection (1) of this section.

(2)   The weapons and ammunition specified in subsections (1) and (1A) of this section (including, in the case of ammunition, any missiles falling within subsection (1A)(g) of this section) are referred to in this Act as 'prohibited weapons' and 'prohibited ammunition' respectively.

(3)   An authority given to a person by the Secretary of State under this section shall be in writing and be subject to conditions specified therein.

(5)   It is an offence for a person to whom an authority is given under this section to fail to comply with any condition of the authority.

(7)   For the purposes of this section and section 5A of this Act—

(a)   any rocket or ammunition which is designed to be capable of being used with a military weapon shall be taken to be for military use;

(b)   references to a missile designed so that a substance contained in the missile will ignite on or immediately before impact include references to any missile containing a substance that ignites on exposure to air; and

(c)   references to a missile's expanding on impact include references to its deforming in any predictable manner on or immediately after impact.

(8)   For the purposes of subsection (1)(aba) and (ac) above, any detachable, folding, retractable or other movable butt-stock shall be disregarded in measuring the length of any firearm.

(9)   Any reference in this section to a muzzle-loading gun is a reference to a gun which is designed to be loaded at the muzzle end of the barrel or chamber with a loose charge and a separate ball (or other missile).

5A.   Exemptions from requirement of authority under section 5

(1)   Subject to subsection (2) below, the authority of the Secretary of State shall not be required by virtue of subsection (1A) of section 5 of this Act for any person to have in his possession, or to purchase, acquire, sell or transfer, any prohibited weapon or ammunition if he is authorised by a certificate under this Act to possess, purchase or acquire that weapon or

ammunition subject to a condition that he does so only for the purpose of its being kept or exhibited as part of a collection.

(2) No sale or transfer may be made under subsection (1) above except to a person who—

    (a) produces the authority of the Secretary of State under section 5 of this Act for his purchase or acquisition; or

    (b) shows that he is, under this section or a licence under the Schedule to the Firearms (Amendment) Act 1988 (museums etc.), entitled to make the purchase or acquisition without the authority of the Secretary of State.

(3) The authority of the Secretary of State shall not be required by virtue of subsection (1A) of section 5 of this Act for any person to have in his possession, or to purchase or acquire, any prohibited weapon or ammunition if his possession, purchase or acquisition is exclusively in connection with the carrying on of activities in respect of which—

    (a) that person; or

    (b) the person on whose behalf he has possession, or makes the purchase or acquisition,

is recognised, for the purposes of the law of another member State relating to firearms, as a collector of firearms or a body concerned in the cultural or historical aspects of weapons.

(4) The authority of the Secretary of State shall not be required by virtue of subsection (1A) of section 5 of this Act for any person to have in his possession, or to purchase or acquire or to sell or transfer, any expanding ammunition or the missile for any such ammunition if—

    (a) he is authorised by a firearm certificate or visitor's firearm permit to possess, or purchase or acquire, any expanding ammunition; and

    (b) the certificate or permit is subject to a condition restricting the use of any expanding ammunition to use in connection with any one or more of the following, namely—

        (i) the lawful shooting of deer;

        (ii) the shooting of vermin or, in the course of carrying on activities in connection with the management of any estate other wildlife;

        (iii) the humane killing of animals;

        (iv) the shooting of animals for the protection of other animals or humans.

(5) The authority of the Secretary of State shall not be required by virtue of subsection (1A) of section 5 of this Act for any person to have in his possession any expanding ammunition or the missile for any such ammunition if—

    (a) he is entitled, under section 10 of this Act, to have a slaughtering instrument and the ammunition for it in his possession; and

    (b) the ammunition or missile in question is designed to be capable of being used with a slaughtering instrument.

(6) The authority of the Secretary of State shall not be required by virtue of subsection (1A) of section 5 of this Act for the sale or transfer of any expanding ammunition or the missile for any such ammunition to any person who produces a certificate by virtue of which he is authorised under subsection (4) above to purchase or acquire it without the authority of the Secretary of State.

(7) The authority of the Secretary of State shall not be required by virtue of subsection (1A) of section 5 of this Act for a person carrying on the business of a firearms dealer, or any servant of his, to have in his possession, or to purchase, acquire, sell or transfer, any expanding ammunition or the missile for any such ammunition in the ordinary course of that business.

(8) In this section—

    (a) references to expanding ammunition are references to any ammunition which . . . incorporates a missile which is designed to expand on impact; and

    (b) references to the missile for any such ammunition are references to anything which, in relation to any such ammunition, falls within section 5(1A)(g) of this Act.

7.   Police permit

(1) A person who has obtained from the chief officer of police for the area in which he resides a permit for the purpose in the prescribed form may, without holding a certificate under this Act, have in his possession a firearm and ammunition in accordance with the terms of the permit.

(2)   It is an offence for a person knowingly or recklessly to make a statement false in any material particular for the purpose of procuring, whether for himself or for another person, the grant of a permit under this section.

16.   Possession of firearm with intent to injure

It is an offence for a person to have in his possession any firearm or ammunition with intent by means thereof to endanger life . . . or to enable another person by means thereof to endanger life . . . whether any injury has been caused or not.

16A.   Possession of firearm with intent to cause fear of violence

It is an offence for a person to have in his possession any firearm or imitation firearm with intent—

(a)   by means thereof to cause, or

(b)   to enable another person by means thereof to cause,

any person to believe that unlawful violence will be used against him or another person.

17.   Use of firearm to resist arrest

(1)   It is an offence for a person to make or attempt to make any use whatsoever of a firearm or imitation firearm with intent to resist or prevent the lawful arrest or detention of himself or another person.

(2)   If a person, at the time of his committing or being arrested for an offence specified in Schedule 1 to this Act, has in his possession a firearm or imitation firearm, he shall be guilty of an offence under this subsection unless he shows that he had it in his possession for a lawful object.

(4)   For purposes of this section, the definition of 'firearm' in section 57(1) of this Act shall apply without paragraphs (b) and (c) of that subsection, and 'imitation firearm' shall be construed accordingly.

18.   Carrying firearm with criminal intent

(1)   It is an offence for a person to have with him a firearm or imitation firearm with intent to commit an indictable offence, or to resist arrest or prevent the arrest of another, in either case while he has the firearm or imitation firearm with him.

(2)   In proceedings for an offence under this section proof that the accused had a firearm or imitation firearm with him and intended to commit an offence, or to resist or prevent arrest, is evidence that he intended to have it with him while doing so.

19.   Carrying firearm in a public place

A person commits an offence if, without lawful authority or reasonable excuse (the proof whereof lies on him) he has with him in a public place—

(a)   a loaded shot gun,

(b)   an air weapon (whether loaded or not),

(c)   any other firearm (whether loaded or not) together with ammunition suitable for use in that firearm, or

(d)   an imitation firearm.

19A.   Having small-calibre pistol outside premises of licensed pistol club

(1)   It is an offence for any person to have a small-calibre pistol with him outside licensed premises of a licensed pistol club.

(2)   It is not an offence for a person to have with him a small-calibre pistol if—

(a)   he is permitted by virtue of any provision of this Act to have the pistol in his possession without holding a firearm certificate or a visitor's firearm permit;

(b)   he is authorised to have the pistol with him by virtue of a permit granted under section 13 of the Firearms (Amendment) Act 1997; or

(c)   he is authorised to have the pistol in his possession by virtue of a firearm certificate or visitor's firearm permit which is not subject to a condition requiring it to be kept at a licensed pistol club.

(3)   In this section 'licensed pistol club' means a pistol club which is licensed under Part II of the Firearms (Amendment) Act 1997 and 'licensed premises' has the meaning given in section 19 of that Act.

20.   Trespassing with firearm

(1)   A person commits an offence if, while he has a firearm or imitation firearm with him, he enters or is in any building or part of a building as a trespasser and without reasonable excuse (the proof whereof lies on him).

(2)   A person commits an offence if, while he has a firearm or imitation firearm with him, he enters or is on any land as a trespasser and without reasonable excuse (the proof whereof lies on him).

(3)   In subsection (2) of this section the expression 'land' includes land covered with water.

22.   Acquisition and possession of firearms by minors

(1)   It is an offence for a person under the age of seventeen to purchase or hire any firearm or ammunition.

(1A) Where a person under the age of eighteen is entitled, as the holder of a certificate under this Act, to have a firearm in his possession, it is an offence for that person to use that firearm for a purpose not authorised by the European weapons directive.

(2)   It is an offence for a person under the age of fourteen to have in his possession any firearm or ammunition to which section 1 of this Act applies, except in circumstances where under section 11 (1), (3) or (4) of this Act or section 15 of the Firearms (Amendment) Act 1988 he is entitled to have possession of it without holding a firearm certificate.

(3)   It is an offence for a person under the age of fifteen to have with him an assembled shot gun except while under the supervision of a person of or over the age of twenty-one, or while the shot gun is so covered with a securely fastened gun cover that it cannot be fired.

(4)   Subject to section 23 below, it is an offence for a person under the age of seventeen to have with him an air weapon or ammunition for an air weapon.

23.   Exceptions from s. 22(4)

(1)   It is not an offence under section 22(4) of this Act for a person to have with him an air weapon or ammunition while he is under the supervision of a person of or over the age of twenty-one; but where a person has with him an air weapon on any premises in circumstances where he would be prohibited from having it with him but for this subsection, it is an offence—

(a)   for him to use it for firing any missile beyond those premises; or

(b)   for the person under whose supervision he is to allow him so to use it.

(2)   It is not an offence under section 22(4) . . . of this Act for a person to have with him an air weapon or ammunition at a time when—

(a)   being a member of a rifle club or miniature rifle club for the time being approved by the Secretary of State for the purposes of this section or section 15 of the Firearms (Amendment) Act 1988, he is engaged as such a member in or in connection with target shooting; or

(b)   he is using the weapon or ammunition at a shooting gallery where the only firearms used are either air weapons or miniature rifles not exceeding 0.23 inch calibre.

(3)   It is not an offence under section 22(4) of this Act for a person of or over the age of fourteen to have with him an air weapon or ammunition on private premises with the consent of the occupier.

(4)   But where a person has with him an air weapon on premises in circumstances where he would be prohibited from having it with him but for subsection (3), it is an offence for him to use it for firing any missile beyond those premises.

24.   Supplying firearms to minors

(1)   It is an offence to sell or let on hire any firearm or ammunition to a person under the age of seventeen.

(2)   It is an offence—

(a)   to make a gift of or lend any firearm or ammunition to which section 1 of this Act applies to a person under the age of fourteen; or

(b)   to part with the possession of any such firearm or ammunition to a person under that age, except in circumstances where that person is entitled under section 11(1), (3) or (4) of this Act or section 15 of the Firearms (Amendment) Act 1988 to have possession thereof without holding a firearm certificate.

(3)   It is an offence to make a gift of a shot gun or ammunition for a shot gun to a person under the age of fifteen.

(4)   It is an offence—

(a)   to make a gift of an air weapon or ammunition for an air weapon to a person under the age of seventeen; or

(b)   to part with the possession of an air weapon or ammunition for an air weapon to a person under the age of seventeen except where by virtue of section 23 of this Act the person is not prohibited from having it with him.

(5)   In proceedings for an offence under any provision of this section it is a defence to prove that the person charged with the offence believed the other person to be of or over the age mentioned in that provision and had reasonable ground for the belief.

25.   Supplying firearm to person drunk or insane

It is an offence for a person to sell or transfer any firearm or ammunition to, or to repair, prove or test any firearm or ammunition for, another person whom he knows or has reasonable cause for believing to be drunk or of unsound mind.

57.   Interpretation

(1)   In this Act, the expression 'firearm' means a lethal barrelled weapon of any description from which any shot, bullet or other missile can be discharged and includes—

(a)   any prohibited weapon, whether it is such a lethal weapon as aforesaid or not; and

(b)   any component part of such a lethal or prohibited weapon; and

(c)   any accessory to any such weapon designed or adapted to diminish the noise or flash caused by firing the weapon;

and so much of section 1 of this Act as excludes any description of firearm from the category of firearms to which that section applies shall be construed as also excluding component parts of, and accessories to, firearms of that description.

(1A) . . .

(2)   In this Act, the expression 'ammunition' means ammunition for any firearm and includes grenades, bombs and other like missiles, whether capable of use with a firearm or not, and also includes prohibited ammunition.

(2A) In this Act 'self-loading' and 'pump-action' in relation to any weapon mean respectively that it is designed or adapted (otherwise than as mentioned in section 5(1)(a)) so that it is automatically re-loaded or that it is so designed or adapted that it is re-loaded by the manual operation of the fore-end or forestock of the weapon.

(2B) In this Act 'revolver', in relation to a smooth-bore gun, means a gun containing a series of chambers which revolve when the gun is fired.

(3)   For purposes of sections 45, 46, 50, 51(4) and 52 of this Act, the offences under this Act relating specifically to air weapons are those under sections 22(4), 22(5), 23(1) and 24(4).

(4)   In this Act—

'acquire' means hire, accept as a gift or borrow and 'acquisition' shall be construed accordingly;

'air weapon' has the meaning assigned to it by section 1(3)(b) of this Act;

'another member State' means a member State other than the United Kingdom, and 'other member States' shall be construed accordingly;

'area' means a police area;

'Article 7 authority' means a document issued by virtue of section 32A(1)(b) or (2) of this Act;

'British Transport Police Force' means the constables appointed under section 53 of the British Transport Commission Act 1949;

'certificate' (except in a context relating to the registration of firearms dealers) and 'certificate under this Act' mean a firearm certificate or a shot gun certificate and—

(a)   'firearm certificate' means a certificate granted by a chief officer of police under this Act in respect of any firearm or ammunition to which section 1 of this Act applies and includes a certificate granted in Northern Ireland under section 1 of the Firearms Act 1920 or under an enactment of the Parliament of Northern Ireland amending or substituted for that section; and

(b)   'shot gun certificate' means a certificate granted by a chief officer of police under this Act and authorising a person to possess shot guns;

'civilian officer' means—

(a)   a person employed by a police authority or the Corporation of the City of London who is under the direction and control of a chief officer of police; . . .

(b)   . . .

'European firearms pass' means a document to which the holder of a certificate under this Act is entitled by virtue of section 32A(1)(a) of this Act;

'European weapons directive' means the directive of the Council of the European Communities No 91/477/EEC (directive on the control of the acquisition and possession of weapons);

'firearms dealer' means a person who, by way of trade or business, manufactures, sells, transfers, repairs, tests or proves firearms or ammunition to which section 1 of this Act applies, or shot guns;

'imitation firearm' means any thing which has the appearance of being a firearm (other than such a weapon as is mentioned in section 5(1)(b) of this Act) whether or not it is capable of discharging any shot, bullet or other missile;

. . .

'premises' includes any land;

'prescribed' means prescribed by rules made by the Secretary of State under section 53 of this Act;

'prohibited weapon' and 'prohibited ammunition' have the meanings assigned to them by section 5(2) of this Act;

'public place' includes any highway and any other premises or place to which at the material time the public have or are permitted to have access, whether on payment or otherwise;

'registered', in relation to a firearms dealer, means registered either—

(a)   in Great Britain, under section 33 of this Act, or

(b)   in Northern Ireland, under section 8 of the Firearms Act 1920 or any enactment of the Parliament of Northern Ireland amending or substituted for that section,

and references to 'the register', 'registration' and a 'certificate of registration' shall be construed accordingly, except in section 40;

'rifle' includes carbine;

'shot gun' has the meaning assigned to it by section 1(3)(a) of this Act and, in sections 3(1) and 45(2) of this Act and in the definition of 'firearms dealer', includes any component part of a shot gun and any accessory to a shot gun designed or adapted to diminish the noise or flash caused by firing the gun;

'slaughtering instrument' means a firearm which is specially designed or adapted for the instantaneous slaughter of animals or for the instantaneous stunning of animals with a view to slaughtering them; and

'transfer' includes let on hire, give, lend and part with possession, and 'transferee' and 'transferor' shall be construed accordingly.

(4A) For the purposes of any reference in this Act to the use of any firearm or ammunition for a purpose not authorised by the European weapons directive, the directive shall be taken to authorise the use of a firearm or ammunition as or with a slaughtering instrument and the use of a firearm and ammunition—

(a)   for sporting purposes;

(b)   for the shooting of vermin, or, in the course of carrying on activities in connection with the management of any estate, of other wildlife; and

(c)   for competition purposes and target shooting outside competitions.

(5)   The definitions in subsections (1) to (3) above apply to the provisions of this Act except where the context otherwise requires.

(6)   For purposes of this Act—

(a)   the length of the barrel of a firearm shall be measured from the muzzle to the point at which the charge is exploded on firing; and

(b)   a shot gun or an air weapon shall be deemed to be loaded if there is ammunition in the chamber or barrel or in any magazine or other device which is in such a position that the ammunition can be fed into the chamber or barrel by the manual or automatic operation of some part of the gun or weapon.

58.   Particular savings

(2)   Nothing in this Act relating to firearms shall apply to an antique firearm which is sold, transferred, purchased, acquired or possessed as a curiosity or ornament.

(3)   The provisions of this Act relating to ammunition shall be in addition to and not in derogation of any enactment relating to the keeping and sale of explosives.

SCHEDULE 1
OFFENCES TO WHICH SECTION 17(2) APPLIES

1.   Offences under section 1 of the Criminal Damage Act 1971

2.   Offences under any of the following provisions of the Offences against the Person Act 1861—
section 20 to 22 (inflicting bodily injury; garrotting; criminal use of stupefying drugs);
section 30 (laying explosive to building etc.);
section 32 (endangering railway passengers by tampering with track);
section 38 (assault with intent to commit felony or resist arrest);
section 47 (criminal assaults);
section 56 (child-stealing and abduction).

2A.   Offences under Part 1 of the Child Abduction Act 1984 (abduction of children).

4.   Theft, robbery, burglary, blackmail and any offence under section 12(1) (taking of motor vehicle or other conveyance without owner's consent) of the Theft Act 1968.

5.   Offences under section 51(1) of the Police Act 1964 or section 41 of the Police (Scotland) Act 1967 (assaulting constable in execution of his duty).

5A.   An offence under section 90(1) of the Criminal Justice Act 1991 (assaulting prisoner custody officer).

5B.   An offence under section 13(1) of the Criminal Justice and Public Order Act 1994 (assaulting secure training centre custody officer).

5C.   An offence under paragraph 4 of Schedule 11 to the Immigration and Asylum Act 1999 (assaulting a detainee custody officer).

6.   Offences under any of the following provisions of the Sexual Offences Act 2003—

(a)   section 1 (rape);

(b)   section 2 (assault by penetration);

(c)   section 4 (causing a person to engage in sexual activity without consent), where the activity caused involved penetration within subsection (4)(a) to (d) of that section;

(d)   section 5 (rape of a child under 13);

(e)   section 6 (assault of a child under 13 by penetration);

(f)   section 8 (causing or inciting a child under 13 to engage in sexual activity), where an activity involving penetration within subsection (3)(a) to (d) of that section was caused;

(g)   section 30 (sexual activity with a person with a mental disorder impeding choice), where the touching involved penetration within subsection (3)(a) to (d) of that section;

(h)   section 31 (causing or inciting a person, with a mental disorder impeding choice, to engage in sexual activity), where an activity involving penetration within subsection (3)(a) to (d) of that section was caused.

8.   Aiding or abetting the commission of any offence specified in paragraphs 1 to 6 of this Schedule.

9.   Attempting to commit any offence so specified.

FOOTBALL (OFFENCES) ACT 1991

1.   Designated football matches

(1)   In this Act a 'designated football match' means an association football match designated, or of a description designated, for the purposes of this Act by order of the Secretary of State.

        Any such order shall be made by statutory instrument which shall be subject to annulment in pursuance of a resolution of either House of Parliament.

(2)   References in this Act to things done at a designated football match include anything done at the ground—

     (a)   within the period beginning two hours before the start of the match or (if earlier) two hours before the time at which it is advertised to start and ending one hour after the end of the match; or

     (b)   where the match is advertised to start at a particular time on a particular day but does not take place on that day, within the period beginning two hours before and ending one hour after the advertised starting time.

2.   Throwing of missiles

It is an offence for a person at a designated football match to throw anything at or towards—

     (a)   the playing area, or any area adjacent to the playing area to which spectators are not generally admitted, or

     (b)   any area in which spectators or other persons are or may be present,

without lawful authority or lawful excuse (which shall be for him to prove).

3.   Indecent or racialist chanting

(1)   It is an offence to engage or take part in chanting of an indecent or racialist nature at a designated football match.

(2)   For this purpose—

     (a)   'chanting' means the repeated uttering of any words or sounds (whether alone or in concert with one or more others); and

     (b)   'of a racialist nature' means consisting of or including matter which is threatening, abusive or insulting to a person by reason of his colour, race, nationality (including citizenship) or ethnic or national origins.

4.   Going onto the playing area

It is an offence for a person at a designated football match to go onto the playing area, or any area adjacent to the playing area to which spectators are not generally admitted, without lawful authority or lawful excuse (which shall be for him to prove).

FORGERY AND COUNTERFEITING ACT 1981

PART I
FORGERY AND KINDRED OFFENCES

1.   The offence of forgery

A person is guilty of forgery if he makes a false instrument, with the intention that he or another shall use it to induce somebody to accept it as genuine, and by reason of so accepting it to do or not to do some act to his own or any other person's prejudice.

2.   The offence of copying a false instrument

It is an offence for a person to make a copy of an instrument which is, and which he knows or believes to be, a false instrument, with the intention that he or another shall use it to induce somebody to accept it as a copy of a genuine instrument, and by reason of so accepting it to do or not to do some act to his own or any other person's prejudice.

3.   The offence of using a false instrument

It is an offence for a person to use an instrument which is, and which he knows or believes to be, false, with the intention of inducing somebody to accept it as genuine, and by reason of so accepting it to do or not to do some act to his own or any other person's prejudice.

4.   The offence of using a copy of a false instrument

It is an offence for a person to use a copy of an instrument which is, and which he knows or believes to be, a false instrument, with the intention of inducing somebody to accept it as a copy of a genuine instrument, and by reason of so accepting it to do or not to do some act to his own or any other person's prejudice.

5.   Offences relating to money orders, share certificates, passports, etc.

(1)   It is an offence for a person to have in his custody or under his control an instrument to which this section applies which is, and which he knows or believes to be, false, with the intention that he or another shall use it to induce somebody to accept it as genuine, and by reason of so accepting it to do or not to do some act to his own or any other person's prejudice.

(2)   It is an offence for a person to have in his custody or under his control, without lawful authority or excuse, an instrument to which this section applies which is, and which he knows or believes to be, false.

(3)   It is an offence for a person to make or to have in his custody or under his control a machine or implement, or paper or any other material, which to his knowledge is or has been specially designed or adapted for the making of an instrument to which this section applies, with the intention that he or another shall make an instrument to which this section applies which is false and that he or another shall use the instrument to induce somebody to accept it as genuine, and by reason of so accepting it to do or not to do some act to his own or any other person's prejudice.

(4)   It is an offence for a person to make or to have in his custody or under his control any such machine, implement, paper or material, without lawful authority or excuse.

(5)   The instruments to which this section applies are—

(a)   money orders;

(b)   postal orders;

(c)   United Kingdom postage stamps;

(d)   Inland Revenue stamps;

(e)   share certificates;

(f)   passports and documents which can be used instead of passports;

(fa)   immigration documents;

(g)   cheques and other bills of exchange;

(h)   travellers' cheques;

(ha)   bankers' drafts;

(hb)   promissory notes;

(j)   cheque cards;

(ja)   debit cards;

(k)   credit cards;

(l)   certified copies relating to an entry in a register of births, adoptions, marriages, civil partnerships or deaths and issued by the Registrar General, the Registrar General for Northern Ireland, a registration officer or a person lawfully authorised to issue certified copies relating to such entries; and

(m)   certificates relating to entries in such registers.

(6)   In subsection (5)(e) above 'share certificate' means an instrument entitling or evidencing the title of a person to a share or interest—

(a)   in any public stock, annuity, fund or debt of any government or state, including a state which forms part of another state; or

(b)   in any stock, fund or debt of a body (whether corporate or unincorporated) established in the United Kingdom or elsewhere.

(7) An instrument is also an instrument to which this section applies if it is a monetary instrument specified for the purposes of this section by an order made by the Secretary of State.

(8) The power under subsection (7) above is exercisable by statutory instrument subject to annulment in pursuance of a resolution of either House of Parliament.

(9) In subsection (5)(fa) 'immigration document' means a card, adhesive label or other instrument which satisfies subsection (10) or (11).

(10) A card, adhesive label or other instrument satisfies this subsection if it—

    (a) is designed to be given, in the exercise of a function under the Immigration Acts (within the meaning of section 44 of the Asylum and Immigration (Treatment of Claimants, etc) Act 2004), to a person who has been granted leave to enter or remain in the United Kingdom, and

    (b) carries information (whether or not wholly or partly electronically) about the leave granted.

(11) A card, adhesive label or other instrument satisfies this subsection if it is given to a person to confirm a right of his under the Community Treaties in respect of entry to or residence in the United Kingdom.

8. Meaning of 'instrument'

(1) Subject to subsection (2) below, in this Part of this Act 'instrument' means—

    (a) any document, whether of a formal or informal character;

    (b) any stamp issued or sold by a postal operator;

    (c) any Inland Revenue stamp; and

    (d) any disc, tape, sound track or other device on or in which information is recorded or stored by mechanical, electronic or other means.

(2) A currency note within the meaning of Part II of this Act is not an instrument for the purposes of this Part of this Act.

(3) A mark denoting payment of postage which a postal operator authorises to be used instead of an adhesive stamp is to be treated for the purposes of this Part of this Act as if it were a stamp issued by the postal operator concerned.

(3A) In this section 'postal operator' has the same meaning as in the Postal Services Act 2000.

9. Meaning of 'false' and 'making'

(1) An instrument is false for the purposes of this Part of this Act—

    (a) if it purports to have been made in the form in which it is made by a person who did not in fact make it in that form; or

    (b) if it purports to have been made in the form in which it is made on the authority of a person who did not in fact authorise its making in that form; or

    (c) if it purports to have been made in the terms in which it is made by a person who did not in fact make it in those terms; or

    (d) if it purports to have been made in the terms in which it is made on the authority of a person who did not in fact authorise its making in those terms; or

    (e) if it purports to have been altered in any respect by a person who did not in fact alter it in that respect; or

    (f) if it purports to have been altered in any respect on the authority of a person who did not in fact authorise the alteration in that respect; or

    (g) if it purports to have been made or altered on a date on which, or at a place at which, or otherwise in circumstances in which, it was not in fact made or altered; or

    (h) if it purports to have been made or altered by an existing person but he did not in fact exist.

(2) A person is to be treated for the purposes of this Part of this Act as making a false instrument if he alters an instrument so as to make it false in any respect (whether or not it is false in some other respect apart from that alteration).

10.   Meaning of 'prejudice' and 'induce'

(1)   Subject to subsections (2) and (4) below, for the purposes of this Part of this Act an act or omission intended to be induced is to a person's prejudice if, and only if, it is one which if it occurs—

(a)   will result—

(i)   in his temporary or permanent loss of property; or

(ii)   in his being deprived of an opportunity to earn remuneration or greater remuneration; or

(iii)   in his being deprived of an opportunity to gain a financial advantage otherwise than by way of remuneration; or

(b)   will result in somebody being given an opportunity—

(i)   to earn remuneration or greater remuneration from him; or

(ii)   to gain a financial advantage from him otherwise than by way of remuneration; or

(c)   will be the result of his having accepted a false instrument as genuine, or a copy of a false instrument as a copy of a genuine one, in connection with his performance of any duty.

(2)   An act which a person has an enforceable duty to do and an omission to do an act which a person is not entitled to do shall be disregarded for the purposes of this Part of this Act.

(3)   In this Part of this Act references to inducing somebody to accept a false instrument as genuine, or a copy of a false instrument as a copy of a genuine one, include references to inducing a machine to respond to the instrument or copy as if it were a genuine instrument or, as the case may be, a copy of a genuine one.

(4)   Where subsection (3) above applies, the act or omission intended to be induced by the machine responding to the instrument or copy shall be treated as an act or omission to a person's prejudice.

(5)   In this section 'loss' includes not getting what one might get as well as parting with what one has.

PART II
COUNTERFEITING AND KINDRED OFFENCES

14.   Offences of counterfeiting notes and coins

(1)   It is an offence for a person to make a counterfeit of a currency note or of a protected coin, intending that he or another shall pass or tender it as genuine.

(2)   It is an offence for a person to make a counterfeit of a currency note or of a protected coin without lawful authority or excuse.

15.   Offences of passing, etc., counterfeit notes and coins

(1)   It is an offence for a person—

(a)   to pass or tender as genuine any thing which is, and which he knows or believes to be, a counterfeit of a currency note or of a protected coin; or

(b)   to deliver to another any thing which is, and which he knows or believes to be, such a counterfeit, intending that the person to whom it is delivered or another shall pass or tender it as genuine.

(2)   It is an offence for a person to deliver to another, without lawful authority or excuse, any thing which is, and which he knows or believes to be, a counterfeit of a currency note or of a protected coin.

16.   Offences involving the custody or control of counterfeit notes and coins

(1)   It is an offence for a person to have in his custody or under his control any thing which is, and which he knows or believes to be, a counterfeit of a currency note or of a protected coin, intending either to pass or tender it as genuine or to deliver it to another with the intention that he or another shall pass or tender it as genuine.

(2) It is an offence for a person to have in his custody or under his control, without lawful authority or excuse, anything which is, and which he knows or believes to be, a counterfeit of a currency note or of a protected coin.

27. Meaning of 'currency note' and 'protected coin'

(1) In this Part of this Act—

'currency note' means—

(a) any note which—

(i) has been lawfully issued in England and Wales, Scotland, Northern Ireland, any of the Channel Islands, the Isle of Man or the Republic of Ireland; and

(ii) is or has been customarily used as money in the country where it was issued; and

(iii) is payable on demand; or

(b) any note which—

(i) has been lawfully issued in some country other than those mentioned in paragraph (a)(i) above; and

(ii) is customarily used as money in that country; and

'protected coin' means any coin which—

(a) is customarily used as money in any country; or

(b) is specified in an order made by the Treasury for the purposes of this Part of this Act.

(2) The power to make an order conferred on the Treasury by subsection (1) above shall be exercisable by statutory instrument.

(3) A statutory instrument containing such an order shall be laid before Parliament after being made.

28. Meaning of 'counterfeit'

(1) For the purposes of this Part of this Act a thing is a counterfeit of a currency note or of a protected coin—

(a) if it is not a currency note or a protected coin but resembles a currency note or protected coin (whether on one side only or on both) to such an extent that it is reasonably capable of passing for a currency note or protected coin of that description; or

(b) if it is currency note or protected coin which has been so altered that it is reasonably capable of passing for a currency note or protected coin of some other description.

(2) For the purposes of this Part of this Act—

(a) a thing consisting of one side only of a currency note, with or without the addition of other material, is a counterfeit of such a note;

(b) a thing consisting—

(i) of parts of two or more currency notes; or

(ii) of parts of a currency note, or of parts of two or more currency notes, with the addition of other material,

is capable of being a counterfeit of a currency note.

(3) References in this Part of this Act to passing or tendering a counterfeit of a currency note or a protected coin are not to be construed as confined to passing or tendering it as legal tender.

GENDER RECOGNITION ACT 2004

9. General

(1) Where a full gender recognition certificate is issued to a person, the person's gender becomes for all purposes the acquired gender (so that, if the acquired gender is the male gender, the person's sex becomes that of a man and, if it is the female gender, the person's sex becomes that of a woman).

(2) Subsection (1) does not affect things done, or events occurring, before the certificate is issued; but it does operate for the interpretation of enactments passed, and instruments and other documents made, before the certificate is issued (as well as those passed or made afterwards).

20.   **Gender-specific offences**

(1)   Where (apart from this subsection) a relevant gender-specific offence could be committed or attempted only if the gender of a person to whom a full gender recognition certificate has been issued were not the acquired gender, the fact that the person's gender has become the acquired gender does not prevent the offence being committed or attempted.

(2)   An offence is a 'relevant gender-specific offence' if—

(a)   either or both of the conditions in subsection (3) are satisfied, and

(b)   the commission of the offence involves the accused engaging in sexual activity.

(3)   The conditions are—

(a)   that the offence may be committed only by a person of a particular gender, and

(b)   that the offence may be committed only on, or in relation to, a person of a particular gender,

and the references to a particular gender include a gender identified by reference to the gender of the other person involved.

HOMICIDE ACT 1957

1.   **Abolition of 'constructive malice'**

(1)   Where a person kills another in the course or furtherance of some other offence, the killing shall not amount to murder unless done with the same malice aforethought (express or implied) as is required for a killing to amount to murder when not done in the course or furtherance of another offence.

(2)   For the purposes of the foregoing subsection, a killing done in the course or for the purpose of resisting an officer of justice, or of resisting or avoiding or preventing a lawful arrest, or of effecting or assisting an escape or rescue from legal custody, shall be treated as a killing in the course or furtherance of an offence.

2.   **Persons suffering from diminished responsibility**

(1)   Where a person kills or is a party to the killing of another, he shall not be convicted of murder if he was suffering from such abnormality of mind (whether arising from a condition of arrested or retarded development of mind or any inherent causes or induced by disease or injury) as substantially impaired his mental responsibility for his acts and omissions in doing or being a party to the killing.

(2)   On a charge of murder, it shall be for the defence to prove that the person charged is by virtue of this section not liable to be convicted of murder.

(3)   A person who but for this section would be liable, whether as a principal or as accessory, to be convicted of murder shall be liable instead to be convicted of manslaughter.

(4)   The fact that one party to a killing is by virtue of this section not liable to be convicted of murder shall not affect the question whether the killing amounted to murder in the case of any other party to it.

3.   **Provocation**

Where on a charge of murder there is evidence on which the jury can find that the person charged was provoked (whether by things done or by things said or by both together) to lose his self-control, the question whether the provocation was enough to make a reasonable man do as he did shall be left to be determined by the jury; and in determining that question the jury shall take into account everything both done and said according to the effect which, in their opinion, it would have on a reasonable man.

4.   **Suicide pacts**

(1)   It shall be manslaughter, and shall not be murder, for a person acting in pursuance of a suicide pact between him and another to kill the other or be a party to the other . . . being killed by a third person.

(2) Where it is shown that a person charged with the murder of another killed the other or was a party to his . . . being killed, it shall be for the defence to prove that the person charged was acting in pursuance of a suicide pact between him and the other.

(3) For the purposes of this section 'suicide pact' means a common agreement between two or more persons having for its object the death of all of them, whether or not each is to take his own life, but nothing done by a person who enters into a suicide pact shall be treated as done by him in pursuance of the pact unless it is done while he has the settled intention of dying in pursuance of the pact.

HUMAN RIGHTS ACT 1998

1.   **The Convention Rights**

(1) In this Act 'the Convention rights' means the rights and fundamental freedoms set out in—

    (a) Articles 2 to 12 and 14 of the Convention,

    (b) Articles 1 to 3 of the First Protocol, and

    (c) Article 1 of the Thirteenth Protocol,

as read with Articles 16 to 18 of the Convention.

(2) Those Articles are to have effect for the purposes of this Act subject to any designated derogation or reservation (as to which see sections 14 and 15).

(3) The Articles are set out in Schedule 1.

2.   **Interpretation of Convention Rights**

(1) A court or tribunal determining a question which has arisen in connection with a Convention right must take into account any—

    (a) judgment, decision, declaration or advisory opinion of the European Court of Human Rights,

    (b) opinion of the Commission given in a report adopted under Article 31 of the Convention,

    (c) decision of the Commission in connection with Article 26 or 27(2) of the Convention, or

    (d) decision of the Committee of Ministers taken under Article 46 of the Convention,

whenever made or given, so far as, in the opinion of the court or tribunal, it is relevant to the proceedings in which that question has arisen.

(2) Evidence of any judgment, decision, declaration or opinion of which account may have to be taken under this section is to be given in proceedings before any court or tribunal in such manner as may be provided by rules.

3.   **Interpretation of legislation**

(1) So far as it is possible to do so, primary legislation and subordinate legislation must be read and given effect in a way which is compatible with the Convention rights.

(2) This section—

    (a) applies to primary legislation and subordinate legislation whenever enacted;

    (b) does not affect the validity, continuing operation or enforcement of any incompatible primary legislation; and

    (c) does not affect the validity, continuing operation or enforcement of any incompatible subordinate legislation if (disregarding any possibility of revocation) primary legislation prevents removal of the incompatibility,

4.   **Declaration of incompatibility**

(1) Subsection (2) applies in any proceedings in which a court determines whether a provision of primary legislation is compatible with a Convention right.

(2) If the court is satisfied that the provision is incompatible with a Convention right, it may make a declaration of that incompatibility.

(3) Subsection (4) applies in any proceedings in which a court determines whether a provision of subordinate legislation, made in the exercise of a power conferred by primary legislation, is compatible with a Convention right.

(4) If the court is satisfied—

    (a) that the provision is incompatible with a Convention right, and

    (b) that (disregarding any possibility of revocation) the primary legislation concerned prevents removal of the incompatibility,

it may make a declaration of that incompatibility.

(5) In this section 'court' means—

    (a) the House of Lords;

    (b) the Judicial Committee of the Privy Council;

    (c) the Courts-Martial Appeal Court;

    (d) in Scotland, the High Court of Justiciary sitting otherwise than as a trial court or the Court of Session;

    (e) in England and Wales or Northern Ireland, the High Court or the Court of Appeal.

(6) A declaration under this section ('a declaration of incompatibility')—

    (a) does not affect the validity, continuing operation or enforcement of the provision in respect of which it is given; and

    (b) is not binding on the parties to the proceedings in which it is made.

SCHEDULE 1
THE ARTICLES

PART I
THE CONVENTION

RIGHTS AND FREEDOMS

Article 2
Right to life

1. Everyone's right to life shall be protected by law. No one shall be deprived of his life intentionally save in the execution of a sentence of a court following his conviction of a crime for which this penalty is provided by law.

2. Deprivation of life shall not be regarded as inflicted in contravention of this Article when it results from the use of force which is no more than absolutely necessary:

    (a) in defence of any person from unlawful violence;

    (b) in order to effect a lawful arrest or to prevent the escape of a person lawfully detained;

    (c) in action lawfully taken for the purpose of quelling a riot or insurrection.

Article 3
Prohibition of torture

No one shall be subjected to torture or to inhuman or degrading treatment or punishment.

Article 4
Prohibition of slavery and forced labour

1. No one shall be held in slavery or servitude.

2. No one shall be required to perform forced or compulsory labour.

3. For the purpose of this Article the term 'forced or compulsory labour' shall not include:

    (a) any work required to be done in the ordinary course of detention imposed according to the provisions of Article 5 of this Convention or during conditional release from such detention;

    (b) any service of a military character or, in case of conscientious objectors in countries where they are recognised, service exacted instead of compulsory military service;

    (c) any service exacted in case of an emergency or calamity threatening the life or well-being of the community;

    (d) any work or service which forms part of normal civic obligations.

Article 5
Right to liberty and security

1.   Everyone has the right to liberty and security of person. No one shall be deprived of his liberty save in the following cases and in accordance with a procedure prescribed by law:

     (a)   the lawful detention of a person after conviction by a competent court;

     (b)   the lawful arrest or detention of a person for non-compliance with the lawful order of a court or in order to secure the fulfilment of any obligation prescribed by law;

     (c)   the lawful arrest or detention of a person effected for the purpose of bringing him before the competent legal authority on reasonable suspicion of having committed an offence or when it is reasonably considered necessary to prevent his committing an offence or fleeing after having-done so;

     (d)   the detention of a minor by lawful order for the purpose of educational supervision or his lawful detention for the purpose of bringing him before the competent legal authority;

     (e)   the lawful detention of persons for the prevention of the spreading of infectious diseases, of persons of unsound mind, alcoholics or drug addicts or vagrants;

     (f)   the lawful arrest or detention of a person to prevent his effecting an unauthorised entry into the country or of a person against whom action is being taken with a view to deportation or extradition.

Article 6
Right to a fair trial

1.   In the determination of his civil rights and obligations or of any criminal charge against him, everyone is entitled to a fair and public hearing within a reasonable time by an independent and impartial tribunal established by law. Judgment shall be pronounced publicly but the press and public may be excluded from all or part of the trial in the interest of morals, public order or national security in a democratic society, where the interests of juveniles or the protection of the private life of the parties so require, or to the extent strictly necessary in the opinion of the court in special circumstances where publicity would prejudice the interests of justice.

2.   Everyone charged with a criminal offence shall be presumed innocent until proved guilty according to law.

Article 7
No punishment without law

1.   No one shall be held guilty of any criminal offence on account of any act or omission which did not constitute a criminal offence under national or international law at the time when it was committed. Nor shall a heavier penalty be imposed than the one that was applicable at the time the criminal offence was committed.

2.   This Article shall not prejudice the trial and punishment of any person for any act or omission which, at the time when it was committed, was criminal according to the general principles of law recognised by civilised nations.

Article 8
Right to respect for private and family life

1.   Everyone has the right to respect for his private and family life, his home and his correspondence.

2.   There shall be no interference by a public authority with the exercise of this right except such as is in accordance with the law and is necessary in a democratic society in the interests of national security, public safety or the economic well being of the country, for the prevention of disorder or crime, for the protection of health or morals, or for the protection of the rights and freedoms of others.

Article 9
Freedom of thought, conscience and religion

1. Everyone has the right to freedom of thought, conscience and religion; this right includes freedom to change his religion or belief and freedom, either alone or in community with others and in public or private, to manifest his religion or belief, in worship, teaching, practice and observance.

2. Freedom to manifest one's religion or beliefs shall he subject only to such limitations as are prescribed by law and are necessary in a democratic society in the interests of public safety, for the protection of public order, health or morals, or for the protection of the rights and freedoms of others.

Article 10
Freedom of expression

1. Everyone has the right to freedom of expression. This right shall include freedom to hold opinions and to receive and impart information and ideas without interference by public authority and regardless of frontiers. This Article shall not prevent States from requiring the licensing of broadcasting television or cinema enterprises.

2. The exercise of these freedoms, since it carries with it duties and responsibilities, may be subject to such formalities, conditions, restrictions or penalties as are prescribed by law and are necessary in a democratic society, in the interests of national security, territorial integrity or public safety, for the prevention of disorder or crime, for the protection of health or morals, for the protection of the reputation or rights of others, for preventing the disclosure of information received in confidence, or for maintaining the authority and impartiality of the judiciary.

Article 11
Freedom of assembly and association

1. Everyone has the right to freedom of peaceful assembly and to freedom of association with others, including the right to form and to join trade unions for the protection of his interests.

2. No restrictions shall be placed on the exercise of these rights other than such as are prescribed by law and are necessary in a democratic society in the interests of national security or public safety, for the prevention of disorder or crime, for the protection of health or morals or for the protection of the rights and freedoms of others. This Article shall not prevent the imposition of lawful restrictions on the exercise of these rights by members of the armed forces, of the police or of the administration of the State.

Article 14
Prohibition of discrimination

The enjoyment of the rights and freedoms set forth in this Convention shall be secured without discrimination on any ground such as sex, race, colour, language, religion, political or other opinion, national or social origin, association with a national minority, property, birth or other status.

Article 16
Restrictions on political activity of aliens

Nothing in Articles 10, 11 and 14 shall be regarded as preventing the High Contracting Parties from imposing restrictions on the political activity of aliens.

Article 17
Prohibition of abuse of rights

Nothing in this Convention may be interpreted as implying for any State, group or person any right to engage in any activity or perform any act aimed at the destruction of any of the rights and freedoms set forth herein or at their limitation to a greater extent than is provided for in the Convention.

Article 18
Limitation on use of restrictions on rights

The restrictions permitted under this Convention to the said rights and freedoms shall not be applied for any purpose other than those for which they have been prescribed.

PART II
THE FIRST PROTOCOL

Article 1
Protection of property

Every natural or legal person is entitled to the peaceful enjoyment of his possessions. No one shall be deprived of his possessions except in the public interest and subject to the conditions provided for by law and by the general principles of international law.

INFANT LIFE (PRESERVATION) ACT 1929

1.   Punishment for child destruction

    (1)   Subject as hereinafter in this subsection provided, any person who, with intent to destroy the life of a child capable of being born alive, by any wilful act causes a child to die before it has an existence independent of its mother, shall be guilty of an offence, to wit, of child destruction, and shall be liable on conviction thereof . . . to imprisonment for life:

        Provided that no person shall be found guilty of an offence under this section unless it is proved that the act which caused the death of the child was not done in good faith for the purpose only of preserving the life of the mother.

    (2)   For the purposes of this Act, evidence that a woman had at any material time been pregnant for a period of twenty-eight weeks or more shall be a prima facie proof that she was at that time pregnant of a child capable of being born alive.

2.   Prosecution of offences

    (2)   Where upon the trial of any person for the murder or manslaughter of any child, or for infanticide, or for an offence under section fifty-eight of the Offences against the Person Act, 1861 (which relates to administering drugs or using instruments to procure abortion), the jury are of opinion that the person charged is not guilty of murder, manslaughter or infanticide, or of an offence under the said section fifty-eight, as the case may be, but that he is shown by the evidence to be guilty of the offence of child destruction, the jury may find him guilty of that offence, and thereupon the person convicted shall be liable to be punished as if he had been convicted upon an indictment for child destruction.

    (3)   Where upon the trial of any person for the offence of child destruction the jury are of opinion that the person charged is not guilty of any offence, but that he is shown by the evidence to be guilty of an offence under the said section fifty-eight of the Offences against the Person Act, 1861, the jury may find him guilty of that offence, and thereupon the person convicted shall be liable to be punished as if he had been convicted upon an indictment under that section.

INFANTICIDE ACT 1938

1.   Offence of infanticide

    (1)   Where a woman by any wilful act or omission causes the death of her child being a child under the age of twelve months, but at the time of the act or omission the balance of her mind was disturbed by reason of her not having fully recovered from the effect of giving birth to the child or by reason of the effect of lactation consequent upon the birth of the child, then, notwithstanding that the circumstances were such that but for this Act the offence would have amounted to murder, she shall be guilty of an offence, to wit of

infanticide, and may for such offence be dealt with and punished as if she had been guilty of the offence of manslaughter of the child.

(2)   Where upon the trial of a woman for the murder of her child, being a child under the age of twelve months, the jury are of opinion that she by any wilful act or omission caused its death, but that at the time of the act or omission the balance of her mind was disturbed by reason of her not having fully recovered from the effect of giving birth to the child or by reason of the effect of lactation consequent upon the birth of the child, then the jury may, notwithstanding that the circumstances were such that but for the provisions of this Act they might have returned a verdict of murder, return in lieu thereof a verdict of infanticide.

(3)   Nothing in this Act shall affect the power of the jury upon an indictment for the murder of a child to return a verdict of manslaughter, or a verdict of guilty but insane . . .

INTERPRETATION ACT 1978

5.   Definitions

In any Act, unless the contrary intention appears, words and expressions listed in Schedule 1 to this Act are to be construed according to that Schedule.

6.   Gender and number

In any Act, unless the contrary intention appears,—

(a)   words importing the masculine gender include the feminine;

(b)   words importing the feminine gender include the masculine;

(c)   words in the singular include the plural and words in the plural include the singular.

15.   Repeal of repeal

Where an Act repeals a repealing enactment, the repeal does not revive any enactment previously repealed unless words are added reviving it.

16.   General savings

(1)   Without prejudice to section 15, where an Act repeals an enactment, the repeal does not, unless the contrary intention appears,—

(a)   revive anything not in force or existing at the time at which the repeal takes effect;

(b)   affect the previous operation of the enactment repealed or anything duly done or suffered under that enactment;

(c)   affect any right, privilege, obligation or liability acquired, accrued, or incurred under that enactment;

(e)   affect any investigation, legal proceeding or remedy in respect of any such right, privilege, obligation, liability, penalty, forfeiture or punishment;

and any such investigation, legal proceeding or remedy may be instituted, continued or enforced, and any such penalty, forefeiture or punishment may be imposed, as if the repealing Act had not been passed.

(2)   This section applies to the expiry of a temporary enactment as if it were repealed by an Act.

18.   Duplicated offences

Where an act or omission constitutes an offence under two or more Acts, or both under an Act and at common law, the offender shall, unless the contrary intention appears, be liable to be prosecuted and punished under either or any of those Acts or at common law, but shall not be liable to be punished more than once for the same offence.

SCHEDULE 1

'Person' includes a body of persons corporate or unincorporate.

Construction of certain expressions relating to offences

In relation to England and Wales—

(a)   'indictable offence' means an offence which, if committed by an adult, is triable on indictment, whether it is exclusively so triable or triable either way;

(b)   'summary offence' means an offence which, if committed by an adult, is triable only summarily;

(c)   'offence triable either way' means an offence which, if committed by an adult, is triable either on indictment or summarily;

and the terms 'indictable', 'summary' and 'triable either way', in their application to offences, are to be construed accordingly.

In the above definitions references to the way or ways in which an offence is triable are to be construed without regard to the effect, if any, of section 22 of the Magistrates' Courts Act 1980 on the mode of trial in a particular case.

INTOXICATING SUBSTANCES (SUPPLY) ACT 1985

1.   **Offence of supplying intoxicating substance**

(1)   It is an offence for a person to supply or offer to supply a substance other than a controlled drug—

     (a)   to a person under the age of eighteen whom he knows, or has reasonable cause to believe, to be under that age; or

     (b)   to a person—

         (i)   who is acting on behalf of a person under that age; and

         (ii)   whom he knows, or has reasonable cause to believe, to be so acting,

   if he knows or has reasonable cause to believe that the substance is, or its fumes are, likely to be inhaled by the person under the age of eighteen for the purpose of causing intoxication.

(2)   In proceedings against any person for an offence under subsection (1) above it is a defence for him to show that at the time he made the supply or offer he was under the age of eighteen and was acting otherwise than in the course of furtherance of a business.

(4)   In this section 'controlled drug' has the same meaning as in the Misuse of Drugs Act 1971.

KNIVES ACT 1997

1.   **Unlawful marketing of knives**

(1)   A person is guilty of an offence if he markets a knife in a way which—

     (a)   indicates, or suggests, that it is suitable for combat; or

     (b)   is otherwise likely to stimulate or encourage violent behaviour involving the use of the knife as a weapon.

(2)   'Suitable for combat' and 'violent behaviour' are defined in section 10.

(3)   For the purposes of this Act, an indication or suggestion that a knife is suitable for combat may, in particular, be given or made by a name or description—

     (a)   applied to the knife;

     (b)   on the knife or on any packaging in which it is contained; or

     (c)   included in any advertisement which, expressly or by implication, relates to the knife.

(4)   For the purposes of this Act, a person markets a knife if—

     (a)   he sells or hires it;

     (b)   he offers, or exposes, it for sale or hire; or

     (c)   he has it in his possession for the purpose of sale or hire.

(5)   A person who is guilty of an offence under this section is liable—

     (a)   on summary conviction to imprisonment for a term not exceeding six months or to a fine not exceeding the statutory maximum, or to both;

     (b)   on conviction on indictment to imprisonment for a term not exceeding two years or to a fine, or to both.

2.   **Publications**

(1)   A person is guilty of an offence if he publishes any written, pictorial or other material in connection with the marketing of any knife and that material—

     (a)   indicates, or suggests, that the knife is suitable for combat; or

      (b)   is otherwise likely to stimulate or encourage violent behaviour involving the use of the knife as a weapon.

(2)   A person who is guilty of an offence under this section is liable—

      (a)   on summary conviction to imprisonment for a term not exceeding six months or to a fine not exceeding the statutory maximum, or to both;

      (b)   on conviction on indictment to imprisonment for a term not exceeding two years or to a fine, or to both.

3. Exempt trades

(1)   It is a defence for a person charged with an offence under section 1 to prove that—

      (a)   the knife was marketed—

           (i)   for use by the armed forces of any country;

           (ii)   as an antique or curio; or

           (iii)   as falling within such other category (if any) as may be prescribed;

      (b)   it was reasonable for the knife to be marketed in that way; and

      (c)   there were no reasonable grounds for suspecting that a person into whose possession the knife might come in consequence of the way in which it was marketed would use it for an unlawful purpose.

(2)   It is a defence for a person charged with an offence under section 2 to prove that—

      (a)   the material was published in connection with marketing a knife—

           (i)   for use by the armed forces of any country;

           (ii)   as an antique or curio; or

           (iii)   as falling within such other category (if any) as may be prescribed.

4. Other defences

(1)   It is a defence for a person charged with an offence under section 1 to prove that he did not know or suspect, and had no reasonable grounds for suspecting, that the way in which the knife was marketed—

      (a)   amounted to an indication or suggestion that the knife was suitable for combat; or

      (b)   was likely to stimulate or encourage violent behaviour involving the use of the knife as a weapon.

(2)   It is a defence for a person charged with an offence under section 2 to prove that he did not know or suspect, and had no reasonable grounds for suspecting, that the material—

      (a)   amounted to an indication or suggestion that the knife was suitable for combat; or

      (b)   was likely to stimulate or encourage violent behaviour involving the use of the knife as a weapon.

(3)   It is a defence for a person charged with an offence under section 1 or 2 to prove that he took all reasonable precautions and exercised all due diligence to avoid committing the offence.

9. Offences by bodies corporate

(1)   If an offence under this Act committed by a body corporate is proved—

      (a)   to have been committed with the consent or connivance of an officer, or

      (b)   to be attributable to any neglect on his part,

he as well as the body corporate is guilty of be offence and liable to be proceeded against and punished accordingly.

(2)   In subsection (1) 'officer', in relation to a body corporate, means a director, manager, secretary or other similar officer of the body, or a person purporting to act in any such capacity.

(3)   If the affairs of a body corporate are managed by its members, subsection (1) applies in relation to the acts and defaults of a member in connection with his functions of management as if he were a director of the body corporate.

10. Interpretation

In this Act—

'the court' means—

(a)   in relation to England and Wales or Northern Ireland, the Crown Court or a magistrate's court;

'knife' means an instrument which has a blade or is sharply pointed;

'marketing' and related expressions are to be read with section 1(4);

'publication' includes a publication in electronic form and, in the case of a publication which is, or may be, produced from electronic data, any medium on which the data are stored;

'suitable for combat' means suitable for use as a weapon for inflicting injury on a person or causing a person to fear injury:

'violent behaviour' means an unlawful act inflicting injury on a person or causing a person to fear injury.

LAW REFORM (YEAR AND A DAY RULE) ACT 1996

1.   Abolition of 'year and a day rule'

The rule known as the 'year and a day rule' (that is, the rule that, for the purposes of offences involving death and of suicide, an act or omission is conclusively presumed not to have caused a person's death if more than a year and a day elapsed before he died) is abolished for all purposes.

2.   Restriction on institution of proceedings for a fatal offence

(1)   Proceedings to which this section applies may only be instituted by or with the consent of the Attorney General.

(2)   This section applies to proceedings against a person for a fatal offence if—

    (a)   the injury alleged to have caused the death was sustained more than three years before the death occurred, or

    (b)   the person has previously been convicted of an offence committed in circumstances alleged to be connected with the death.

(3)   In subsection (2) 'fatal offence' means—

    (a)   murder, manslaughter, infanticide or any other offence of which one of the elements is causing a person's death,

    (b)   the offence of aiding, abetting, counselling or procuring a person's suicide, or

    (c)   an offence under section 5 of the Domestic Violence, Crime and Victims Act 2004 (causing or allowing the death of a child or vulnerable adult).

3.   Commencement etc.

(2)   Section 1 does not affect the continued application of the rule referred to in that section to a case where the act or omission (or the last of the acts or omissions) which caused the death occurred before the day on which this Act is passed.

MAGISTRATES' COURTS ACT 1980

44.   Aiders and abettors

(1)   A person who aids, abets, counsels or procures the commission by another person of a summary offence shall be guilty of the like offence and may be tried (whether or not he is charged as a principal) either by a court having jurisdiction to try that other person or by a court having by virtue of his own offence jurisdiction to try him.

(2)   Any offence consisting in aiding, abetting, counselling or procuring the commission of an offence triable either way (other than an offence listed in Schedule 1 to this Act) shall by virtue of this subsection be triable either way.

45.   Incitement

(1)   Any offence consisting in the incitement to commit a summary offence shall be triable only summarily.

(2)   Subsection (1) above is without prejudice to any other enactment by virtue of which any offence is triable only summarily.

(3)   On conviction of an offence consisting in the incitement to commit a summary offence a person shall be liable to the same penalties as he would be liable to on conviction of the last-mentioned offence.

MALICIOUS COMMUNICATIONS ACT 1988

1.   Offence of sending letters etc. with intent to cause distress or anxiety

(1)   Any person who sends to another person—
  (a)   a letter, electronic communication of any description which conveys—
      (i)   a message which is indecent or grossly offensive;
      (ii)   a threat; or
      (iii) information which is false and known or believed to be false by the sender; or
  (b)   any article or electronic communication which is, in whole or part, of an indecent or grossly offensive nature,
is guilty of an offence if his purpose, or one of his purposes, in sending it is that it should, so far as falling within paragraph (a) or (b) above, cause distress or anxiety to the recipient or to any other person to whom he intends that it or its contents or nature should be communicated.

(2)   A person is not guilty of an offence by virtue of subsection (1)(a)(ii) above if he shows—
  (a)   that the threat was used to reinforce a demand made by him on reasonable grounds; and
  (b)   that he believed, and had reasonable grounds for believing that the use of the threat was a proper means of reinforcing the demand.

(2A) In this section 'electronic communication' includes—
  (a)   any oral or other communication by means of a telecommunication system (within the meaning of the Telecommunications Act 1984); and
  (b)   any communication (however sent) that is in electronic form.

(3)   In this section references to sending include references to delivering or transmitting and to causing to be sent, delivered or transmitted and 'sender' shall be construed accordingly.

MISUSE OF DRUGS ACT 1971

2.   Controlled drugs and their classification for purposes of this Act

(1)   In this Act—
  (a)   the expression 'controlled drug' means any substance or product for the time being specified in Part I, II or III of Schedule 2 to this Act; and
  (b)   the expressions 'Class A drug', 'Class B drug', and 'Class C drug' mean any of the substances and products for the time being specified respectively in Part I, Part II and Part III of that Schedule;
and the provisions of Part IV of that Schedule shall have effect with respect to the meanings of expressions used in that Schedule.

3.   Restriction of importation and exportation of controlled drugs

(1)   Subject to subsection (2) below—
  (a)   the importation of a controlled drug; and
  (b)   the exportation of a controlled drug,
are hereby prohibited.

(2)   Subsection (1) above does not apply—
  (a)   to the importation or exportation of a controlled drug which is for the time being excepted from paragraph (a) or, as the case may be, paragraph (b) of subsection (1) above by regulations under section 7 of this Act; or
  (b)   to the importation or exportation of a controlled drug under and in accordance with the terms of a licence issued by the Secretary of State and in compliance with any conditions attached thereto.

4. **Restriction of production and supply of controlled drugs**

(1) Subject to any regulations under section 7 of this Act for the time being in force, it shall not be lawful for a person—

    (a) to produce a controlled drug; or

    (b) to supply or offer to supply a controlled drug to another.

(2) Subject to section 28 of this Act, it is an offence for a person—

    (a) to produce a controlled drug in contravention of subsection (1) above; or

    (b) to be concerned in the production of such a drug in contravention of that subsection by another.

(3) Subject to section 28 of this Act, it is an offence for a person—

    (a) to supply or offer to supply a controlled drug to another in contravention of subsection (1) above; or

    (b) to be concerned in the supplying of such a drug to another in contravention of that subsection; or

    (c) to be concerned in the making to another in contravention of that subsection of an offer to supply such a drug.

4A. **Aggravation of offence of supply of controlled drug**

(1) This section applies if—

    (a) a court is considering the seriousness of an offence under section 4(3) of this Act, and

    (b) at the time the offence was committed the offender had attained the age of 18.

(2) If either of the following conditions is met the court—

    (a) must treat the fact that the condition is met as an aggravating factor (that is to say, a factor that increases the seriousness of the offence), and

    (b) must state in open court that the offence is so aggravated.

(3) The first condition is that the offence was committed on or in the vicinity of school premises at a relevant time.

(4) The second condition is that in connection with the commission of the offence the offender used a courier who, at the time the offence was committed, was under the age of 18.

(5) In subsection (3), a relevant time is—

    (a) any time when the school premises are in use by persons under the age of 18;

    (b) one hour before the start and one hour after the end of any such time.

(6) For the purposes of subsection (4), a person uses a courier in connection with an offence under section 4(3) of this Act if he causes or permits another person (the courier)—

    (a) to deliver a controlled drug to a third person, or

    (b) to deliver a drug related consideration to himself or a third person.

(7) For the purposes of subsection (6), a drug related consideration is a consideration of any description which—

    (a) is obtained in connection with the supply of a controlled drug, or

    (b) is intended to be used in connection with obtaining a controlled drug.

(8) In this section—

'school premises' means land used for the purposes of a school excluding any land occupied solely as a dwelling by a person employed at the school; and

'school' has the same meaning—

    (a) in England and Wales, as in section 4 of the Education Act 1996;

    (b) in Scotland, as in section 135(1) of the Education (Scotland) Act 1980;

    (c) in Northern Ireland, as in Article 2(2) of the Education and Libraries (Northern Ireland) Order 1986.

5. **Restriction of possession of controlled drugs**

(1) Subject to any regulations under section 7 of this Act for the time being in force, it shall not be lawful for a person to have a controlled drug in his possession.

(2) Subject to section 28 of this Act and to subsection (4) below, it is an offence for a person to have a controlled drug in his possession in contravention of subsection (1) above.

(3) Subject to section 28 of this Act, it is an offence for a person to have a controlled drug in his possession, whether lawfully or not, with intent to supply it to another in contravention of section 4(1) of this Act.

(4) In any proceedings for an offence under subsection (2) above in which it is proved that the accused had a controlled drug in his possession, it shall be a defence for him to prove—

    (a) that, knowing or suspecting it to be a controlled drug, he took possession of it for the purpose of preventing another from committing or continuing to commit an offence in connection with that drug and that as soon as possible after taking possession of it he took all such steps as were reasonably open to him to destroy the drug or to deliver it into the custody of a person lawfully entitled to take custody of it; or

    (b) that, knowing or suspecting it to be a controlled drug, he took possession of it for the purpose of delivering it into the custody of a person lawfully entitled to take custody of it and that as soon as possible after taking possession of it he took all such steps as were reasonably open to him to deliver it into the custody of such a person.

(6) Nothing in subsection (4) above shall prejudice any defence which is open to a person charged with an offence under this section to raise apart from that subsection.

6. Restriction of cultivation of cannabis plants

(1) Subject to any regulations under section 7 of this Act for the time being in force, it shall not be lawful for a person to cultivate any plant of the genus Cannabis.

(2) Subject to section 28 of this Act, it is an offence to cultivate any such plant in contravention of subsection (1) above.

7. Authorisation of activities otherwise unlawful under foregoing provisions

(1) The Secretary of State may by regulations—

    (a) except from section 3(1)(a) or (b), 4(1)(a) or (b) or 5(1) of this Act such controlled drugs as may be specified in the regulations; and

    (b) make such other provision as he thinks fit for the purpose of making it lawful for persons to do things which under any of the following provisions of this Act, that is to say sections 4(1), 5(1) and 6(1), it would otherwise be unlawful for them to do.

(2) Without prejudice to the generality of paragraph (b) of subsection (1) above, regulations under that subsection authorising the doing of any such thing as is mentioned in that paragraph may in particular provide for the doing of that thing to be lawful—

    (a) if it is done under and in accordance with the terms of a licence or other authority issued by the Secretary of State and in compliance with any conditions attached thereto; or

    (b) if it is done in compliance with such conditions as may be prescribed.

(3) Subject to subsection (4) below, the Secretary of State shall so exercise his power to make regulations under subsection (1) above as to secure—

    (a) that it is not unlawful under section 4(1) of this Act for a doctor, dentist, veterinary practitioner or veterinary surgeon, acting in his capacity as such, to prescribe, administer, manufacture, compound or supply a controlled drug, or for a pharmacist or a person lawfully conducting a retail pharmacy business, acting in either case in his capacity as such, to manufacture, compound or supply a controlled drug; and

    (b) that it is not unlawful under section 5(1) of this Act for a doctor, dentist, veterinary practitioner, veterinary surgeon, pharmacist or person lawfully conducting a retail pharmacy business to have a controlled drug in his possession for the purpose of acting in his capacity as such.

(4) If in the case of any controlled drug the Secretary of State is of the opinion that it is in the public interest—

    (a) for production, supply and possession of that drug to be either wholly unlawful or unlawful except for purposes of research or other special purposes; or

    (b) for it to be unlawful for practitioners, pharmacists and persons lawfully conducting retail pharmacy business to do in relation to that drug any of the things mentioned in subsection (3) above except under a licence or other authority issued by the Secretary of State,

he may by order designate that drug as a drug to which this subsection applies; and while there is in force an order under this subsection designating a controlled drug as one to which this subsection applies subsection (3) above shall not apply as regards that drug.

(8)   References in this section to a person's 'doing' things include references to his having things in his possession.

8.   Occupiers etc., of premises to be punishable for permitting certain activities to take place there

A person commits an offence if, being the occupier or concerned in the management of any premises, he knowingly permits or suffers any of the following activities to take place on those premises, that is to say—

(a)   producing or attempting to produce a controlled drug in contravention of section 4(1) of this Act;

(b)   supplying or attempting to supply a controlled drug to another in contravention of section 4(1) of this Act, or offering to supply a controlled drug to another in contravention of section 4(1);

(c)   preparing opium for smoking;

(d)   administering or using a controlled drug which is unlawfully in any person's possession at or immediately before the time when it is administered or used.

9.   Prohibition of certain activities etc., relating to opium

Subject to section 28 of this Act, it is an offence for a person—

(a)   to smoke or otherwise use prepared opium; or

(b)   to frequent a place used for the purpose of opium smoking; or

(c)   to have in his possession—

(i)   any pipes or other utensils made or adapted for use in connection with the smoking of opium, being pipes or utensils which have been used by him or with his knowledge and permission in that connection or which he intends to use or permit others to use in that connection; or

(ii)   any utensils which have been used by him or with his knowledge and permission in connection with the preparation of opium for smoking.

9A.   Prohibition of supply etc., of articles for administering or preparing controlled drugs

(1)   A person who supplies or offers to supply any article which may be used or adapted to be used (whether by itself or in combination with another article or other articles) in the administration by any person of a controlled drug to himself or another, believing that the article (or the article as adapted) is to be so used in circumstances where the administration is unlawful, is guilty of an offence.

(2)   It is not an offence under subsection (1) above to supply or offer to supply a hypodermic syringe, or any part of one.

(3)   A person who supplies or offers to supply any article which may be used to prepare a controlled drug for administration by any person to himself or another believing that the article is to be so used in circumstances where the administration is unlawful is guilty of an offence.

(4)   For the purposes of this section, any administration of a controlled drug is unlawful except—

(a)   the administration by any person of a controlled drug to another in circumstances where the administration of the drug is not unlawful under section 4(1) of this Act, or

(b)   the administration by any person of a controlled drug to himself in circumstances where having the controlled drug in his possession is not unlawful under section 5(1) of this Act.

(5)   In this section, references to administration by any person of a controlled drug to himself include a reference to his administering it to himself with the assistance of another.

19.   Attempts etc., to commit offences

It is an offence for a person . . . to incite another to commit such an offence.

20.   Assisting in or inducing commission outside United Kingdom of offence punishable under a corresponding law

A person commits an offence if in the United Kingdom he assists in or induces the commission in any place outside the United Kingdom of an offence punishable under the provisions of a corresponding law in force in that place.

28.   Proof of lack of knowledge etc., to be a defence in proceedings for certain offences

(1)   This section applies to offences under any of the following provisions of this Act; that is to say section 4(2) and (3), section 5(2) and (3), section 6(2) and section 9.

(2)   Subject to subsection (3) below, in any proceedings for an offence to which this section applies it shall be a defence for the accused to prove that he neither knew of nor suspected nor had reason to suspect the existence of some fact alleged by the prosecution which is necessary for the prosecution to prove if he is to be convicted of the offence charged.

(3)   Where in any proceedings for an offence to which this section applies it is necessary, if the accused is to be convicted of the offence charged, for the prosecution to prove that some substance or product involved in the alleged offence was the controlled drug which the prosecution alleges it to have been, and it is proved that the substance or product in question was that controlled drug, the accused—

    (a)   shall not be acquitted of the offence charged by reason only of proving that he neither knew or suspected nor had reason to suspect that the substance or product in question was the particular controlled drug alleged; but

    (b)   shall be acquitted thereof—

       (i)   if he proves that he neither believed nor suspected nor had reason to suspect that the substance or product in question was a controlled drug; or

      (ii)   if he proves that he believed the substance or product in question to be a controlled drug, or a controlled drug of a description, such that, if it had in fact been that controlled drug or a controlled drug of that description, he would not at the material time have been committing any offence to which this section applies.

(4)   Nothing in this section shall prejudice any defence which it is open to a person charged with an offence to which this section applies to raise apart from this section.

36.   Meaning of 'corresponding law', and evidence of certain matters by certificate

(1)   In this Act the expression 'corresponding law' means a law stated in a certificate purporting to be issued by or on behalf of the government of a country outside the United Kingdom to be a law providing for the control and regulation in that country of the production, supply, use, export and import of drugs and other substances in accordance with the provisions of the Single Convention on Narcotic Drugs signed at New York on 30th March 1961 or a law providing for the control and regulation in that country of the production, supply, use, export and import of dangerous or otherwise harmful drugs in pursuance of any treaty, convention or other agreement or arrangement to which the government of that country and Her Majesty's Government in the United Kingdom are for the time being parties.

37.   Interpretation

(1)   In this Act, except in so far as the context otherwise requires, the following expressions have the meanings hereby assigned to them respectively, that is to say:—

'produce', where the reference is to producing a controlled drug, means producing it by manufacture, cultivation or any other method and 'production' has a corresponding meaning;

'supplying' includes distributing;

(2)   References in this Act to misusing a drug are references to misusing it by taking it; and the reference in the foregoing provision to the taking of a drug is a reference to the taking of it

by a human being by way of any form of self administration, whether or not involving assistance by another.

(3) For the purposes of this Act the things which a person has in his possession shall be taken to include any thing subject to his control which is in the custody of another.

MOBILE TELEPHONES (RE-PROGRAMMING) ACT 2002

1.   Re-programming mobile telephone etc.

(1) A person commits an offence if—
     (a)   he changes a unique device identifier, or
     (b)   he interferes with the operation of a unique device identifier.

(2) A unique device identifier is an electronic equipment identifier which is unique to a mobile wireless communications device.

(3) But a person does not commit an offence under this section if—
     (a)   he is the manufacturer of the device, or
     (b)   he does the act mentioned in subsection (1) with the written consent of the manufacturer of the device.

2.   Possession or supply of anything for re-programming purposes

(1) A person commits an offence if—
     (a)   he has in his custody or under his control anything which may be used for the purpose of changing or interfering with the operation of a unique device identifier, and
     (b)   he intends to use the thing unlawfully for that purpose or to allow it to be used unlawfully for that purpose.

(2) A person commits an offence if—
     (a)   he supplies anything which may be used for the purpose of changing or interfering with the operation of a unique device identifier, and
     (b)   he knows or believes that the person to whom the thing is supplied intends to use it unlawfully for that purpose or to allow it to be used unlawfully for that purpose.

(3) A person commits an offence if—
     (a)   he offers to supply anything which may be used for the purpose of changing or interfering with the operation of a unique device identifier, and
     (b)   he knows or believes that the person to whom the thing is offered intends if it is supplied to him to use it unlawfully for that purpose or to allow it to be used unlawfully for that purpose.

(4) A unique device identifier is an electronic equipment identifier which is unique to a mobile wireless communications device.

(5) A thing is used by a person unlawfully for a purpose if in using it for that purpose he commits an offence under section 1.

OBSCENE PUBLICATIONS ACT 1959

1.   Test of obscenity

(1) For the purpose of this Act an article shall be deemed to be obscene if its effect or (where the article comprises two or more distinct items) the effect of any one of its items is, if taken as a whole, such as to tend to deprave and corrupt persons who are likely, having regard to all relevant circumstances, to read, see or hear the matter contained or embodied in it.

(2) In this Act 'article' means any description of article containing or embodying matter to be read or looked at or both, and sound record, and any film or other record of a picture or pictures.

(3) For the purposes of this Act a person publishes an article who—
     (a)   distributes, circulates, sells, lets on hire, gives, or lends it, or who offers it for sale or for letting on hire; or

(b)   in the case of an article containing or embodying matter to be looked at or a record, shows, plays or projects it, or, where the matter is data stored electronically, transmits that data.

(4)   For the purposes of this Act a person also publishes an article to the extent that any matter recorded on it is included by him in a programme included in a programme service.

(5)   Where the inclusion of any matter in a programme so included would, if that matter were recorded matter, constitute the publication of an obscene article for the purposes of this Act by virtue of subsection (4) above, this Act shall have effect in relation to the inclusion of that matter in the programme as if it were recorded matter.

(6)   In this section 'programme' and 'programme service' have the same meaning as in the Broadcasting Act 1990.

2.   Prohibition of publication of obscene matter

(1)   Subject as hereinafter provided, any person who, whether for gain or not publishes an obscene article or who has an obscene article for publication for gain (whether gain to himself or gain to another) shall be liable—

   (a)   on summary conviction to a fine not exceeding the prescribed sum or to imprisonment for a term not exceeding six months;

   (b)   on conviction on indictment to a fine or to imprisonment for a term not exceeding three years or both.

(3)   A prosecution for an offence against this section shall not be commenced more than two years after the commission of the offence.

(3A)   Proceedings for an offence under this section shall not be instituted except by or with the consent of the Director of Public Prosecutions in any case where the article in question is a moving picture film of a width of not less than sixteen millimetres and the relevant publication or the only other publication which followed or could reasonably have been expected to follow from the relevant publication took place or (as the case may be) was to take place in the course of an exhibition of a film; and in this subsection 'the relevant publication' means—

   (a)   in the case of any proceedings under this section for publishing an obscene article, the publication in respect of which the defendant would be charged if the proceedings were brought; and

   (b)   in the case of any proceedings under this section for having an obscene article for publication for gain, the publication which, if the proceedings were brought, the defendant would be alleged to have had in contemplation.

(4)   A person publishing an article shall not be proceeded against for an offence at common law consisting of the publication of any matter contained or embodied in the article where it is of the essence of the offence that the matter is obscene.

(4A)   Without prejudice to subsection (4) above, a person shall not be proceeded against for an offence at common law—

   (a)   in respect of an exhibition of a film or anything said or done in the course of an exhibition of a film, where it is of the essence of the common law offence that the exhibition or, as the case may be, what was said or done was obscene, indecent, offensive, disgusting or injurious to morality; or

   (b)   in respect of an agreement to give an exhibition of a film or to cause anything to be said or done in the course of such an exhibition where the common law offence consists of conspiring to corrupt public morals or to do any act contrary to public morals or decency.

(5)   A person shall not be convicted of an offence against this section if he proves that he had not examined the article in respect of which he is charged and had no reasonable cause to suspect that it was such that his publication of it would make him liable to be convicted of an offence against this section.

(6)   In any proceedings against a person under this section the question whether an article is obscene shall be determined without regard to any publication by another person unless it

could reasonably have been expected that the publication by the other person would follow from publication by the person charged.

(7)   In this section, 'exhibition of a film' has the meaning given in paragraph 15 of Schedule 1 to the Licensing Act 2003.

3.   Powers of search and seizure

(1)   If a justice of the peace is satisfied by information on oath that there is reasonable ground for suspecting that, in any premises . . . or on any stall or vehicle in that area, being premises or a stall or vehicle specified in the information, obscene articles are, or are from time to time kept for publication for gain, the justice may issue a warrant under his hand empowering any constable to enter (if need be by force) and search the premises, or to search the stall or vehicle, and to sieze and remove any articles found therein or thereon which the constable has reason to believe to be obscene articles and to be kept for publication for gain.

(2)   A warrant under the foregoing subsection shall, if any obscene articles are seized under the warrant, also empower the seizure and removal of any documents found in the premises or, as the case may be, on the stall or vehicle which relate to a trade or business carried on at the premises or from the stall or vehicle.

(3)   Subject to subsection (3A) of this section any articles seized under subsection (1) of this section shall be brought before a justice of the peace acting in the local justice area in which the articles were seized, who may thereupon issue a summons to the occupier of the premises or, as the case may be, the user of the stall or vehicle to appear on a day specified in the summons before a magistrates' court acting in that local justice area to show cause why the articles or any of them should not be forfeited; and if the court is satisfied, as respects any of the articles, that at the time when they were seized they were obscene articles kept for publication for gain, the court shall order those articles to be forfeited:

       Provided that if the person summoned does not appear, the court shall not make an order unless service of the summons is proved; Provided also that this subsection does not apply in relation to any article seized under subsection (1) of this section which is returned to the occupier of the premises or, as the case may be, to the user of the stall or vehicle in or on which it was found.

(3A) Without prejudice to the duty of a court to make an order for the forfeiture of an article where section 1(4) of the Obscene Publications Act 1964 applies (order made on conviction), in a case where by virtue of subsection (3A) of section 2 of this Act proceedings under the said section 2 for having an article for publication for gain could not be instituted except by or with the consent of the Director of Public Prosecutions; no order for the forfeiture of the article shall be made under this section unless the warrant under which the article was seized was issued on an information laid by or on behalf of the Director of Public Prosecutions.

(4)   In addition to the person summoned, any other person being the owner, author or maker of any of the articles brought before the court, or any other person through whose hands they had passed before being seized, shall be entitled to appear before the court on the day specified in the summons to show cause why they should not be forfeited.

(7)   For the purposes of this section the question whether an article is obscene shall be determined on the assumption that copies of it would be published in any manner likely having regard to the circumstances in which it was found, but in no other manner.

4.   Defence of public good

(1)   Subject to subsection (1A) of this section a person shall not be convicted of an offence against section two of this Act, and an order for forfeiture shall not be made under the foregoing section, if it is proved that publication of the article in question is justified as being for the public good on the ground that it is in the interests of science, literature, art or learning, or of other objects of general concern.

(1A) Subsection (1) of this section shall not apply where the article in question is a moving picture film or soundtrack, but—

(a) a person shall not be convicted of an offence against section 2 of this Act in relation to any such film or soundtrack, and

(b) an order for forfeiture of any such film or soundtrack shall not be made under section 3 of this Act,

if it is proved that publication of the film or soundtrack is justified as being for the public good on the grounds that it is in the interests of drama, opera, ballet or any other art, or of literature or learning.

(2) It is hereby declared that the opinion of experts as to the literary, artistic, scientific or other merits of an article may be admitted in any proceedings under this Act either to establish or to negative the said ground.

(3) In this section 'moving picture soundtrack' means any sound record designed for playing with a moving picture film, whether incorporated with the film or not.

OBSCENE PUBLICATIONS ACT 1964

1. **Obscene articles intended for publication for gain**

(2) For the purpose of any proceedings for an offence against the said section 2 a person shall be deemed to have an article for publication for gain if with a view to such publication he has the article in his ownership, possession or control.

(3) In proceedings brought against a person under the said section 2 for having an obscene article for publication for gain the following provisions shall apply in place of subsections (5) and (6) of that section, that is to say,—

(a) he shall not be convicted of that offence if he proves that he had not examined the article and had no reasonable cause to suspect that it was such that his having it would make him liable to be convicted of an offence against that section; and

(b) the question whether the article is obscene shall be determined by reference to such publication for gain of the article as in the circumstances it may reasonably be inferred he had in contemplation and to any further publication that could reasonably be expected to follow from it, but not to any other publication.

(4) Where articles are seized under section 3 of the Obscene Publications Act 1959 (which provides for the seizure and forfeiture of obscene articles kept for publication for gain), and a person is convicted under section 2 of that Act of having them for publication for gain, the court on his conviction shall order the forfeiture of those articles:

Provided that an order made by virtue of this subsection (including an order so made on appeal) shall not take effect until the expiration of the ordinary time within which an appeal in the matter of the proceedings in which the order was made may be instituted or, where such an appeal is duly instituted, until the appeal is finally decided or abandoned; and for this purpose—

(a) an application for a case to be stated or for leave to appeal shall be treated as the institution of an appeal; and

(b) where a decision on appeal is subject to a further appeal, the appeal shall not be deemed to be finally decided until the expiration of the ordinary time within which a further appeal is duly instituted, until the further appeal is finally decided or abandoned.

(5) References in section 3 of the Obscene Publications Act 1959 and this section to publication for gain shall apply to any publication with a view to gain, whether the gain is to accrue by way of consideration for the publication or in any other way.

2. **Negatives, etc. for production of obscene articles**

(1) The Obscene Publications Act 1959 (as amended by this Act) shall apply in relation to anything which is intended to be used, either alone or as one of a set, for the reproduction or manufacture therefrom of articles containing or embodying matter to be read, looked at or listened to, as if it were an article containing or embodying that matter so far as that matter is to be derived from it or from the set.

(2) For the purposes of the Obscene Publications Act 1959 (as so amended) an article shall be deemed to be had or kept for publication if it is had or kept for the reproduction or manufacture therefrom of articles for publication; and the question whether an article so had or kept is obscene shall—

(a) for the purposes of section 2 of the Act be determined in accordance with section 1(3)(b) above as if any reference there to publication of the article were a reference to publication of articles reproduced or manufactured from it; and

(b) for purposes of section 3 of the Act be determined on the assumption that articles reproduced or manufactured from it would be published in any manner likely having regard to the circumstances in which it was found, but in no other manner.

OFFENCES AGAINST THE PERSON ACT 1861

4. Soliciting to commit murder

Whosoever shall solicit, encourage, persuade, or endeavour to persuade, or shall propose to any person, to murder any other person, whether he be a subject of Her Majesty or not, and whether he be within the Queen's dominions or not, shall be guilty of an offence, and being convicted thereof shall be liable to imprisonment for life.

9. Murder or manslaughter abroad

Where any murder or manslaughter shall be committed on land out of the United Kingdom, whether within the Queen's dominions or without, and whether the person killed were a subject of Her Majesty or not, every offence committed by any subject of Her Majesty in respect of any such case, whether the same shall amount to the offence of murder or of manslaughter, . . . may be dealt with, inquired of, tried, determined, and punished . . . in England or Ireland . . .

10. Provision for the trial of murder and manslaughter where the death or cause of death only happens in England or Ireland

Where any person being criminally stricken, poisoned, or otherwise hurt upon the sea, or at any place out of England or Ireland, shall die of such stroke, poisoning, or hurt in England or Ireland, or, being criminally stricken, poisoned or otherwise hurt in any place in England or Ireland, shall die of such stroke, poisoning, or hurt upon the sea, or at any place out of England or Ireland, every offence committed in respect of any such case, whether the same shall amount to the offence of murder or of manslaughter, . . . may be dealt with, inquired of, tried, determined, and punished . . . in England or Ireland . . .

16. Threats to kill

A person who without lawful excuse makes to another a threat, intending that that other would fear it would be carried out, to kill that other or a third person, shall be guilty of an offence and liable on conviction on indictment to imprisonment for a term not exceeding ten years.

17. Impeding a person endeavouring to save himself or another from shipwreck

Whosoever shall unlawfully and maliciously prevent or impede any person, being on board of or having quitted any ship or vessel which shall be in distress, or wrecked, stranded, or cast on shore, in his endeavour to save his life, or shall unlawfully and maliciously prevent or impede any person in his endeavour to save the life of any such person as in this section first aforesaid, shall be guilty of an offence, and being convicted thereof shall be liable . . . to imprisonment for life.

18. Wounding, or causing grievous bodily harm with intent to do grievous bodily harm, or to resist apprehension

Whosoever shall unlawfully and maliciously by any means whatsoever wound or cause any grievous bodily harm to any person . . . with intent . . . to do some . . . grievous bodily harm to any person, or with intent to resist or prevent the lawful apprehension or detainer of any person, shall be guilty of an offence, and being convicted thereof shall be liable . . . to imprisonment for life . . .

20.   Inflicting bodily injury with or without a weapon

Whosoever shall unlawfully and maliciously wound or inflict any grievous bodily harm upon any other person, either with or without any weapon or instrument, shall be guilty of an offence, and being convicted thereof shall be liable . . . to imprisonment for a term not exceeding five years.

21.   Attempting to choke, etc., in order to commit or assist in the committing of any indictable offence

Whosoever shall, by any means whatsoever, attempt to choke, suffocate, or strangle any other person, or shall by any means calculated to choke, suffocate, or strangle, attempt to render any other person insensible, unconscious, or incapable of resistance, with intent in any of such cases thereby to enable himself or any other person to commit, or with intent in any of such cases thereby to assist any other person in committing any indictable offence, shall be guilty of an offence, and being convicted thereof shall be liable . . . to imprisonment for life . . .

22.   Using chloroform, etc., to commit or assist in the committing of any indictable offence

Whosoever shall unlawfully apply or administer to or cause to be taken by, or attempt to apply or administer to or attempt to cause to be administered to or taken by, any person, any chloroform, laudanum, or other stupefying or overpowering drug, matter, or thing, with intent in any of such cases thereby to enable himself or any other person to commit, or with intent in any of such cases thereby to assist any other person in committing any indictable offence, shall be guilty of an offence, and being convicted thereof shall be liable . . . to imprisonment for life . . .

23.   Maliciously administering poison, etc., so as to endanger life or inflict grievous bodily harm

Whosoever shall unlawfully and maliciously administer to or cause to be administered to or taken by any other person any poison or other destructive or noxious thing, so as thereby to endanger the life of such person, or so as thereby to inflict upon such person any grievous bodily harm, shall be guilty of an offence, and being convicted thereof shall be liable . . . to imprisonment for any term not exceeding ten years . . .

24.   Maliciously administering poison, etc., with intent to injure, aggrieve, or annoy any other person

Whosoever shall unlawfully and maliciously administer to or cause to be administered to or taken by any other person any poison or other destructive or noxious thing, with intent to injure, aggrieve, or annoy such person, shall be guilty of an offence, and being . . . convicted thereof shall be liable to imprisonment for a term not exceeding five years.

26.   Not providing apprentices or servants with food, etc., or doing bodily harm, whereby life is endangered, or health permanently injured

Whosoever, being legally liable, either as a master or mistress, to provide for any apprentice or servant necessary food, clothing, or lodging, shall wilfully and without lawful excuse refuse or neglect to provide the same, or shall unlawfully and maliciously do or cause to be done any bodily harm to any such apprentice or servant, so that the life of such apprentice or servant shall be endangered, or the health of such apprentice or servant shall be likely to be permanently injured, shall be guilty of an offence, and being convicted thereof shall be liable . . . to imprisonment for a term not exceeding five years.

27.   Exposing child, whereby life is endangered, or health permanently injured

Whosoever shall unlawfully abandon or expose any child, being under the age of two years, whereby the life of such child shall be endangered, or the health of such child shall have been or shall be likely to be permanently injured, shall be guilty of an offence, and being convicted thereof shall be liable to imprisonment for a term not exceeding five years.

28.   Causing bodily injury by gunpowder

Whosoever shall unlawfully and maliciously, by the explosion of gunpowder or other explosive substance, burn, maim, disfigure, disable, or do any grievous bodily harm to any person, shall be guilty of an offence, and being convicted thereof shall be liable, at the discretion of the court, to imprisonment for life.

29. Causing gunpowder to explode, or sending to any person an explosive substance, or throwing corrosive fluid on a person, with intent to grievous bodily harm

Whosoever shall unlawfully and maliciously cause any gunpowder or other explosive substance to explode, or send or deliver to or cause to be taken or received by any person any explosive substance or any other dangerous or noxious thing, or put or lay at any place, or cast or throw at or upon or otherwise apply to any person, any corrosive fluid or any destructive or explosive substance, with intent in any of the cases aforesaid to burn, maim, disfigure, or disable any person, or to do some grievous bodily harm to any person, shall, whether any bodily injury be effected or not, be guilty of an offence, and being convicted thereof shall be liable, at the discretion of the court, to imprisonment for life.

30. Placing gunpowder near a building etc., with intent to do bodily injury to any person

Whosoever shall unlawfully and maliciously place or throw in, into, upon, against, or near any building, ship, or vessel any gunpowder or other explosive substance, with intent to do any bodily injury to any person, shall, whether or not any explosion take place, and whether or not any bodily injury be effected, be guilty of an offence, and being convicted thereof shall be liable, at the discretion of the court, to imprisonment for any term not exceeding fourteen years.

31. Setting or allowing to remain spring guns, etc., with intent to inflict grievous bodily harm

Whosoever shall set or place, or cause to be set or placed, any spring gun, man trap, or other engine calculated to destroy human life or inflict grievous bodily harm, with the intent that the same or whereby the same may destroy or inflict grievous bodily harm upon a trespasser or other person coming in contact therewith, shall be guilty of an offence, and being convicted thereof shall be liable . . . to imprisonment for a term not exceeding five years; and whosoever shall knowingly and wilfully permit any such spring gun, man trap, or other engine which may have been set or placed in any place then being in or afterwards coming into his possession or occupation by some other person to continue so set or placed, shall be deemed to have set and placed such gun, trap, or engine with such intent as aforesaid: Provided, that nothing in this section contained shall extend to make it illegal to set or place any gun or trap such as may have been or may be usually set or placed with the intent of destroying vermin: Provided also, that nothing in this section shall be deemed to make it unlawful to set or place, or cause to be set or placed, or to be continued set or placed, from sunset to sunrise, any spring gun, man trap, or other engine which shall be set or placed, or caused or continued to be set or placed, in a dwelling-house, for the protection thereof.

32. Placing wood, etc., on railway, taking up rails, showing or hiding signals, etc., with intent to endanger passengers

Whosoever shall unlawfully and maliciously put or throw upon or across any railway any wood, stone, or other matter or thing, or shall unlawfully and maliciously take up, remove, or displace any rail, sleeper, or other matter or thing belonging to any railway, or shall unlawfully and maliciously turn, move or divert any points or other machinery belonging to any railway, or shall unlawfully and maliciously make or show, hide or remove, any signal or light upon or near to any railway, or shall unlawfully and maliciously do or cause to be done any other matter or thing, with intent, in any of the cases aforesaid, to endanger the safety of any person travelling or being upon such railway, shall be guilty of an offence, and being convicted thereof shall be liable, at the discretion of the court, to imprisonment for life.

33. Casting stone, etc., upon a railway carriage, with intent to endanger the safety of any person therein, or in any part of the same train

Whosoever shall unlawfully and maliciously throw, or cause to fall or strike, at, against, into, or upon any engine, tender, carriage, or truck used upon any railway, any wood, stone, or other matter or thing, with intent to injure or endanger the safety of any person being in or upon such engine, tender, carriage, or truck, or in or upon any other any other engine, tender, carriage, or truck of any train of which such first-mentioned engine, tender, carriage, or truck shall form part, shall be guilty of an offence, and being convicted thereof shall be liable . . . to imprisonment for life.

34.   Doing or omitting anything so as to endanger passengers by railway

Whosoever, by any unlawful act, or by any wilful omission or neglect, shall endanger or cause to be endangered the safety of any person conveyed or being in or upon a railway, or shall aid or assist therein, shall be guilty of an offence, and being convicted thereof shall be liable, at the discretion of the court, to be imprisoned for any term not exceeding two years.

35.   Drivers of carriages injuring persons by furious driving

Whosoever, having the charge of any carriage or vehicle, shall by wanton or furious driving or racing, or other wilful misconduct, or by wilful neglect, do or cause to be done any bodily harm to any person whatsoever, shall be guilty of an offence, and being convicted thereof shall be liable, at the discretion of the court, to be imprisoned for any term not exceeding two years.

36.   Obstructing or assaulting a clergyman or other minister in the discharge of his duties in place of worship or burial place, or on his way thither

Whosoever shall, by threats or force, obstruct or prevent or endeavour to obstruct or prevent, any clergyman or other minister in or from celebrating divine service or otherwise officiating in any church, chapel, meeting house, or other place of divine worship, or in or from the performance of his duty in the lawful burial of the dead in any churchyard or other burial place, or shall strike or offer any violence to, or shall, upon any civil process, or under the pretence of executing any civil process, arrest any clergyman or other minister who is engaged in, or to the knowledge of the offender is about to engage in, any of the rites or duties in this section aforesaid, or who to the knowledge of the offender shall be going to perform the same or returning from the performance thereof, shall be guilty of an offence, and being convicted thereof shall be liable to a term of imprisonment not exceeding two years.

37.   Assaulting a magistrate, etc., on account of his preserving wreck

Whosoever shall assault and strike or wound any magistrate, officer, or other person whatsoever lawfully authorized, in or on account of the exercise of his duty in or concerning the preservation of any vessel in distress, or of any vessel, goods, or effects wrecked, stranded, or cast on shore, or lying under water, shall be guilty of an offence, and being convicted thereof shall be liable . . . to be a term of imprisonment not exceeding seven years . . .

38.   Assault with intent to resist arrest

Whosoever . . . shall assault any person with intent to resist or prevent the lawful apprehension or detainer of himself or of any other person for any offence, shall be guilty of an offence, and being convicted thereof shall be liable, at the discretion of the court, to be imprisoned for any term not exceeding two years.

47.   Assault occasioning bodily harm

Whosoever shall be convicted upon an indictment of any assault occasioning actual bodily harm shall be liable . . . to be imprisoned for any term not exceeding five years.

57.   Bigamy

Whosoever, being married, shall marry any other person during the life of the former husband or wife, whether the second marriage shall have taken place in England or Ireland or elsewhere, shall be guilty of an offence, and being convicted thereof shall be liable to a term of imprisonment not exceeding seven years . . .:

Provided, that nothing in this section contained shall extend to any second marriage contracted elsewhere than in England and Ireland by any other than a subject of Her Majesty, or to any person marrying a second time whose husband or wife shall have been continually absent from such person for the space of seven years then last past, and shall not have been known by such person to be living within that time, or shall extend to any person who, at the time of such second marriage, shall have been divorced from the bond of the first marriage, or to any person whose former marriage shall have been declared void by the sentence of any court of competent jurisdiction.

58.　Administering drugs or using instruments to procure abortion

Every woman, being with child, who, with intent to procure her own miscarriage, shall unlawfully administer to herself any poison or other noxious thing, or shall unlawfully use any instrument or other means whatsoever with the like intent, and whosoever, with intent to procure the miscarriage of any woman, whether she be or be not with child, shall unlawfully administer to her or cause to be taken by her any poison or other noxious thing, or shall unlawfully use any instrument or other means whatsoever with the like intent, shall be guilty of an offence, and being convicted thereof shall be liable . . . to imprisonment for life . . .

59.　Procuring drugs, etc., to cause abortion

Whosoever shall unlawfully supply or procure any poison or other noxious thing, or any instrument or thing whatsoever, knowing that the same is intended to be unlawfully used or employed with intent to procure the miscarriage of any woman, whether she be or be not with child, shall be guilty of an offence, and being convicted thereof shall be liable . . . to a term of imprisonment not exceeding five years . . .

60.　Concealing the birth of a child

If any woman shall be delivered of a child, every person who shall, by any secret disposition of the dead body of the said child, whether such child died before, at, or after its birth, endeavour to conceal the birth thereof, shall be guilty of an offence, and being convicted thereof shall be liable, at the discretion of the court, to be imprisoned for any term not exceeding two years.

64.　Making or having anything with intent to commit an offence in this Act

Whosoever shall knowingly have in his possession, or make or manufacture, any gunpowder, explosive substance, or any dangerous or noxious thing, or any machine, engine, instrument, or thing, with intent by means thereof to commit, or for the purpose of enabling any other person to commit, any of the offences in this Act mentioned shall be guilty of an offence, and being convicted thereof shall be liable, at the discretion of the court, to be imprisoned for any term not exceeding two years . . .

OFFICIAL SECRETS ACT 1911

1.　Penalties for spying

(1)　If any person for any purpose prejudicial to the safety or interests of the State—

   (a)　approaches, inspects, passes over or is in the neighbourhood of, or enters any prohibited place within the meaning of this Act; or

   (b)　makes any sketch, plan, model, or note which is calculated to be or might be or is intended to be directly or indirectly useful to an enemy; or

   (c)　obtains, collects, records, or publishes, or communicates to any other person any secret official code word or pass word, or any sketch, plan, model, article, or note, or other document or information which is directly or indirectly useful to an enemy;

   he shall be guilty of an offence . . .

(2)　On a prosecution under this section, it shall not be necessary to show that the accused person was guilty of any particular act tending to show a purpose prejudicial to the safety or interests of the State, and, notwithstanding that no such act is proved against him, he may be convicted if, from the circumstances of the case, or his conduct, or his known character as proved, it appears that his purpose was a purpose prejudicial to the safety or interests of the State; and if any sketch, plan, model, article, note, document, or information relating to or used in any prohibited place within the meaning of this Act, or anything in such a place or any secret official code word or pass word, is made, obtained, collected, recorded, published, or communicated by any person other than a person acting under lawful authority, it shall be deemed to have been made, obtained, collected, recorded, published or communicated for a purpose prejudicial to the safety or interests of the State unless the contrary is proved.

3.   **Definition of prohibited place**

For the purposes of this Act, the expression 'prohibited place' means—

(a)   any work of defence, arsenal, naval or air force establishment or station, factory, dockyard, mine, minefield, camp, ship, or aircraft belonging to or occupied by or on behalf of His Majesty, or any telegraph, telephone, wireless or signal station, or office so belonging or occupied, and any place belonging to or occupied by or on behalf of His Majesty and used for the purpose of building, repairing, making or storing any munitions of war, or any sketches, plans, models or documents relating thereto, or for the purpose of getting any metals, oil or minerals of use in time of war;

(b)   any place not belonging to His Majesty where any munitions of war, or any sketches, models, plans or documents relating thereto, are being made, repaired, gotten or stored under contract with, or with any person on behalf of, His Majesty, or otherwise on behalf of His Majesty; and

(c)   any place belonging to or used for the purposes of His Majesty which is for the time being declared by order of a Secretary of State to be a prohibited place for the purposes of this section on the ground that information with respect thereto, or damage thereto, would be useful to an enemy; and

(d)   any railway, road, way, or channel, or other means of communication by land or water (including any works or structures being part thereof or connected therewith), or any place used for gas, water, or electricity works or other works for purposes of a public character, or any place where any munitions of war, or any sketches, models, plans, or documents relating thereto, are being made, repaired, or stored otherwise than on behalf of His Majesty, which is for the time being declared by order of a Secretary of State to be a prohibited place for the purposes of this section, on the ground that information with respect thereto, or the destruction or obstruction thereof, or interference therewith, would be useful to an enemy.

7.   **Penalty for harbouring spies**

If any person knowingly harbours any person whom he knows, or has reasonable grounds for supposing, to be a person who is about to commit or who has committed an offence under this Act, or knowingly permits to meet or assemble in any premises in his occupation or under his control any such persons, or if any person having harboured any such person, or permitted to meet or assemble in any premises in his occupation or under his control any such person, wilfully omits or refuses to disclose to a superintendent of police any information which it is in his power to give in relation to any such person he shall be guilty of an offence . . .

OFFICIAL SECRETS ACT 1989

1.   **Security and intelligence**

(1)   A person who is or has been—

(a)   a member of the security and intelligence services; or

(b)   a person notified that he is subject to the provisions of this subsection,

is guilty of an offence if without lawful authority he discloses any information, document or other article relating to security or intelligence which is or has been in his possession by virtue of his position as a member of any of those services or in the course of his work while the notification is or was in force.

(2)   The reference in subsection (1) above to disclosing information relating to security or intelligence includes a reference to making any statement which purports to be a disclosure of such information or is intended to be taken by those to whom it is addressed as being such a disclosure.

(3)   A person who is or has been a Crown servant or government contractor is guilty of an offence if without lawful authority he makes a damaging disclosure of any information,

document or other article relating to security or intelligence which is or has been in his possession by virtue of his position as such but otherwise than as mentioned in subsection (1) above.

(4) For the purposes of subsection (3) above a disclosure is damaging if—

(a) it causes damage to the work of, or of any part of, the security and intelligence services; or

(b) it is of information or a document or other article which is such that its unauthorised disclosure would be likely to cause such damage or which falls within a class or description of information, documents or articles the unauthorised disclosure of which would be likely to have that effect.

(5) It is a defence for a person charged with an offence under this section to prove that at the time of the alleged offence he did not know, and had no reasonable cause to believe, that the information, document or article in question related to security or intelligence or, in the case of an offence under subsection (2), that the disclosure would be damaging within the meaning of that subsection.

(6) Notification that a person is subject to subsection (1) above shall be effected by a notice in writing served on him by a Minister of the Crown; and such a notice may be served if, in the Minister's opinion, the work undertaken by the person in question is or includes work connected with the security and intelligence services and its nature is such that the interests of national security require that he should be subject to the provisions of that subsection.

(7) Subject to subsection (8) below, a notification for the purposes of subsection (1) above shall be in force for the period of five years beginning with the day on which it is served but may be renewed by further notices under subsection (6) above for periods of five years at a time.

(8) A notification for the purposes of subsection (1) above may at any time be revoked by a further notice in writing served by the Minister on the person concerned; and the Minister shall serve such a further notice as soon as, in his opinion, the work undertaken by that person ceases to be such as is mentioned in subsection (6) above.

(9) In this section 'security or intelligence' means the work of, or in support of, the security and intelligence services or any part of them, and references to information relating to security or intelligence include references to information held or transmitted by those services or by persons in support of, or of any part of, them.

2. **Defence**

(1) A person who is or has been a Crown servant or government contractor is guilty of an offence if without lawful authority he makes a damaging disclosure of any information, document or other article relating to defence which is or has been in his possession by virtue of his position as such.

(2) For the purposes of subsection (1) above a disclosure is damaging if—

(a) it damages the capability of, or of any part of, the armed forces of the Crown to carry out their tasks or leads to loss of life or injury to members of those forces or serious damage to the equipment or installations of those forces; or

(b) otherwise than as mentioned in paragraph (a) above, it endangers the interests of the United Kingdom abroad, seriously obstructs the promotion or protection by the United Kingdom of those interests or endangers the safety of British citizens abroad; or

(c) it is of information or of a document or article which is such that its unauthorised disclosure would be likely to have any of those effects.

(3) It is a defence for a person charged with an offence under this section to prove that at the time of the alleged offence he did not know, and had no reasonable cause to believe, that the information, document or article in question related to defence or that its disclosure would be damaging within the meaning of subsection (1) above.

(4) In this section 'defence' means—

(a) the size, shape, organisation, logistics, order of battle, deployment, operations, state of readiness and training of the armed forces of the Crown;

(b) the weapons, stores or other equipment of those forces and the invention, development, production and operation of such equipment and research relating to it;

(c) defence policy and strategy and military planning and intelligence;

(d) plans and measures for the maintenance of essential supplies and services that are or would be needed in time of war.

3. International relations

(1) A person who is or has been a Crown servant or government contractor is guilty of an offence if without lawful authority he makes a damaging disclosure of—

(a) any information, document or other article relating to international relations; or

(b) any confidential information, document or other article which was obtained from a State other than the United Kingdom or an international organisation,

being information or a document or article which is or has been in his possession by virtue of his position as a Crown servant or government contractor.

(2) For the purposes of subsection (1) above a disclosure is damaging if—

(a) it endangers the interests of the United Kingdom abroad, seriously obstructs the promotion or protection by the United Kingdom of those interests or endangers the safety of British citizens abroad; or

(b) it is of information or of a document or article which is such that its unauthorised disclosure would be likely to have any of those effects.

(3) In the case of information or a document or article within subsection (1)(b) above—

(a) the fact that it is confidential, or

(b) its nature or contents,

may be sufficient to establish for the purposes of subsection (2)(b) above that the information, document or article is such that its unauthorised disclosure would be likely to have any of the effects there mentioned.

(4) It is a defence for a person charged with an offence under this section to prove that at the time of the alleged offence he did not know, and had no reasonable cause to believe, that the information, document or article in question was such as is mentioned in subsection (1) above or that its disclosure would be damaging within the meaning of that subsection.

(5) In this section 'international relations' means the relations between States, between international organisations or between one or more States and one or more such organisations and includes any matter relating to a State other than the United Kingdom or to an international organisation which is capable of affecting the relations of the United Kingdom with another State or with an international organisation.

(6) For the purposes of this section any information, document or article obtained from a State or organisation is confidential at any time while the terms on which it was obtained require it to be held in confidence or while the circumstances in which it was obtained make it reasonable for the State or organisation to expect that it would be so held.

4. Crime and special investigation powers

(1) A person who is or has been a Crown servant or government contractor is guilty of an offence if without lawful authority he discloses any information, document or other article to which this section applies and which is or has been in his possession by virtue of his position as such.

(2) This section applies to any information, document or other article—

(a) the disclosure of which—

(i) results in the commission of an offence; or

(ii) facilitates an escape from legal custody or the doing of any other act prejudicial to the safekeeping of persons in legal custody; or

(iii) impedes the prevention or detection of offences or the apprehension or prosecution of suspected offenders; or

(b) which is such that its unauthorised disclosure would be likely to have any of those effects.

(3) This section also applies to—

(a) any information obtained by reason of the interception of any communication in obedience to a warrant issued under section 2 of the Interception of Communications

Act 1985, or under the authority of an interception warrant under section 5 of the Regulation of Investigatory Powers Act 2000, any information relating to the obtaining of information by reason of any such interception and any document or other article which is or has been used or held for use in, or has been obtained by reason of, any such interception; and

(b)   any information obtained by reason of action authorised by a warrant issued under section 3 of the Security Service Act 1989 or under section 5 of the Intelligence Services Act 1994 or by an authorisation given under section 7 of that Act, any information relating to the obtaining of information by reason of any such action and any document or other article which is or has been used or held for use in, or has been otained by reason of, any such action.

(4)   It is a defence for a person charged with an offence under this section in respect of a disclosure falling within subsection (2)(a) above to prove that at the time of the alleged offence he did not know, and had no reasonable cause to believe, that the disclosure would have any of the effects there mentioned.

(5)   It is a defence for a person charged with an offence under this section in respect of any other disclosure to prove that at the time of the alleged offence he did not know, and had no reasonable cause to believe, that the information, document or article in question was information or a document or article to which this section applies.

(6)   In this section 'legal custody' includes detention in pursuance of any enactment or any instrument made under an enactment.

5.   Information resulting from unauthorised disclosures or entrusted in confidence

(1)   Subsection (2) below applies where—
(a)   any information, document or other article protected against disclosure by the foregoing provisions of this Act has come into a person's possession as a result of having been—
(i)   disclosed (whether to him or another) by a Crown servant or government contractor without lawful authority; or
(ii)   entrusted to him by a Crown servant or government contractor on terms requiring it to be held in confidence or in circumstances in which the Crown servant or government contractor could reasonably expect that it would be so held; or
(iii) disclosed (whether to him or another) without lawful authority by a person to whom it was entrusted as mentioned in sub-paragraph (ii) above; and
(b)   the disclosure without lawful authority of the information, document or article by the person into whose possession it has come is not an offence under any of those provisions.

(2)   Subject to subsections (3) and (4) below, the person into whose possession the information, document or article has come is guilty of an offence if he discloses it without lawful authority knowing, or having reasonable cause to believe, that it is protected against disclosure by the foregoing provisions of this Act and that it has come into his possession as mentioned in subsection (1) above.

(3)   In the case of information or a document or article protected against disclosure by sections 1 to 3 above, a person does not commit an offence under subsection (2) above unless—
(a)   the disclosure by him is damaging; and
(b)   he makes it knowing, or having reasonable cause to believe, that it would be damaging;
and the question whether a disclosure is damaging shall be determined for the purposes of this subsection as it would be in relation to a disclosure of that information, document or article by a Crown servant in contravention of section 1(3), 2(1) or 3(1) above.

(4)   A person does not commit an offence under subsection (2) above in respect of information or a document or other article which has come into his possession as a result of having been disclosed—
(a)   as mentioned in subsection (1)(a)(i) above by a government contractor; or
(b)   as mentioned in subsection (1)(a)(iii) above,

unless that disclosure was by a British citizen or took place in the United Kingdom, in any of the Channel Islands or in the Isle of Man or a colony.

(5) For the purposes of this section information or a document or article is protected against disclosure by the foregoing provisions of this Act if—

(a) it relates to security or intelligence, defence or international relations within the meaning of section 1, 2 or 3 above or is such as is mentioned in section 3(1)(b) above; or

(b) it is information or a document or article to which section 4 above applies;

and information or a document or article is protected against disclosure by sections 1 to 3 above if it falls within paragraph (a) above.

(6) A person is guilty of an offence if without lawful authority he discloses any information, document or other article which he knows, or has reasonable cause to believe, to have come into his possession as a result of a contravention of section 1 of the Official Secrets Act 1911.

6. Information entrusted in confidence to other States or international organisations

(1) This section applies where—

(a) any information, document or other article which—

(i) relates to security or intelligence, defence or international relations; and

(ii) has been communicated in confidence by or on behalf of the United Kingdom to another State or to an international organisation,

has come into a person's possession as a result of having been disclosed (whether to him or another) without the authority of that State or organisation or, in the case of an organisation, of a member of it; and

(b) the disclosure without lawful authority of the information, document or article by the person into whose possession it has come is not an offence under any of the foregoing provisions of this Act.

(2) Subject to subsection (3) below, the person into whose possession the information, document or article has come is guilty of an offence if he makes a damaging disclosure of it knowing, or having reasonable cause to believe, that it is such as is mentioned in subsection (1) above, that it has come into his possession as there mentioned and that its disclosure would be damaging.

(3) A person does not commit an offence under subsection (2) above if the information, document or article is disclosed by him with lawful authority or has previously been made available to the public with the authority of the State or organisation concerned or, in the case of an organisation, of a member of it.

(4) For the purposes of this section 'security or intelligence', 'defence' and 'international relations' have the same meaning as in sections 1, 2 and 3 above and the question whether a disclosure is damaging shall be determined as it would be in relation to a disclosure of the information, document or article in question by a Crown servant in contravention of sections 1(3), 2(1) and 3(1) above.

(5) For the purposes of this section information or a document or article is communicated in confidence if it is communicated on terms requiring it to be held in confidence or in circumstances in which the person communicating it could reasonably expect that it would be so held.

7. Authorised disclosures

(1) For the purposes of this Act a disclosure by—

(a) a Crown servant; or

(b) a person, not being a Crown servant or government contractor, in whose case a notification for the purposes of section 1(1) above is in force,

is made with lawful authority if, and only if, it is made in accordance with his official duty.

(2) For the purposes of this Act a disclosure by a government contractor is made with lawful authority if, and only if, it is made—

(a) in accordance with an official authorisation; or

(b)   for the purposes of the functions by virtue of which he is a government contractor and without contravening an official restriction.

(3)   For the purposes of this Act a disclosure made by any other person is made with lawful authority if, and only if, it is made—

(a)   to a Crown servant for the purposes of his functions as such; or

(b)   in accordance with an official authorisation.

(4)   It is a defence for a person charged with an offence under any of the foregoing provisions of this Act to prove that at the time of the alleged offence he believed that he had lawful authority to make the disclosure in question and had no reasonable cause to believe otherwise.

(5)   In this section 'official authorisation' and 'official restriction' mean, subject to subsection (6) below, an authorisation or restriction duly given or imposed by a Crown servant or government contractor or by or on behalf of a prescribed body or a body of a prescribed class.

(6)   In relation to section 6 above 'official authorisation' includes an authorisation duly given by or on behalf of the State or organisation concerned or, in the case of an organisation, a member of it.

8.   **Safeguarding of information**

(1)   Where a Crown servant or government contractor, by virtue of his position as such, has in his possession or under his control any document or other article which it would be an offence under any of the foregoing provisions of this Act for him to disclose without lawful authority he is guilty of an offence if—

(a)   being a Crown servant, he retains the document or article contrary to his official duty; or

(b)   being a government contractor, he fails to comply with an official direction for the return or disposal of the document or article,

or if he fails to take such care to pevent the unauthorised disclosure of the document or article as a person in his position may reasonably be expected to take.

(2)   It is a defence for a Crown servant charged with an offence under subsection (1)(a) above to prove that at the time of the alleged offence he believed that he was acting in accordance with his official duty and had no reasonable cause to believe otherwise.

(3)   In subsections (1) and (2) above references to a Crown servant include any person, not being a Crown servant or government contractor, in whose case a notification for the purposes of section 1(1) above is in force.

(4)   Where a person has in his possession or under his control any document or other article which it would be an offence under section 5 above for him to disclose without lawful authority, he is guilty of an offence if—

(a)   he fails to comply with an official direction for its return or disposal; or

(b)   where he obtained it from a Crown servant or government contractor on terms requiring it to be held in confidence or in circumstances in which that servant or contractor could reasonably expect that it would be so held, he fails to take such care to prevent its unauthorised disclosure as a person in his position may reasonably be expected to take.

(5)   Where a person has in his possession or under his control any document or other article which it would be an offence under section 6 above for him to disclose without lawful authority, he is guilty of an offence if he fails to comply with an official direction for its return or disposal.

(6)   A person is guilty of an offence if he discloses any official information, document or other article which can be used for the purpose of obtaining access to any information, document or other article protected against disclosure by the foregoing provisions of this Act and the circumstances in which it is disclosed are such that it would be reasonable to expect that it might be used for that purpose without authority.

(7)   For the purposes of subsection (6) above a person discloses information or a document or article which is official if—

(a) he has or has had it in his possession by virtue of his position as a Crown servant or government contractor; or

(b) he knows or has reasonable cause to believe that a Crown servant or government contractor has or has had it in his possession by virtue of his position as such.

(8) Subsection (5) of section 5 above applies for the purposes of subsection (6) above as it applies for the purposes of that section.

(9) In this section 'official direction' means a direction duly given by a Crown servant or government contractor or by or on behalf of a prescribed body or a body of a prescribed class.

12. 'Crown servant' and 'government contractor'

(1) In this Act 'Crown servant' means—

    (a) a Minister of the Crown;

    (aa) a member of the Scottish Executive or a junior Scottish Minister;

    (b) ...

    (c) any person employed in the civil service of the Crown, including Her Majesty's Diplomatic Service, Her Majesty's Overseas Civil Service, the civil service of Northern Ireland and the Northern Ireland Court Service;

    (d) any member of the naval, military or air forces of the Crown, including any person employed by an association established for the purposes of Part XI of the Reserve Forces Act 1996;

    (e) any constable and any other person employed or appointed in or for the purposes of any police force (including the Police Service of Northern Ireland and the Police Service of Northern Ireland Reserve) or of the Serious Organised Crime Agency;

    (f) any person who is a member or employee of a prescribed body or a body of a prescribed class and either is prescribed for the purposes of this paragraph or belongs to a prescribed class of members or employees of any such body;

    (g) any person who is the holder of a prescribed office or who is an employee of such a holder and either is prescribed for the purposes of this paragraph or belongs to a prescribed class of such employees.

(2) In this Act 'government contractor' means, subject to subsection (3) below, any person who is not a Crown servant but who provides, or is employed in the provision of, goods or services—

    (a) for the purposes of any Minister or person mentioned in paragraph (a) or (b) of subsection (1) above, of any office holder in the Scottish Administration, of any of the services, forces or bodies mentioned in that subsection or of the holder of any office prescribed under that subsection;

    (aa) for the purposes of the National Assembly for Wales; or

    (b) under an agreement or arrangement certified by the Secretary of State as being one to which the government of a State other than the United Kingdom or an international organisation is a party or which is subordinate to, or made for the purposes of implementing, any such agreement or arrangement.

(3) Where an employee or class of employees of any body, or of any holder of an office, is prescribed by an order made for the purposes of subsection (1) above—

    (a) any employee of that body, or of the holder of that office, who is not prescribed or is not within the prescribed class; and

    (b) any person who does not provide, or is not employed in the provision of, goods or services for the purposes of the performance of those functions of the body or the holder of the office in connection with which the employee or prescribed class of employees is engaged,

shall not be a government contractor for the purposes of this Act.

13. Other interpretation provisions

(1) In this Act—

'disclose' and 'disclosure', in relation to a document or other article, include parting with possession of it;

'international organisation' means, subject to subsections (2) and (3) below, an organisation of which only States are members and includes a reference to any organ of such an organisation;

'prescribed' means prescribed by an order made by the Secretary of State;

'State' includes the government of a State and any organ of its government and references to a State other than the United Kingdom include references to any territory outside the United Kingdom.

(2)   In section 12(2)(b) above the reference to an international organisation includes a reference to any such organisation whether or not one of which only States are members and includes a commercial organisation.

(3)   In determining for the purposes of subsection (1) above whether only States are members of an organisation, any member which is itself an organisation of which only States are members, or which is an organ of such an organisation, shall be treated as a State.

15.   Acts done abroad

(1)   Any act—

(a)   done by a British citizen or Crown servant; or

(b)   done by any person in any of the Channel Islands or the Isle of Man or any colony,

shall, if it would be an offence by that person under any provision of this Act other than section 8(1), (4) or (5) when done by him in the United Kingdom, be an offence under that provision.

PERJURY ACT 1911

1.   Perjury

(1)   If any person lawfully sworn as a witness or as an interpreter in a judicial proceeding wilfully makes a statement material in that proceeding, which he knows to be false or does not believe to be true, he shall be guilty of perjury, and shall, on conviction thereof on indictment, be liable to imprisonment for a term not exceeding seven years . . . or to a fine or to both . . . imprisonment and a fine.

(2)   The expression 'judicial proceeding' includes a proceeding before any court, tribunal, or person having by law power to hear, receive, and examine evidence on oath.

(3)   Where a statement made for the purposes of a judicial proceeding is not made before the tribunal itself, but is made on oath before a person authorised by law to administer an oath to the person who makes the statement, and to record or authenticate the statement, it shall, for the purposes of this section, be treated as having been made in a judicial proceeding.

(4)   A statement made by a person lawfully sworn in England for the purposes of a judical proceeding—

(a)   in another part of Her Majesty's dominions; or

(b)   in a British tribunal lawfully constituted in any place by sea or land outside Her Majesty's dominions; or

(c)   in a tribunal of any foreign state,

shall, for the purposes of this section, be treated as a statement made in a judicial proceeding in England.

(5)   Where for the purposes of a judicial proceeding in England, a person is lawfully sworn under the authority of an Act of Parliament—

(a)   in any other part of Her Majesty's dominions; or

(b)   before a British tribunal or a British officer in a foreign country, or within the jurisdiction of the Admiralty of England;

a statement made by such person so sworn as aforesaid (unless the Act of Parliament under which it was made otherwise specifically provides) shall be treated for the purposes of this section as having been made in the judicial proceeding in England for the purposes whereof it was made.

(6) The question whether a statement on which perjury is assigned was material is a question of law to be determined by the court of trial.

1A. False unsworn statement under Evidence (Proceedings in other Jurisdictions) Act 1975

If any person in giving any testimony (either orally or in writing) otherwise than on oath, where required to do so by an order under section 2 of the Evidence (Proceedings in other Jurisdictions) Act 1975, makes a statement—

(a) which he knows to be false in a material particular, or

(b) which is false in a material particular and which he does not believe to be true,

he shall be guilty of an offence and shall be liable on conviction on indictment to imprisonment for a term not exceeding two years or a fine or both.

7. Aiders, abettors, suborners, etc.

(1) Every person who aids, abets, counsels, procures, or suborns another person to commit an offence against this Act shall be liable to be proceeded against, indicted, tried and punished as if he were a principal offender.

(2) Every person who incites another person to commit an offence against this Act shall be guilty of an offence, and on conviction thereof on indictment, shall be liable to imprisonment, or to a fine, or to both such imprisonment and fine.

15. Interpretation, etc.

(1) For the purposes of this Act, the forms and ceremonies used in administering an oath are immaterial, if the court or person before whom the oath is taken has power to administer an oath for the purpose of verifying the statement in question, and if the oath has been administered in a form and with ceremonies which the person taking the oath has accepted without objection, or has declared to be binding on him.

(2) In this Act—

The expression 'oath' includes 'affirmation' and 'declaration', and the expression 'swear' includes 'affirm' and 'declare'; and

The expression 'statutory declaration' means a declaration made by virtue of the Statutory Declarations Act, 1835, or of any Act, Order in Council, rule or regulation applying or extending the provisions thereof.

POLICE ACT 1996

89. Assaults on constables

(1) Any person who assaults a constable in the execution of his duty, or a person assisting a constable in the execution of his duty, shall be guilty of an offence and liable on summary conviction to imprisonment for a term not exceeding six months or to a fine not exceeding level 5 on the standard scale, or to both.

(2) Any person who resists or wilfully obstructs a constable in the execution of his duty, or a person assisting a constable in the execution of his duty shall be guilty of an offence and liable on summary conviction to imprisonment for a term not exceeding 51 weeks or to a fine not exceeding level 3 on the standard scale, or to both.

90. Impersonation, etc.

(1) Any person who with intent to deceive impersonates a member of a police force or special constable, or makes any statement or does any act calculated falsely to suggest that he is such a member or constable, shall be guilty of an offence and liable on summary conviction to imprisonment for a term not exceeding six months or to a fine not exceeding level 5 on the standard scale, or to both.

(2) Any person who, not being a constable, wears any article of police uniform in circumstances where it gives him an appearance so nearly resembling that of a member of a police force as

to be calculated to deceive shall be guilty of an offence and liable on summary conviction to a fine not exceeding level 3 on the standard scale.

(3)   Any person who, not being a member of a police force or special constable, has in his possession any article of police uniform shall, unless he proves that he obtained possession of that article lawfully and has possession of it for a lawful purpose, be guilty of an offence and liable on summary conviction to a fine not exceeding level 1 on the standard scale.

(4)   In this section—

    (a)   'article of police uniform' means any article of uniform or any distinctive badge or mark or document of identification usually issued to members of police forces or special constables, or anything having the appearance of such an article, badge, mark or document; and

    (aa)   'member of a police force' includes a member of the British Transport Police Force; and

    (b)   'special constable' means a special constable appointed for a police area.

PREVENTION OF CRIME ACT 1953

1.   Prohibition of the carrying of offensive weapons without lawful authority or reasonable excuse

(1)   Any person who without lawful authority or reasonable excuse, the proof whereof shall lie on him, has with him in any public place any offensive weapon shall be guilty of an offence, and shall be liable—

    (a)   on summary conviction, to imprisonment for a term not exceeding six months or a fine not exceeding the prescribed sum or both;

    (b)   on conviction on indictment, to imprisonment for a term not exceeding four years or a fine . . . or both.

(2)   Where any person is convicted of an offence under subsection (1) of this section the court may make an order for the forfeiture or disposal of any weapon in respect of which the offence was committed.

(4)   In this section 'public place' includes any highway and any other premises or place to which at the material time the public have or are permitted to have access, whether on payment or otherwise; and 'offensive weapon' means any article made or adapted for use for causing injury to the person, or intended by the person having it with him for such use by him or by some other person.

PREVENTION OF TERRORISM ACT 2005

9   Offences

(1)   A person who, without reasonable excuse, contravenes an obligation imposed on him by a control order is guilty of an offence.

(2)   A person is guilty of an offence if—

    (a)   a control order by which he is bound at a time when he leaves the United Kingdom requires him, whenever he enters the United Kingdom, to report to a specified person that he is or has been the subject of such an order;

    (b)   he re-enters the United Kingdom after the order has ceased to have effect;

    (c)   the occasion on which he re-enters the United Kingdom is the first occasion on which he does so after leaving while the order was in force; and

    (d)   on that occasion he fails, without reasonable excuse, to report to the specified person in the manner that was required by the order.

(3)   A person is guilty of an offence if he intentionally obstructs the exercise by any person of a power conferred by section 7(9).

PRISON SECURITY ACT 1992

1. Offence of prison mutiny

(1) Any prisoner who takes part in a prison mutiny shall be guilty of an offence and liable, on conviction on indictment, to imprisonment for a term not exceeding ten years or to a fine or to both.

(2) For the purposes of this section there is a prison mutiny where two or more prisoners, while on the premises of any prison, engage in conduct which is intended to further a common purpose of overthrowing lawful authority in that prison.

(3) For the purposes of this section the intentions and common purpose of prisoners may be inferred from the form and circumstances of their conduct and it shall be immaterial that conduct falling within subsection (2) above takes a different form in the case of different prisoners.

(4) Where there is a prison mutiny, a prisoner who has or is given a reasonable opportunity of submitting to lawful authority and fails, without reasonable excuse, to do so shall be regarded for the purposes of this section as taking part in the mutiny.

(6) In this section—

'conduct' includes acts and omissions;

'prison' means any prison or young offender institution . . . which is under the general superintendence of, or is provided by, the Secretary of State under the Prison Act 1952, including a contracted out prison within the meaning of Part IV of the Criminal Justice Act 1991;

'prisoner' means any person for the time being in a prison as a result of any requirement imposed by a court or otherwise that he be detained in legal custody.

PROTECTION OF CHILDREN ACT 1978

1. Indecent photographs of children

(1) Subject to sections 1A and 1B, it is an offence for a person—

(a) to take, or permit to be taken or to make, any indecent photograph or pseudo-photograph of a child . . . ; or

(b) to distribute or show such indecent photographs or pseudo-photographs; or

(c) to have in his possession such indecent photographs or pseudo-photographs, with a view to their being distributed or shown by himself or others; or

(d) to publish or cause to be published any advertisement likely to be understood as conveying that the advertiser distributes or shows such indecent photographs or pseudo-photographs, or intends to do so.

(2) For purposes of this Act, a person is to be regarded as distributing an indecent photograph or pseudo-photograph if he parts with possession of it to, or exposes or offers it for acquisition by, another person.

(4) Where a person is charged with an offence under subsection (1)(b) or (c), it shall be a defence for him to prove—

(a) that he had a legitimate reason for distributing or showing the photographs or pseudo-photographs or (as the case may be) having them in his possession; or

(b) that he had not himself seen the photographs or pseudo-photographs and did not know, nor had any cause to suspect, them to be indecent.

1A. Marriage and other relationships

(1) This section applies where, in proceedings for an offence under section 1(1)(a) of taking or making an indecent photograph of a child, or for an offence under section 1(1)(b) or (c) relating to an indecent photograph of a child, the defendant proves that the photograph was of the child aged 16 or over, and that at the time of the offence charged the child and he—

(a) were married or civil partners of each other, or

(b) lived together as partners in an enduring family relationship.

(2) Subsections (5) and (6) also apply where, in proceedings for an offence under section 1(1)(b) or (c) relating to an indecent photograph of a child, the defendant proves that the photograph was of the child aged 16 or over, and that at the time when he obtained it the child and he—

    (a) were married or civil partners of each other, or

    (b) lived together as partners in an enduring family relationship.

(3) This section applies whether the photograph showed the child alone or with the defendant, but not if it showed any other person.

(4) In the case of an offence under section 1(1)(a), if sufficient evidence is adduced to raise an issue as to whether the child consented to the photograph being taken or made, or as to whether the defendant reasonably believed that the child so consented, the defendant is not guilty of the offence unless it is proved that the child did not so consent and that the defendant did not reasonably believe that the child so consented.

(5) In the case of an offence under section 1(1)(b), the defendant is not guilty of the offence unless it is proved that the showing or distributing was to a person other than the child.

(6) In the case of an offence under section 1(1)(c), if sufficient evidence is adduced to raise an issue both—

    (a) as to whether the child consented to the photograph being in the defendant's possession, or as to whether the defendant reasonably believed that the child so consented, and

    (b) as to whether the defendant had the photograph in his possession with a view to its being distributed or shown to anyone other than the child,

the defendant is not guilty of the offence unless it is proved either that the child did not so consent and that the defendant did not reasonably believe that the child so consented, or that the defendant had the photograph in his possession with a view to its being distributed or shown to a person other than the child.

1B.   Exception for criminal proceedings, investigations etc.

(1) In proceedings for an offence under section 1(1)(a) of making an indecent photograph or pseudo-photograph of a child, the defendant is not guilty of the offence if he proves that—

    (a) it was necessary for him to make the photograph or pseudo-photograph for the purposes of the prevention, detection or investigation of crime, or for the purposes of criminal proceedings, in any part of the world,

    (b) at the time of the offence charged he was a member of the Security Service, and it was necessary for him to make the photograph or pseudo-photograph for the exercise of any of the functions of the Service, or

    (c) at the time of the offence charged he was a member of GCHQ, and it was necessary for him to make the photograph or pseudo-photograph for the exercise of any of the functions of GCHQ.

(2) In this section 'GCHQ' has the same meaning as in the Intelligence Services Act 1994.

2.   Evidence

(3) In proceedings under this Act relating to indecent photographs of children a person is to be taken as having been a child at any material time if it appears from the evidence as a whole that he was then under the age of 18.

3.   Offences by corporations

(1) Where a body corporate is guilty of an offence under this Act and it is proved that the offence occurred with the consent or connivance of, or was attributable to any neglect on the part of, any director, manager, secretary or other officer of the body, or any person who was purporting to act in any such capacity he, as well as the body corporate, shall be deemed to be guilty of that offence and shall be liable to be proceeded against and punished accordingly.

(2) Where the affairs of a body corporate are managed by its members, subsection (1) shall apply in relation to the acts and defaults of a member in connection with his functions of management as if he were a director of the body corporate.

7. **Interpretation**

(1) The following subsections apply for the interpretation of this Act.

(2) References to an indecent photograph include an indecent film, a copy of an indecent photograph or film, and an indecent photograph comprised in a film.

(3) Photographs (including those comprised in a film) shall, if they show children and are indecent, be treated for all purposes of this Act as indecent photographs of children and so as respects pseudo-photographs.

(4) References to a photograph include—

   (a) the negative as well as the positive version; and

   (b) data stored on a computer disc or by other electronic means which is capable of conversion into a photograph.

(5) 'Film' includes any form of video-recording.

(6) 'Child', subject to subsection (8), means a person under the age of 18.

(7) 'Pseudo-photograph' means an image, whether made by computer-graphics or otherwise howsoever, which appears to be a photograph.

(8) If the impression conveyed by a pseudo-photograph is that the person shown is a child, the pseudo-photograph shall be treated for all purposes of this Act as showing a child and so shall a pseudo- photograph where the predominant impression conveyed is that the person shown is a child notwithstanding that some of the physical characteristics shown are those of an adult.

(9) References to an indecent pseudo-photograph include—

   (a) a copy of an indecent pseudo-photograph; and

   (b) data stored on a computer disc or by other electronic means which is capable of conversion into a pseudo-photograph.

PROTECTION FROM HARASSMENT ACT 1997

1. **Prohibition of harassment**

(1) A person must not pursue a course of conduct—

   (a) which amounts to harassment of another, and

   (b) which he knows or ought to know amounts to harassment of the other.

(1A) A person must not pursue a course of conduct—

   (a) which involves harassment of two or more persons, and

   (b) which he knows or ought to know involves harassment of those persons, and

   (c) by which he intends to persuade any person (whether or not one of those mentioned above)—

      (i) not to do something that he is entitled or required to do, or

      (ii) to do something that he is not under any obligation to do.

(2) For the purposes of this section, the person whose course of conduct is in question ought to know that it amounts to or involves harassment of another if a reasonable person in possession of the same information would think the course of conduct amounted to or involved harassment of the other.

(3) Subsection (1) or (1A) does not apply to a course of conduct if the person who pursued it shows—

   (a) that it was pursued for the purpose of preventing or detecting crime,

   (b) that it was pursued under any enactment or rule of law or to comply with any condition or requirement imposed by any person under any enactment, or

   (c) that in the particular circumstances the pursuit of the course of conduct was reasonable.

2. **Offence of harassment**

(1) A person who pursues a course of conduct in breach of section 1(1) or (1A) is guilty of an offence.

4.   **Putting people in fear of violence**

(1)   A person whose course of conduct causes another to fear, on at least two occasions, that violence will be used against him is guilty of an offence if he knows or ought to know that his course of conduct will cause the other so to fear on each of those occasions.

(2)   For the purposes of this section, the person whose course of conduct is in question ought to know that it will cause another to fear that violence will be used against him on any occasion if a reasonable person in possession of the same information would think the course of conduct would cause the other so to fear on that occasion.

(3)   It is a defence for a person charged with an offence under this section to show that—

    (a)   his course of conduct was pursued for the purpose of preventing or detecting crime,

    (b)   his course of conduct was pursued under any enactment or rule of law or to comply with any condition or requirement imposed by any person under any enactment, or

    (c)   the pursuit of his course of conduct was reasonable for the protection of himself or another or for the protection of his or another's property.

7.   **Interpretation of this group of sections**

(1)   This section applies for the interpretation of sections 1 to 5A.

(2)   References to harassing a person include alarming the person or causing the person distress.

(3)   A 'course of conduct' must involve—

    (a)   in the case of conduct in relation to a single person (see section 1(1)), conduct on at least two occasions in relation to that person, or

    (b)   in the case of conduct in relation to two or more persons (see section 1(1A)), conduct on at least one occasion in relation to each of those persons.

(3A) A person's conduct on any occasion shall be taken, if aided, abetted, counselled or procured by another—

    (a)   to be conduct on that occasion of the other (as well as conduct of the person whose conduct it is); and

    (b)   to be conduct in relation to which the other's knowledge and purpose, and what he ought to have known, are the same as they were in relation to what was contemplated or reasonably foreseeable at the time of the aiding, abetting, counselling or procuring.

(4)   'Conduct' includes speech.

(5)   References to a person, in the context of the harassment of a person, are references to a person who is an individual.

PUBLIC ORDER ACT 1936

1.   **Prohibition of uniforms in connection with political objects**

(1)   Subject as hereinafter provided, any person who in any public place or at any public meeting wears uniform signifying his association with any political organisation or with the promotion of any political object shall be guilty of an offence:

     Provided that, if the chief officer of police is satisfied that the wearing of any such uniform as aforesaid on any ceremonial, anniversary, or other special occasion will not be likely to involve risk of public disorder, he may, with the consent of a Secretary of State, by order permit the wearing of such uniform on that occasion either absolutely or subject to such conditions as may be specified in the order.

(2)   Where any person is charged before any court with an offence under this section, no further proceedings in respect thereof shall be taken against him without the consent of the Attorney-General except such as are authorised by section 6 of the Prosecution of Offences Act 1979 so, however, that if that person is remanded in custody he shall, after the expiration of a period of eight days from the date on which he was so remanded, be entitled to be released on bail without sureties unless within that period the Attorney-General has consented to such further proceedings as aforesaid.

2.   **Prohibition of quasi-military organisations**

(1) If the members or adherents of any association of persons, whether incorporated or not, are—

(a) organised or trained or equipped for the purpose of enabling them to be employed in usurping the functions of the police or of the armed forces of the Crown; or

(b) organised and trained or organised and equipped either for the purpose of enabling them to be employed for the use or display of physical force in promoting any political object, or in such manner as to arouse reasonable apprehension that they are organised and either trained or equipped for that purpose;

then any person who takes part in the control or management of the association, or in so organising or training as aforesaid any members or adherents thereof, shall be guilty of an offence under this section:

Provided that in any proceedings against a person charged with the offence of taking part in the control or management of such an association as aforesaid it shall be a defence to that charge to prove the he neither consented to nor connived at the organisation, training, or equipment of members or adherents of the association in contravention of the provisions of this section.

(2) No prosecution shall be instituted under this section without the consent of the Attorney-General.

(3) If upon application being made by the Attorney-General it appears to the High Court that any association is an association of which members or adherents are organised, trained, or equipped in contravention of the provisions of this section, the Court may make such order as appears necessary to prevent any disposition without the leave of the Court of property held by or for the association and in accordance with rules of court may direct an inquiry and report to be made as to any such property as aforesaid and as to the affairs of the association and make such further orders as appear to the Court to be just and equitable for the application of such property in or towards the discharge of the liabilities of the association lawfully incurred before the date of the application or since that date with the approval of the Court, in or towards the repayment of moneys to persons who became subscribers or contributors to the association in good faith and without knowledge of any such contravention as aforesaid, and in or towards any costs incurred in connection with any such inquiry and report as aforesaid or in winding-up or dissolving the association, and may order that any property which is not directed by the Court to be so applied as aforesaid shall be forfeited to the Crown.

(4) In any criminal or civil proceedings under this section proof of things done or of words written, spoken or published (whether or not in the presence of any party to the proceedings) by any person taking part in the control or management of an association or in organising, training or equipping members or adherents of an association shall be admissible as evidence of the purposes for which, or the manner in which, members or adherents of the association (whether those persons or others) were organised, or trained, or equipped.

(5) If a judge of the High Court is satisfied by information on oath that there is reasonable ground for suspecting that an offence under this section has been committed, and that evidence of the commission thereof is to be found at any premises or place specified in the information, he may, on an application made by an officer of police of a rank not lower than that of inspector, grant a search warrant authorising any such officer as aforesaid named in the warrant and any other officers of police to enter the premises or place at any time within three months from the date of the warrant, if necessary by force, and to search the premises or place and every person found therein, and to seize anything found on the premises or place or on any such person which the officer has reasonable ground for suspecting to be evidence of the commission of such an offence as aforesaid:

Provided that no woman shall, in pursuance of a warrant issued under this subsection, be searched except by a woman.

(6) Nothing in this section shall be construed as prohibiting the employment of a reasonable number or persons as stewards to assist in the preservation of order at any public meeting

held upon private premises, or the making of arrangements for that purpose or the instruction of the persons to be so employed in their lawful duties as such stewards, or their being furnished with badges or other distinguishing signs.

PUBLIC ORDER ACT 1986

PART I

1.   Riot

(1)   Where 12 or more persons who are present together use or threaten unlawful violence for a common purpose and the conduct of them (taken together) is such as would cause a person of reasonable firmness present at the scene to fear for his personal safety, each of the persons using unlawful violence for the common purpose is guilty of riot.

(2)   It is immaterial whether or not the 12 or more use or threaten unlawful violence simultaneously.

(3)   The common purpose may be inferred from conduct.

(4)   No person of reasonable firmness need actually be, or be likely to be, present at the scene.

(5)   Riot may be committed in private as well as in public places.

(6)   A person guilty of riot is liable on conviction on indictment to imprisonment for a term not exceeding ten years or a fine or both.

2.   Violent disorder

(1)   Where 3 or more persons who are present together use or threaten unlawful violence and the conduct of them (taken together) is such as would cause a person of reasonable firmness present at the scene to fear for his personal safety, each of the persons using or threatening unlawful violence is guilty of violent disorder.

(2)   It is immaterial whether or not the 3 or more use or threaten unlawful violence simultaneously.

(3)   No person of reasonable firmness need actually be, or be likely to be, present at the scene.

(4)   Violent disorder may be committed in private as well as in public places.

(5)   A person guilty of violent disorder is liable on conviction on indictment to imprisonment for a term not exceeding 5 years or a fine or both, or on summary conviction to imprisonment for a term not exceeding 6 months or a fine not exceeding the statutory maximum or both.

3.   Affray

(1)   A person is guilty of affray if he uses or threatens unlawful violence towards another and his conduct is such as would cause a person of reasonable firmness present at the scene to fear for his personal safety.

(2)   Where 2 or more persons use or threaten the unlawful violence, it is the conduct of them taken together that must be considered for the purposes of subsection (1).

(3)   For the purposes of this section a threat cannot be made by the use of words alone.

(4)   No person of reasonable firmness need actually be, or be likely to be, present at the scene.

(5)   Affray may be committed in private as well as in public places.

(7)   A person guilty of affray is liable on conviction on indictment to imprisonment for a term not exceeding 3 years or a fine or both, or on summary conviction to imprisonment for a term not exceeding 6 months or a fine not exceeding the statutory maximum or both.

4.   Fear or provocation of violence

(1)   A person is guilty of an offence if he—

(a)   uses towards another person threatening, abusive or insulting words or behaviour; or

(b)   distributes or displays to another person any writing, sign or other visible representation which is threatening, abusive or insulting,

with intent to cause that person to believe that immediate unlawful violence will be used against him or another by any person, or to provoke the immediate use of unlawful violence by that person or another, or whereby that person is likely to believe that such violence will be used or it is likely that such violence will be provoked.

(2)   An offence under this section may be committed in a public or a private place, except that no offence is committed where the words or behaviour are used, or the writing, sign or other visible representation is distributed or displayed, by a person inside a dwelling and the other person is also inside that or another dwelling.

(4)   A person guilty of an offence under this section is liable on summary conviction to imprisonment for a term not exceeding 6 months or a fine not exceeding level 5 on the standard scale or both.

4A.   Intentional harassment, alarm or distress

(1)   A person is guilty of an offence if, with intent to cause a person harassment, alarm or distress, he—

(a)   uses threatening, abusive or insulting words or behaviour, or disorderly behaviour, or

(b)   displays any writing, sign or other visible representation which is threatening, abusive or insulting,

thereby causing that or another person harassment, alarm or distress.

(2)   An offence under this section may be committed in a public or a private place, except that no offence is committed where the words or behaviour are used, or the writing, sign or other visible representation is displayed, by a person inside a dwelling and the person who is harassed, alarmed or distressed is also inside that or another dwelling.

(3)   It is a defence for the accused to prove—

(a)   that he was inside a dwelling and had no reason to believe that the words or behaviour used, or the writing, sign or other visible representation displayed would be heard or seen by a person outside that or any other dwelling, or

(b)   that his conduct was reasonable.

(5)   A person guilty of an offence under this section is liable on summary conviction to imprisonment for a term not exceeding 6 months or a fine not exceeding level 5 on the standard scale or both.

5.   Harassment, alarm or distress

(1)   A person is guilty of an offence if he—

(a)   uses threatening, abusive or insulting words or behaviour, or disorderly behaviour, or

(b)   displays any writing, sign or other visible representation which is threatening, abusive or insulting,

within the hearing or sight of a person likely to be caused harassment, alarm or distress thereby.

(2)   An offence under this section may be committed in a public or a private place, except that no offence is committed where the words or behaviour are used, or the writing, sign or other visible representation is displayed, by a person inside a dwelling and the other person is also inside that or another dwelling.

(3)   It is a defence for the accused to prove—

(a)   that he had no reason to believe that there was any person within hearing or sight who was likely to be caused harassment, alarm or distress, or

(b)   that he was inside a dwelling and had no reason to believe that the words or behaviour used, or the writing, sign or other visible representation displayed, would be heard or seen by a person outside that or any other dwelling, or

(c)   that his conduct was reasonable.

(6)   A person guilty of an offence under this section is liable on summary conviction to a fine not exceeding level 3 on the standard scale.

6.   Mental element: miscellaneous

(1)   A person is guilty of riot only if he intends to use violence or is aware that his conduct may be violent.

(2)   A person is guilty of violent disorder or affray only if he intends to use or threaten violence or is aware that his conduct may be violent or threaten violence.

(3) A person is guilty of an offence under section 4 only if he intends his words or behaviour, or the writing, sign or other visible representation, to be threatening, abusive or insulting, or is aware that it may be threatening, abusive or insulting.

(4) A person is guilty of an offence under section 5 only if he intends his words or behaviour, or the writing, sign or other visible representation, to be threatening, abusive or insulting, or is aware that it may be threatening, abusive or insulting or (as the case may be) he intends his behaviour to be or is aware that it may be disorderly.

(5) For the purposes of this section a person whose awareness is impaired by intoxication shall be taken to be aware of that of which he would be aware if not intoxicated, unless he shows either that his intoxication was not self-induced or that it was caused solely by the taking or administration of a substance in the course of medical treatment.

(6) In subsection (5) 'intoxication' means any intoxication, whether caused by drink, drugs or other means, or by a combination of means.

(7) Subsections (1) and (2) do not affect the determination for the purposes of riot or violent disorder of the number of persons who use or threaten violence.

8.   Interpretation

In this Part—

'dwelling' means any structure or part of a structure occupied as a person's home or as other living accommodation (whether the occupation is separate or shared with others) but does not include any part not so occupied, and for this purpose 'structure' includes a tent, caravan, vehicle, vessel or other temporary or movable structure;

'violence' means any violent conduct, so that—

(a) except in the context of affray, it includes violent conduct towards property as well as violent conduct towards persons, and

(b) it is not restricted to conduct causing or intended to cause injury or damage but includes any other violent conduct (for example, throwing at or towards a person a missile of a kind capable of causing injury which does not hit or falls short).

PART III

17.   Meaning of 'racial hatred'

In this Part 'racial hatred' means hatred against a group of persons . . . defined by reference to colour, race, nationality (including citizenship) or ethnic or national origins.

18.   Use of words or behaviour or display of written material

(1) A person who uses threatening, abusive or insulting words or behaviour, or displays any written material which is threatening, abusive or insulting, is guilty of an offence if—

(a)   he intends thereby to stir up racial hatred, or

(b)   having regard to all the circumstances racial hatred is likely to be stirred up thereby.

(2) An offence under this section may be committed in a public or a private place, except that no offence is committed where the words or behaviour are used, or the written material is displayed, by a person inside a dwelling and are not heard or seen except by other persons in that or another dwelling.

(4) In proceedings for an offence under this section it is a defence for the accused to prove that he was inside a dwelling and had no reason to believe that the words or behaviour used, or the written material displayed, would be heard or seen by a person outside that or any other dwelling.

(5) A person who is not shown to have intended to stir up racial hatred is not guilty of an offence under this section if he did not intend his words or behaviour, or the written material, to be, and was not aware that it might be, threatening, abusive or insulting.

(6) This section does not apply to words or behaviour used, or written material displayed, solely for the purpose of being included in a programme included in a programme service.

19.   Publishing or distributing written material

(1) A person who publishes or distributes written material which is threatening, abusive or insulting is guilty of an offence if—

(a)   he intends thereby to stir up racial hatred, or

(b)   having regard to all the circumstances racial hatred is likely to be stirred up thereby.

(2)   In proceedings for an offence under this section it is a defence for an accused who is not shown to have intended to stir up racial hatred to prove that he was not aware of the content of the material and did not suspect, and had no reason to suspect, that it was threatening, abusive or insulting.

(3)   References in this Part to the publication or distribution of written material are to its publication or distribution to the public or a section of the public.

PART V

38.   Contamination of or interference with goods with intention of causing public alarm or anxiety, etc.

(1)   It is an offence for a person, with the intention—

(a)   of causing public alarm or anxiety, or

(b)   of causing injury to members of the public consuming or using the goods, or

(c)   of causing economic loss to any person by reason of the goods being shunned by members of the public, or

(d)   of causing economic loss to any person by reason of steps taken to avoid any such alarm or anxiety, injury or loss

to contaminate or interfere with goods, or make it appear that goods have been contaminated or interfered with, or to place goods which have been contaminated or interfered with, or which appear to have been contaminated and interfered with, in a place where goods of that description are consumed, used, sold or otherwise supplied.

(2)   It is also an offence for a person, with any such intention as is mentioned in paragraph (a), (c) or (d) of subsection (1), to threaten that he or another will do, or claim that he or another has done, any of the acts mentioned in that subsection.

(3)   It is an offence for a person to be in possession of any of the following articles with a view to the commission of an offence under subsection (1)—

(a)   materials to be used for contaminating or interfering with goods or making it appear that goods have been contaminated or interfered with, or

(b)   goods which have been contaminated or interfered with, or which appear to have been contaminated or interfered with.

(4)   A person guilty of an offence under this section is liable—

(a)   on conviction on indictment to imprisonment for a term not exceeding 10 years or a fine or both, or

(b)   on summary conviction to imprisonment for a term not exceeding six months or a fine not exceeding the statutory maximum or both.

(5)   In this section 'goods' includes substances whether natural or manufactured and whether or not incorporated in or mixed with other goods.

(6)   The reference in subsection (2) to a person claiming that certain acts have been committed does not include a person who in good faith reports or warns that such acts have been, or appear to have been, committed.

ROAD TRAFFIC ACT 1988

1.   Causing death by dangerous driving

A person who causes the death of another person by driving a mechanically propelled vehicle dangerously on a road or other public place is guilty of an offence.

2.   Dangerous driving

A person who drives a mechanically propelled vehicle dangerously on a road or other public place is guilty of an offence.

2A.   **Meaning of dangerous driving**

(1)   For the purposes of sections 1 and 2 above a person is to be regarded as driving dangerously if (and, subject to subsection (2) below, only if)—

    (a)   the way he drives falls far below what would be expected of a competent and careful driver, and

    (b)   it would be obvious to a competent and careful driver that driving in that way would be dangerous.

(2)   A person is also to be regarded as driving dangerously for the purposes of sections 1 and 2 above if it would be obvious to a competent and careful driver that driving the vehicle in its current state would be dangerous.

(3)   In subsections (1) and (2) above 'dangerous' refers to danger either of injury to any person or of serious damage to property; and in determining for the purposes of those subsections what would be expected of, or obvious to, a competent and careful driver in a particular case, regard shall be had not only to the circumstances of which he could be expected to be aware but also to any circumstances shown to have been within the knowledge of the accused.

(4)   In determining for the purposes of subsection (2) above the state of a vehicle, regard may be had to anything attached to or carried on or in it and to the manner in which it is attached or carried.

3.   **Careless, and inconsiderate, driving**

If a person drives a mechanically propelled vehicle on a road or other public place without due care and attention, or without reasonable consideration for other persons using the road or place, he is guilty of an offence.

3A.   **Causing death by careless driving when under influence of drink or drugs**

(1)   If a person causes the death of another person by driving a mechanically propelled vehicle on a road or other public place without due care and attention, or without reasonable consideration for other persons using the road or place, and—

    (a)   he is, at the time when he is driving, unfit to drive through drink or drugs, or

    (b)   he has consumed so much alcohol that the proportion of it in his breath, blood or urine at that time exceeds the prescribed limit, or

    (c)   he is, within 18 hours after that time, required to provide a specimen in pursuance of section 7 of this Act, but without reasonable excuse fails to provide it,

he is guilty of an offence.

(2)   For the purposes of this section a person shall be taken to be unfit to drive at any time when his ability to drive properly is impaired.

(3)   Subsection (1)(b) and (c) above shall not apply in relation to a person driving a mechanically propelled vehicle other than a motor vehicle.

4.   **Driving, or being in charge, when under influence of drink or drugs**

(1)   A person who, when driving or attempting to drive a mechanically propelled vehicle on a road or other public place, is unfit to drive through drink or drugs is guilty of an offence.

(2)   Without prejudice to subsection (1) above, a person who, when in charge of a mechanically propelled vehicle which is on a road or other public place, is unfit to drive through drink or drugs is guilty of an offence.

(3)   For the purposes of subsection (2) above, a person shall be deemed not to have been in charge of a mechanically propelled vehicle if he proves that at the material time the circumstances were such that there was no likelihood of his driving it so long as he remained unfit to drive through drink or drugs.

(4)   The court may, in determining whether there was such a likelihood as is mentioned in subsection (3) above, disregard any injury to him and any damage to the vehicle.

(5)   For the purposes of this section, a person shall be taken to be unfit to drive if his ability to drive properly is for the time being impaired.

5.   Driving or being in charge of a motor vehicle with alcohol concentration above prescribed limit

(1)   If a person—

(a)   drives or attempts to drive a motor vehicle on a road or other public place, or

(b)   is in charge of a motor vehicle on a road or other public place,

after consuming so much alcohol that the proportion of it in his breath, blood or urine exceeds the prescribed limit he is guilty of an offence.

(2)   It is a defence for a person charged with an offence under subsection (1)(b) above to prove that at the time he is alleged to have committed the offence the circumstances were such that there was no likelihood of his driving the vehicle whilst the proportion of alcohol in his breath, blood or urine remained likely to exceed the prescribed limit.

(3)   The court may, in determining whether there was such a likelihood as is mentioned in subsection (2) above, disregard any injury to him and any damage to the vehicle.

12.   Motor racing on public ways

(1)   A person who promotes or takes part in a race or trial of speed between motor vehicles on a public way is guilty of an offence.

(2)   In this section 'public way' means, in England and Wales, a public highway . . .

13.   Regulation of motoring events on public ways

(1)   A person who promotes or takes part in a competition or trial (other than a race or trial of speed) involving the use of motor vehicles on a public way is guilty of an offence unless the competition or trial—

(a)   is authorised, and

(b)   is conducted in accordance with any conditions imposed,

by or under regulations under this section.

(4)   In this section 'public way' means, in England and Wales, a public highway . . .

13A.   Disapplication of sections 1 to 3 for authorised motoring events

(1)   A person shall not be guilty of an offence under sections 1, 2 or 3 of this Act by virtue of driving a vehicle in a public place other than a road if he shows that he was driving in accordance with an authorisation for a motoring event given under regulations made by the Secretary of State.

14.   Seat belts: adults

(1)   The Secretary of State may make regulations requiring, subject to such exceptions as may be prescribed, persons who are driving or riding in motor vehicles on a road to wear seat belts of such description as may be prescribed.

(3)   A person who drives or rides in a motor vehicle in contravention of regulations under this section is guilty of an offence; but, notwithstanding any enactment or rule of law, no person other than the person actually committing the contravention is guilty of an offence by reason of the contravention.

(6)   Regulations under this section requiring the wearing of seat belts by persons riding in motor vehicles shall not apply to children under the age of fourteen years.

15.   Restriction on carrying children not wearing seat belts in motor vehicles

(1)   Except as provided by regulations, where a child under the age of fourteen years is in the front of a motor vehicle, a person must not without reasonable excuse drive the vehicle on a road unless the child is wearing a seat belt in conformity with regulations.

(2)   It is an offence for a person to drive a motor vehicle in contravention of subsection (1) above.

(3)   Except as provided by regulations, where a child under the age of fourteen years is in the rear of a motor vehicle and any seat belt is fitted in the rear of that vehicle, a person must not without reasonable excuse drive the vehicle on a road unless the child is wearing a seat belt in conformity with regulations.

(4) It is an offence for a person to drive a motor vehicle in contravention of subsection (3) above.

(9) In this section—

'regulations' means regulations made by the Secretary of State under this section, and 'seat belt' includes any description of restraining device for a child and any reference to wearing a seat belt is to be construed accordingly.

16. Wearing of protective headgear

(1) The Secretary of State may make regulations requiring, subject to such exceptions as may be specified in the regulations, persons driving or riding (otherwise than in side-cars) on motor cycles of any class specified in the regulations to wear protective headgear of such description as may be so specified.

(2) A requirement imposed by regulations under this section shall not apply to any follower of the Sikh religion while he is wearing a turban.

(4) A person who drives or rides a motor cycle in contravention of regulations under this section is guilty of an offence; but notwithstanding any enactment or rule of law no person other than the person actually committing the contravention is guilty of an offence by reason of the contravention unless the person actually committing the contravention is a child under the age of sixteen years.

SERIOUS ORGANISED CRIME AND POLICE ACT 2005

128. Offence of trespassing on designated site

(1) A person commits an offence if he enters, or is on, any protected site in England and Wales or Northern Ireland as a trespasser.

(1A) In this section 'protected site' means—

    (a) a nuclear site; or

    (b) a designated site.

(1B) In this section 'nuclear site' means—

    (a) so much of any premises in respect of which a nuclear site licence (within the meaning of the Nuclear Installations Act 1965) is for the time being in force as lies within the outer perimeter of the protection provided for those premises; and

    (b) so much of any other premises of which premises falling within paragraph (a) form a part as lies within that outer perimeter.

(1C) For this purpose—

    (a) the outer perimeter of the protection provided for any premises is the line of the outermost fences, walls or other obstacles provided or relied on for protecting those premises from intruders; and

    (b) that line shall be determined on the assumption that every gate, door or other barrier across a way through a fence, wall or other obstacle is closed.

(2) A 'designated site' means a site—

    (a) specified or described (in any way) in an order made by the Secretary of State, and

    (b) designated for the purposes of this section by the order.

(3) The Secretary of State may only designate a site for the purposes of this section if—

    (a) it is comprised in Crown land; or

    (b) it is comprised in land belonging to Her Majesty in Her private capacity or to the immediate heir to the Throne in his private capacity; or

    (c) it appears to the Secretary of State that it is appropriate to designate the site in the interests of national security.

(4) It is a defence for a person charged with an offence under this section to prove that he did not know, and had no reasonable cause to suspect, that the site in relation to which the offence is alleged to have been committed was a protected site.

(7) For the purposes of this section a person who is on any protected site as a trespasser does not cease to be a trespasser by virtue of being allowed time to leave the site.

(8) In this section—

    (a) 'site' means the whole or part of any building or buildings, or any land, or both;

    (b) 'Crown land' means land in which there is a Crown interest or a Duchy interest.

(9) For this purpose—

'Crown interest' means an interest belonging to Her Majesty in right of the Crown, and 'Duchy interest' means an interest belonging to Her Majesty in right of the Duchy of Lancaster or belonging to the Duchy of Cornwall.

132. Demonstrating without authorisation in designated area

(1) Any person who—

    (a) organises a demonstration in a public place in the designated area, or

    (b) takes part in a demonstration in a public place in the designated area, or

    (c) carries on a demonstration by himself in a public place in the designated area,

is guilty of an offence if, when the demonstration starts, authorisation for the demonstration has not been given under section 134(2).

(2) It is a defence for a person accused of an offence under subsection (1) to show that he reasonably believed that authorisation had been given.

(3) Subsection (1) does not apply if the demonstration is—

    (a) a public procession of which notice is required to be given under subsection (1) of section 11 of the Public Order Act 1986, or of which (by virtue of subsection (2) of that section) notice is not required to be given, or

    (b) a public procession for the purposes of section 12 or 13 of that Act.

(4) Subsection (1) also does not apply in relation to any conduct which is lawful under section 220 of the Trade Union and Labour Relations (Consolidation) Act 1992.

(5) If subsection (1) does not apply by virtue of subsection (3) or (4), nothing in sections 133 to 136 applies either.

(6) Section 14 of the Public Order Act 1986 (imposition of conditions on public assemblies) does not apply in relation to a public assembly which is also a demonstration in a public place in the designated area.

(7) In this section and in sections 133 to 136—

    (a) 'the designated area' means the area specified in an order under section 138,

    (b) 'public place' means any highway or any place to which at the material time the public or any section of the public has access, on payment or otherwise, as of right or by virtue of express or implied permission,

    (c) references to any person organising a demonstration include a person participating in its organisation,

    (d) references to any person organising a demonstration do not include a person carrying on a demonstration by himself,

    (e) references to any person or persons taking part in a demonstration (except in subsection (1) of this section) include a person carrying on a demonstration by himself.

138. The designated area

(1) The Secretary of State may by order specify an area as the designated area for the purposes of sections 132 to 137.

(2) The area may be specified by description, by reference to a map or in any other way.

(3) No point in the area so specified may be more than one kilometre in a straight line from the point nearest to it in Parliament Square.

145. Interference with contractual relationships so as to harm animal research organisation

(1) A person (A) commits an offence if, with the intention of harming an animal research organisation, he—

    (a) does a relevant act, or

    (b) threatens that he or somebody else will do a relevant act, in circumstances in which that act or threat is intended or likely to cause a second person (B) to take any of the steps in subsection (2).

(2) The steps are—

    (a) not to perform any contractual obligation owed by B to a third person (C) (whether or not such non-performance amounts to a breach of contract);

    (b) to terminate any contract B has with C;

    (c) not to enter into a contract with C

(3) For the purposes of this section, a 'relevant act' is—

    (a) an act amounting to a criminal offence, or

    (b) a tortious act causing B to suffer loss or damage of any description;

but paragraph (b) does not include an act which is actionable on the ground only that it induces another person to break a contract with B.

(4) For the purposes of this section, 'contract' includes any other arrangement (and 'contractual' is to be read accordingly).

(5) For the purposes of this section, to 'harm' an animal research organisation means—

    (a) to cause the organisation to suffer loss or damage of any description, or

    (b) to prevent or hinder the carrying out by the organisation of any of its activities.

(6) This section does not apply to any act done wholly or mainly in contemplation or furtherance of a trade dispute.

(7) In subsection (6) 'trade dispute' has the same meaning as in Part 4 of the Trade Union and Labour Relations (Consolidation) Act 1992, except that section 218 of that Act shall be read as if—

    (a) it made provision corresponding to section 244(4) of that Act, and

    (b) in subsection (5), the definition of 'worker' included any person falling within paragraph (b) of the definition of 'worker' in section 244(5).

146. Intimidation of persons connected with animal research organisation

(1) A person (A) commits an offence if, with the intention of causing a second person (B) to abstain from doing something which B is entitled to do (or to do something which B is entitled to abstain from doing)—

    (a) A threatens B that A or somebody else will do a relevant act, and

    (b) A does so wholly or mainly because B is a person falling within subsection (2).

(2) A person falls within this subsection if he is—

    (a) an employee or officer of an animal research organisation;

    (b) a student at an educational establishment that is an animal research organisation;

    (c) a lessor or licensor of any premises occupied by an animal research organisation;

    (d) a person with a financial interest in, or who provides financial assistance to, an animal research organisation;

    (e) a customer or supplier of an animal research organisation;

    (f) a person who is contemplating becoming someone within paragraph (c), (d) or (e);

    (g) a person who is, or is contemplating becoming, a customer or supplier of someone within paragraph (c), (d), (e) or (f);

    (h) an employee or officer of someone within paragraph (c), (d), (e), (f) or (g);

    (i) a person with a financial interest in, or who provides financial assistance to, someone within paragraph (c), (d), (e), (f) or (g);

    (j) a spouse, civil partner, friend or relative of, or a person who is known personally to, someone within any of paragraphs (a) to (i);

    (k) a person who is, or is contemplating becoming, a customer or supplier of someone within paragraph (a), (b), (h), (i) or (j); or

    (l) an employer of someone within paragraph (j).

(3) For the purposes of this section, an 'officer' of an animal research organisation or a person includes—

    (a) where the organisation or person is a body corporate, a director, manager or secretary;

    (b) where the organisation or person is a charity, a charity trustee (within the meaning of the Charities Act 1993);

(c) where the organisation or person is a partnership, a partner.

(4) For the purposes of this section—

(a) a person is a customer or supplier of another person if he purchases goods, services or facilities from, or (as the case may be) supplies goods, services or facilities to, that other; and

(b) 'supplier' includes a person who supplies services in pursuance of any enactment that requires or authorises such services to be provided.

(5) For the purposes of this section, a 'relevant act' is—

(a) an act amounting to a criminal offence, or

(b) a tortious act causing B or another person to suffer loss or damage of any description.

(6) The Secretary of State may by order amend this section so as to include within subsection (2) any description of persons framed by reference to their connection with—

(a) an animal research organisation, or

(b) any description of persons for the time being mentioned in that subsection.

(7) This section does not apply to any act done wholly or mainly in contemplation or furtherance of a trade dispute.

(8) In subsection (7) 'trade dispute' has the meaning given by section 145(7).

148. Animal research organisations

(1) For the purposes of sections 145 and 146 'animal research organisation' means any person or organisation falling within subsection (2) or (3).

(2) A person or organisation falls within this subsection if he or it is the owner, lessee or licensee of premises constituting or including—

(a) a place specified in a licence granted under section 4 or 5 of the 1986 Act,

(b) a scientific procedure establishment designated under section 6 of that Act, or

(c) a breeding or supplying establishment designated under section 7 of that Act.

(3) A person or organisation falls within this subsection if he or it employs, or engages under a contract for services, any of the following in his capacity as such—

(a) the holder of a personal licence granted under section 4 of the 1986 Act,

(b) the holder of a project licence granted under section 5 of that Act,

(c) a person specified under section 6(5) of that Act, or

(d) a person specified under section 7(5) of that Act.

(4) The Secretary of State may by order amend this section so as to include a reference to any description of persons whom he considers to be involved in, or to have a direct connection with persons who are involved in, the application of regulated procedures.

(5) In this section—

'the 1986 Act' means the Animals (Scientific Procedures) Act 1986;

'organisation' includes any institution, trust, undertaking or association of persons;

'premises' includes any place within the meaning of the 1986 Act;

'regulated procedures' has the meaning given by section 2 of the 1986 Act.

SEXUAL OFFENCES ACT 1956

33. Keeping a brothel

It is an offence for a person to keep a brothel, or to manage, or act or assist in the management of, a brothel.

33A. Keeping a brothel used for prostitution

(1) It is an offence for a person to keep, or to manage, or act or assist in the management of, a brothel to which people resort for practices involving prostitution (whether or not also for other practices).

(2) In this section 'prostitution' has the meaning given by section 51(2) of the Sexual Offences Act 2003.

34.   Landlord letting premises for use as brothel

It is an offence for the lessor or landlord of any premises or his agent to let the whole or part of the premises with the knowledge that it is to be used, in whole or in part, as a brothel, or, where the whole or part of the premises is used as a brothel, to be wilfully a party to that use continuing.

35.   Tenant permitting premises to be used as a brothel

(1)   It is an offence for the tenant or occupier, or person in charge, of any premises knowingly to permit the whole or part of the premises to be used as a brothel.

(2)   Where the tenant or occupier of any premises is convicted (whether under this section or, for an offence committed before the commencement of this Act, under section thirteen of the Criminal Law Amendment Act 1885) of knowingly permitting the whole or part of the premises to be used as a brothel, the First Schedule to this Act shall apply to enlarge the rights of the lessor or landlord with respect to the assignment or determination of the lease or other contract under which the premises are held by the person convicted.

(3)   Where the tenant or occupier of any premises is so convicted, or was so convicted under the said section thirteen before the commencement of this Act, and either—

(a)   the lessor or landlord, after having the conviction brought to his notice, fails or failed to exercise his statutory rights in relation to the lease or contract under which the premises are or were held by the person convicted; or

(b)   the lessor or landlord, after exercising his statutory rights so as to determine that lease or contract, grants or granted a new lease or enters or entered into a new contract of tenancy of the premises to, with or for the benefit of the same person, without having all reasonable provisions to prevent the recurrence of the offence inserted in the new lease or contract;

then, if subsequently an offence under this section is committed in respect of the premises during the subsistence of the lease or contract referred to in paragraph (a) of this subsection or (where paragraph (b) applies) during the subsistence of the new lease or contract, the lessor or landlord shall be deemed to be a party to that offence unless he shows that he took all reasonable steps to prevent the recurrence of the offence.

36.   Tenant permitting premises to be used for prostitution

It is an offence for the tenant or occupier of any premises knowingly to permit the whole or part of the premises to be used for the purposes of habitual prostitution (whether any prostitute involved is male or female).

SEXUAL OFFENCES ACT 1967

6.   Premises resorted to for homosexual practices

Premises shall be treated for purposes of sections 33 to 35 of the Act of 1956 as a brothel if people resort to it for the purpose of lewd homosexual practices in circumstances in which resort thereto for lewd heterosexual practices would have led to its being treated as a brothel for the purposes of those sections.

SEXUAL OFFENCES ACT 1985

1.   Kerb-crawling

1) A person commits an offence if he solicits another person (or different persons) for the purpose of prostitution—

(a)   from a motor vehicle while it is in a street or public place; or

(b)   in a street or public place while in the immediate vicinity of a motor vehicle that he has just got out of or off,

persistently or . . . in such manner or in such circumstances as to be likely to cause annoyance to the person (or any of the persons) solicited, or nuisance to other persons in the neighbourhood.

2. **Persistent soliciting**

(1) A person commits an offence if in a street or public place he persistently solicits another person (or different persons) for the purpose of prostitution.

4. **Interpretation**

(1) References in this Act to a person soliciting another person for the purpose of prostitution are references to his soliciting that person for the purpose of obtaining that person's services as a prostitute.

(4) For the purposes of this Act 'street' includes any bridge, road, lane, footway, subway, square, court, alley or passage, whether a thoroughfare or not, which is for the time being open to the public; and the doorways and entrances of premises abutting on a street (as hereinbefore defined), and any ground adjoining and open to a street, shall be treated as forming part of the street.

SEXUAL OFFENCES ACT 1993

1. **Abolition of presumption of sexual incapacity**

The presumption of criminal law that a boy under the age of fourteen is incapable of sexual intercourse is hereby abolished.

SEXUAL OFFENCES ACT 2003

1. **Rape**

(1) A person (A) commits an offence if—
  (a) he intentionally penetrates the vagina, anus or mouth of another person (B) with his penis,
  (b) B does not consent to the penetration, and
  (c) A does not reasonably believe that B consents.
(2) Whether a belief is reasonable is to be determined having regard to all the circumstances, including any steps A has taken to ascertain whether B consents.
(3) Sections 75 and 76 apply to an offence under this section.

2. **Assault by penetration**

(1) A person (A) commits an offence if—
  (a) he intentionally penetrates the vagina or anus of another person (B) with a part of his body or anything else,
  (b) the penetration is sexual,
  (c) B does not consent to the penetration, and
  (d) A does not reasonably believe that B consents.
(2) Whether a belief is reasonable is to be determined having regard to all the circumstances, including any steps A has taken to ascertain whether B consents.
(3) Sections 75 and 76 apply to an offence under this section.

3. **Sexual assault**

(1) A person (A) commits an offence if—
  (a) he intentionally touches another person (B),
  (b) the touching is sexual,
  (c) B does not consent to the touching, and
  (d) A does not reasonably believe that B consents.
(2) Whether a belief is reasonable is to be determined having regard to all the circumstances, including any steps A has taken to ascertain whether B consents.
(3) Sections 75 and 76 apply to an offence under this section.

4. **Causing a person to engage in sexual activity without consent**

(1) A person (A) commits an offence if—

        (a)   he intentionally causes another person (B) to engage in an activity,

        (b)   the activity is sexual,

        (c)   B does not consent to engaging in the activity, and

        (d)   A does not reasonably believe that B consents.

(2)   Whether a belief is reasonable is to be determined having regard to all the circumstances, including any steps A has taken to ascertain whether B consents.

(3)   Sections 75 and 76 apply to an offence under this section.

(4)   A person guilty of an offence under this section, if the activity caused involved—

        (a)   penetration of B's anus or vagina,

        (b)   penetration of B's mouth with a person's penis,

        (c)   penetration of a person's anus or vagina with a part of B's body or by B with anything else, or

        (d)   penetration of a person's mouth with B's penis,

is liable, on conviction on indictment, to imprisonment for life.

5. Rape of a child under 13

(1)   A person commits an offence if—

        (a)   he intentionally penetrates the vagina, anus or mouth of another person with his penis, and

        (b)   the other person is under 13.

6. Assault of a child under 13 by penetration

(1)   A person commits an offence if—

        (a)   he intentionally penetrates the vagina or anus of another person with a part of his body or anything else,

        (b)   the penetration is sexual, and

        (c)   the other person is under 13.

7. Sexual assault of a child under 13

(1)   A person commits an offence if—

        (a)   he intentionally touches another person,

        (b)   the touching is sexual, and

        (c)   the other person is under 13.

8. Causing or inciting a child under 13 to engage in sexual activity

(1)   A person commits an offence if—

        (a)   he intentionally causes or incites another person (B) to engage in an activity,

        (b)   the activity is sexual, and

        (c)   B is under 13.

(2)   A person guilty of an offence under this section, if the activity caused or incited involved—

        (a)   penetration of B's anus or vagina,

        (b)   penetration of B's mouth with a person's penis,

        (c)   penetration of a person's anus or vagina with a part of B's body or by B with anything else, or

        (d)   penetration of a person's mouth with B's penis,

is liable, on conviction on indictment, to imprisonment for life.

9. Sexual activity with a child

(1)   A person aged 18 or over (A) commits an offence if—

        (a)   he intentionally touches another person (B),

        (b)   the touching is sexual, and

        (c)   either—

            (i)   B is under 16 and A does not reasonably believe that B is 16 or over, or

            (ii)   B is under 13.

(2)   A person guilty of an offence under this section, if the touching involved—

        (a)   penetration of B's anus or vagina with a part of A's body or anything else,

        (b)   penetration of B's mouth with A's penis,

(c)   penetration of A's anus or vagina with a part of B's body, or

(d)   penetration of A's mouth with B's penis,

is liable, on conviction on indictment, to imprisonment for a term not exceeding 14 years.

10.   Causing or inciting a child to engage in sexual activity

(1)   A person aged 18 or over (A) commits an offence if—

    (a)   he intentionally causes or incites another person (B) to engage in an activity,

    (b)   the activity is sexual, and

    (c)   either—

        (i)   B is under 16 and A does not reasonably believe that B is 16 or over, or

        (ii)   B is under 13.

(2)   A person guilty of an offence under this section, if the activity caused or incited involved—

    (a)   penetration of B's anus or vagina,

    (b)   penetration of B's mouth with a person's penis,

    (c)   penetration of a person's anus or vagina with a part of B's body or by B with anything else, or

    (d)   penetration of a person's mouth with B's penis,

is liable, on conviction on indictment, to imprisonment for a term not exceeding 14 years.

11.   Engaging in sexual activity in the presence of a child

(1)   A person aged 18 or over (A) commits an offence if—

    (a)   he intentionally engages in an activity,

    (b)   the activity is sexual,

    (c)   for the purpose of obtaining sexual gratification, he engages in it—

        (i)   when another person (B) is present or is in a place from which A can be observed, and

        (ii)   knowing or believing that B is aware, or intending that B should be aware, that he is engaging in it, and

    (d)   either—

        (i)   B is under 16 and A does not reasonably believe that B is 16 or over, or

        (ii)   B is under 13.

12.   Causing a child to watch a sexual act

(1)   A person aged 18 or over (A) commits an offence if—

    (a)   for the purpose of obtaining sexual gratification, he intentionally causes another person (B) to watch a third person engaging in an activity, or to look at an image of any person engaging in an activity,

    (b)   the activity is sexual, and

    (c)   either—

        (i)   B is under 16 and A does not reasonably believe that B is 16 or over, or

        (ii)   B is under 13.

13.   Child sex offences committed by children or young persons

(1)   A person under 18 commits an offence if he does anything which would be an offence under any of sections 9 to 12 if he were aged 18.

14.   Arranging or facilitating commission of a child sex offence

(1)   A person commits an offence if—

    (a)   he intentionally arranges or facilitates something that he intends to do, intends another person to do, or believes that another person will do, in any part of the world, and

    (b)   doing it will involve the commission of an offence under any of sections 9 to 13.

(2)   A person does not commit an offence under this section if—

    (a)   he arranges or facilitates something that he believes another person will do, but that he does not intend to do or intend another person to do, and

    (b)   any offence within subsection (1)(b) would be an offence against a child for whose protection he acts.

(3)   For the purposes of subsection (2), a person acts for the protection of a child if he acts for the purpose of—
    (a)   protecting the child from sexually transmitted infection,
    (b)   protecting the physical safety of the child,
    (c)   preventing the child from becoming pregnant, or
    (d)   promoting the child's emotional well-being by the giving of advice,
and not for the purpose of obtaining sexual gratification or for the purpose of causing or encouraging the activity constituting the offence within subsection (1)(b) or the child's participation in it.

15.   Meeting a child following sexual grooming etc.

(1)   A person aged 18 or over (A) commits an offence if—
    (a)   having met or communicated with another person (B) on at least two earlier occasions, he—
        (i)   intentionally meets B, or
        (ii)   travels with the intention of meeting B in any part of the world,
    (b)   at the time, he intends to do anything to or in respect of B, during or after the meeting and in any part of the world, which if done will involve the commission by A of a relevant offence,
    (c)   B is under 16, and
    (d)   A does not reasonably believe that B is 16 or over.
(2)   In subsection (1)—
    (a)   the reference to A having met or communicated with B is a reference to A having met B in any part of the world or having communicated with B by any means from, to or in any part of the world;
    (b)   'relevant offence' means—
        (i)   an offence under this Part,
        (ii)   an offence within any of paragraphs 61 to 92 of Schedule 3, or
        (iii) anything done outside England and Wales and Northern Ireland which is not an offence within sub-paragraph (i) or (ii) but would be an offence within sub-paragraph (i) if done in England and Wales.

16.   Abuse of position of trust: sexual activity with a child

(1)   A person aged 18 or over (A) commits an offence if—
    (a)   he intentionally touches another person (B),
    (b)   the touching is sexual,
    (c)   A is in a position of trust in relation to B,
    (d)   where subsection (2) applies, A knows or could reasonably be expected to know of the circumstances by virtue of which he is in a position of trust in relation to B, and
    (e)   either—
        (i)   B is under 18 and A does not reasonably believe that B is 18 or over, or
        (ii)   B is under 13.
(2)   This subsection applies where A—
    (a)   is in a position of trust in relation to B by virtue of circumstances within section 21(2), (3), (4) or (5), and
    (b)   is not in such a position of trust by virtue of other circumstances.
(3)   Where in proceedings for an offence under this section it is proved that the other person was under 18, the defendant is to be taken not to have reasonably believed that that person was 18 or over unless sufficient evidence is adduced to raise an issue as to whether he reasonably believed it.
(4)   Where in proceedings for an offence under this section—
    (a)   it is proved that the defendant was in a position of trust in relation to the other person by virtue of circumstances within section 21(2), (3), (4) or (5), and
    (b)   it is not proved that he was in such a position of trust by virtue of other circumstances,

it is to be taken that the defendant knew or could reasonably have been expected to know of the circumstances by virtue of which he was in such a position of trust unless sufficient evidence is adduced to raise an issue as to whether he knew or could reasonably have been expected to know of those circumstances.

17.   Abuse of position of trust: causing or inciting a child to engage in sexual activity

(1)   A person aged 18 or over (A) commits an offence if—

(a)   he intentionally causes or incites another person (B) to engage in an activity,

(b)   the activity is sexual,

(c)   A is in a position of trust in relation to B,

(d)   where subsection (2) applies, A knows or could reasonably be expected to know of the circumstances by virtue of which he is in a position of trust in relation to B, and

(e)   either—

(i)   B is under 18 and A does not reasonably believe that B is 18 or over, or

(ii)   B is under 13.

(2)   This subsection applies where A—

(a)   is in a position of trust in relation to B by virtue of circumstances within section 21(2), (3), (4) or (5), and

(b)   is not in such a position of trust by virtue of other circumstances.

(3)   Where in proceedings for an offence under this section it is proved that the other person was under 18, the defendant is to be taken not to have reasonably believed that that person was 18 or over unless sufficient evidence is adduced to raise an issue as to whether he reasonably believed it.

(4)   Where in proceedings for an offence under this section—

(a)   it is proved that the defendant was in a position of trust in relation to the other person by virtue of circumstances within section 21(2), (3), (4) or (5), and

(b)   it is not proved that he was in such a position of trust by virtue of other circumstances,

it is to be taken that the defendant knew or could reasonably have been expected to know of the circumstances by virtue of which he was in such a position of trust unless sufficient evidence is adduced to raise an issue as to whether he knew or could reasonably have been expected to know of those circumstances.

18.   Abuse of position of trust: sexual activity in the presence of a child

(1)   A person aged 18 or over (A) commits an offence if—

(a)   he intentionally engages in an activity,

(b)   the activity is sexual,

(c)   for the purpose of obtaining sexual gratification, he engages in it—

(i)   when another person (B) is present or is in a place from which A can be observed, and

(ii)   knowing or believing that B is aware, or intending that B should be aware, that he is engaging in it,

(d)   A is in a position of trust in relation to B,

(e)   where subsection (2) applies, A knows or could reasonably be expected to know of the circumstances by virtue of which he is in a position of trust in relation to B, and

(f)   either—

(i)   B is under 18 and A does not reasonably believe that B is 18 or over, or

(ii)   B is under 13.

(2)   This subsection applies where A—

(a)   is in a position of trust in relation to B by virtue of circumstances within section 21(2), (3), (4) or (5), and

(b)   is not in such a position of trust by virtue of other circumstances.

(3)   Where in proceedings for an offence under this section it is proved that the other person was under 18, the defendant is to be taken not to have reasonably believed that that person was 18 or over unless sufficient evidence is adduced to raise an issue as to whether he reasonably believed it.

(4)   Where in proceedings for an offence under this section—

    (a)   it is proved that the defendant was in a position of trust in relation to the other person by virtue of circumstances within section 21(2), (3), (4) or (5), and

    (b)   it is not proved that he was in such a position of trust by virtue of other circumstances,

it is to be taken that the defendant knew or could reasonably have been expected to know of the circumstances by virtue of which he was in such a position of trust unless sufficient evidence is adduced to raise an issue as to whether he knew or could reasonably have been expected to know of those circumstances.

19.   Abuse of position of trust: causing a child to watch a sexual act

(1)   A person aged 18 or over (A) commits an offence if—

    (a)   for the purpose of obtaining sexual gratification, he intentionally causes another person (B) to watch a third person engaging in an activity, or to look at an image of any person engaging in an activity,

    (b)   the activity is sexual,

    (c)   A is in a position of trust in relation to B,

    (d)   where subsection (2) applies, A knows or could reasonably be expected to know of the circumstances by virtue of which he is in a position of trust in relation to B, and

    (e)   either—

        (i)   B is under 18 and A does not reasonably believe that B is 18 or over, or

        (ii)   B is under 13.

(2)   This subsection applies where A—

    (a)   is in a position of trust in relation to B by virtue of circumstances within section 21(2), (3), (4) or (5), and

    (b)   is not in such a position of trust by virtue of other circumstances.

(3)   Where in proceedings for an offence under this section it is proved that the other person was under 18, the defendant is to be taken not to have reasonably believed that that person was 18 or over unless sufficient evidence is adduced to raise an issue as to whether he reasonably believed it.

(4)   Where in proceedings for an offence under this section—

    (a)   it is proved that the defendant was in a position of trust in relation to the other person by virtue of circumstances within section 21(2), (3), (4) or (5), and

    (b)   it is not proved that he was in such a position of trust by virtue of other circumstances,

it is to be taken that the defendant knew or could reasonably have been expected to know of the circumstances by virtue of which he was in such a position of trust unless sufficient evidence is adduced to raise an issue as to whether he knew or could reasonably have been expected to know of those circumstances.

20.   Abuse of position of trust: acts done in Scotland

Anything which, if done in England and Wales or Northern Ireland, would constitute an offence under any of sections 16 to 19 also constitutes that offence if done in Scotland.

21.   Positions of trust

(1)   For the purposes of sections 16 to 19, a person (A) is in a position of trust in relation to another person (B) if—

    (a)   any of the following subsections applies, or

    (b)   any condition specified in an order made by the Secretary of State is met.

(2)   This subsection applies if A looks after persons under 18 who are detained in an institution by virtue of a court order or under an enactment, and B is so detained in that institution.

(3)   This subsection applies if A looks after persons under 18 who are resident in a home or other place in which—

    (a)   accommodation and maintenance are provided by an authority under section 23(2) of the Children Act 1989 (c 41), or

    (b)   accommodation is provided by a voluntary organisation under section 59(1) of that Act, and B is resident, and is so provided with accommodation and maintenance or accommodation, in that place.

(4) This subsection applies if A looks after persons under 18 who are accommodated and cared for in one of the following institutions—

    (a) a hospital,

    (b) an independent clinic,

    (c) a care home, residential care home or private hospital,

    (d) a community home, voluntary home or children's home,

    (e) a home provided under section 82(5) of the Children Act 1989, or

    (f) a residential family centre,

and B is accommodated and cared for in that institution.

(5) This subsection applies if A looks after persons under 18 who are receiving education at an educational institution and B is receiving, and A is not receiving, education at that institution.

(7) This subsection applies if A is engaged in the provision of services under, or pursuant to anything done under—

    (a) sections 8 to 10 of the Employment and Training Act 1973, or

    (b) section 114 of the Learning and Skills Act 2000,

and, in that capacity, looks after B on an individual basis.

(8) This subsection applies if A regularly has unsupervised contact with B (whether face to face or by any other means)—

    (a) in the exercise of functions of a local authority under section 20 or 21 of the Children Act 1989,

(9) This subsection applies if A, as a person who is to report to the court under section 7 of the Children Act 1989 on matters relating to the welfare of B, regularly has unsupervised contact with B (whether face to face or by any other means).

(10) This subsection applies if A is a personal adviser appointed for B under—

    (a) section 23B(2) of, or paragraph 19C of Schedule 2 to, the Children Act 1989,

and, in that capacity, looks after B on an individual basis.

(11) This subsection applies if—

    (a) B is subject to a care order, a supervision order or an education supervision order, and

    (b) in the exercise of functions conferred by virtue of the order on an authorised person or the authority designated by the order, A looks after B on an individual basis.

(12) This subsection applies if A—

    (a) is an officer of the Service or Welsh family proceedings officer (within the meaning given by section 35 of the Children Act 2004) appointed for B under section 41(1) of the Children Act 1989,

    (b) is appointed a children's guardian of B under rule 6 or rule 18 of the Adoption Rules 1984, or

    (c) is appointed to be the guardian ad litem of B under rule 9.5 of the Family Proceedings Rules 1991,

and, in that capacity, regularly has unsupervised contact with B (whether face to face or by any other means).

(13) This subsection applies if—

    (a) B is subject to requirements imposed by or under an enactment on his release from detention for a criminal offence, or is subject to requirements imposed by a court order made in criminal proceedings, and

    (b) A looks after B on an individual basis in pursuance of the requirements.

22.   Positions of trust: interpretation

(1) The following provisions apply for the purposes of section 21.

(2) Subject to subsection (3), a person looks after persons under 18 if he is regularly involved in caring for, training, supervising or being in sole charge of such persons.

(3) A person (A) looks after another person (B) on an individual basis if—

    (a) A is regularly involved in caring for, training or supervising B, and

      (b)   in the course of his involvement, A regularly has unsupervised contact with B (whether face to face or by any other means).

(4)   A person receives education at an educational institution if—

      (a)   he is registered or otherwise enrolled as a pupil or student at the institution, or

      (b)   he receives education at the institution under arrangements with another educational institution at which he is so registered or otherwise enrolled.

(5)   In section 21—

'authority'—

      (a)   in relation to England and Wales, means a local authority;

'care home' means an establishment which is a care home for the purposes of the Care Standards Act 2000 (c 14);

'care order' has—

      (a)   in relation to England and Wales, the same meaning as in the Children Act 1989,

'children's home' has—

      (a)   in relation to England and Wales, the meaning given by section 1 of the Care Standards Act 2000,

'community home' has the meaning given by section 53 of the Children Act 1989;

'education supervision order' has—

      (a)   in relation to England and Wales, the meaning given by section 36 of the Children Act 1989,

'hospital'—

      (a)   in relation to England and Wales, means a hospital within the meaning given by section 128(1) of the National Health Service Act 1977, or any other establishment which is a hospital within the meaning given by section 2(3) of the Care Standards Act 2000;

'independent clinic' has—

      (a)   in relation to England and Wales, the meaning given by section 2 of the Care Standards Act 2000;

'supervision order' has—

      (a)   in relation to England and Wales, the meaning given by section 31(11) of the Children Act 1989,

'voluntary home' has—

      (a)   in relation to England and Wales, the meaning given by section 60(3) of the Children Act 1989,

23.   **Sections 16 to 19: exception for spouses or civil partners**

(1)   Conduct by a person (A) which would otherwise be an offence under any of sections 16 to 19 against another person (B) is not an offence under that section if at the time—

      (a)   B is 16 or over, and

      (b)   A and B are lawfully married or civil partners of each other.

(2)   In proceedings for such an offence it is for the defendant to prove that A and B were at the time lawfully married or civil partners of each other.

24.   **Sections 16 to 19: sexual relationships which pre-date position of trust**

(1)   Conduct by a person (A) which would otherwise be an offence under any of sections 16 to 19 against another person (B) is not an offence under that section if, immediately before the position of trust arose, a sexual relationship existed between A and B.

(2)   Subsection (1) does not apply if at that time sexual intercourse between A and B would have been unlawful.

(3)   In proceedings for an offence under any of sections 16 to 19 it is for the defendant to prove that such a relationship existed at that time.

25.   **Sexual activity with a child family member**

(1)   A person (A) commits an offence if—

      (a)   he intentionally touches another person (B),

      (b)   the touching is sexual,

    (c)   the relation of A to B is within section 27,

    (d)   A knows or could reasonably be expected to know that his relation to B is of a description falling within that section, and

    (e)   either—

        (i)   B is under 18 and A does not reasonably believe that B is 18 or over, or

        (ii)   B is under 13.

(2)   Where in proceedings for an offence under this section it is proved that the other person was under 18, the defendant is to be taken not to have reasonably believed that that person was 18 or over unless sufficient evidence is adduced to raise an issue as to whether he reasonably believed it.

(3)   Where in proceedings for an offence under this section it is proved that the relation of the defendant to the other person was of a description falling within section 27, it is to be taken that the defendant knew or could reasonably have been expected to know that his relation to the other person was of that description unless sufficient evidence is adduced to raise an issue as to whether he knew or could reasonably have been expected to know that it was.

(4)   A person guilty of an offence under this section, if aged 18 or over at the time of the offence, is liable—

    (a)   where subsection (6) applies, on conviction on indictment to imprisonment for a term not exceeding 14 years;

    (b)   in any other case—

        (i)   on summary conviction, to imprisonment for a term not exceeding 6 months or a fine not exceeding the statutory maximum or both;

        (ii)   on conviction on indictment, to imprisonment for a term not exceeding 14 years.

(6)   This subsection applies where the touching involved—

    (a)   penetration of B's anus or vagina with a part of A's body or anything else,

    (b)   penetration of B's mouth with A's penis,

    (c)   penetration of A's anus or vagina with a part of B's body, or

    (d)   penetration of A's mouth with B's penis.

26.   **Inciting a child family member to engage in sexual activity**

(1)   A person (A) commits an offence if—

    (a)   he intentionally incites another person (B) to touch, or allow himself to be touched by, A,

    (b)   the touching is sexual,

    (c)   the relation of A to B is within section 27,

    (d)   A knows or could reasonably be expected to know that his relation to B is of a description falling within that section, and

    (e)   either—

        (i)   B is under 18 and A does not reasonably believe that B is 18 or over, or

        (ii)   B is under 13.

(2)   Where in proceedings for an offence under this section it is proved that the other person was under 18, the defendant is to be taken not to have reasonably believed that that person was 18 or over unless sufficient evidence is adduced to raise an issue as to whether he reasonably believed it.

(3)   Where in proceedings for an offence under this section it is proved that the relation of the defendant to the other person was of a description falling within section 27, it is to be taken that the defendant knew or could reasonably have been expected to know that his relation to the other person was of that description unless sufficient evidence is adduced to raise an issue as to whether he knew or could reasonably have been expected to know that it was.

(4)   A person guilty of an offence under this section, if he was aged 18 or over at the time of the offence, is liable—

    (a)   where subsection (6) applies, on conviction on indictment to imprisonment for a term not exceeding 14 years;

    (b)   in any other case—

(i)   on summary conviction, to imprisonment for a term not exceeding 6 months or a fine not exceeding the statutory maximum or both;

(ii)   on conviction on indictment, to imprisonment for a term not exceeding 14 years.

(6)   This subsection applies where the touching to which the incitement related involved—

(a)   penetration of B's anus or vagina with a part of A's body or anything else,

(b)   penetration of B's mouth with A's penis,

(c)   penetration of A's anus or vagina with a part of B's body, or

(d)   penetration of A's mouth with B's penis.

27.   Family relationships

(1)   The relation of one person (A) to another (B) is within this section if—

(a)   it is within any of subsections (2) to (4), or

(b)   it would be within one of those subsections but for section 67 of the Adoption and Children Act 2002 (c 38) (status conferred by adoption).

(2)   The relation of A to B is within this subsection if—

(a)   one of them is the other's parent, grandparent, brother, sister, half-brother, half-sister, aunt or uncle, or

(b)   A is or has been B's foster parent.

(3)   The relation of A to B is within this subsection if A and B live or have lived in the same household, or A is or has been regularly involved in caring for, training, supervising or being in sole charge of B, and—

(a)   one of them is or has been the other's step-parent,

(b)   A and B are cousins,

(c)   one of them is or has been the other's stepbrother or stepsister, or

(d)   the parent or present or former foster parent of one of them is or has been the other's foster parent.

(4)   The relation of A to B is within this subsection if—

(a)   A and B live in the same household, and

(b)   A is regularly involved in caring for, training, supervising or being in sole charge of B.

(5)   For the purposes of this section—

(a)   'aunt' means the sister or half-sister of a person's parent, and 'uncle' has a corresponding meaning;

(b)   'cousin' means the child of an aunt or uncle;

(c)   a person is a child's foster parent if—

(i)   he is a person with whom the child has been placed under section 23(2)(a) or 59(1)(a) of the Children Act 1989 (fostering for local authority or voluntary organisation), or

(ii)   he fosters the child privately, within the meaning given by section 66(1)(b) of that Act;

(d)   a person is another's partner (whether they are of different sexes or the same sex) if they live together as partners in an enduring family relationship;

(e)   'step-parent' includes a parent's partner and 'stepbrother' and 'stepsister' include the child of a parent's partner.

28.   Sections 25 and 26: exception for spouses and civil partners

(1)   Conduct by a person (A) which would otherwise be an offence under section 25 or 26 against another person (B) is not an offence under that section if at the time—

(a)   B is 16 or over, and

(b)   A and B are lawfully married or civil partners of each other.

(2)   In proceedings for such an offence it is for the defendant to prove that A and B were at the time lawfully married or civil partners of each other.

29.   Sections 25 and 26: sexual relationships which pre-date family relationships

(1)   Conduct by a person (A) which would otherwise be an offence under section 25 or 26 against another person (B) is not an offence under that section if—

(a)   the relation of A to B is not within subsection (2) of section 27,

(b) it would not be within that subsection if section 67 of the Adoption and Children Act 2002 did not apply, and

(c) immediately before the relation of A to B first became such as to fall within section 27, a sexual relationship existed between A and B.

(2) Subsection (1) does not apply if at the time referred to in subsection (1)(c) sexual intercourse between A and B would have been unlawful.

(3) In proceedings for an offence under section 25 or 26 it is for the defendant to prove the matters mentioned in subsection (1)(a) to (c).

30. Sexual activity with a person with a mental disorder impeding choice

(1) A person (A) commits an offence if—
   (a) he intentionally touches another person (B),
   (b) the touching is sexual,
   (c) B is unable to refuse because of or for a reason related to a mental disorder, and
   (d) A knows or could reasonably be expected to know that B has a mental disorder and that because of it or for a reason related to it B is likely to be unable to refuse.

(2) B is unable to refuse if—
   (a) he lacks the capacity to choose whether to agree to the touching (whether because he lacks sufficient understanding of the nature or reasonably foreseeable consequences of what is being done, or for any other reason), or
   (b) he is unable to communicate such a choice to A.

(3) A person guilty of an offence under this section, if the touching involved—
   (a) penetration of B's anus or vagina with a part of A's body or anything else,
   (b) penetration of B's mouth with A's penis,
   (c) penetration of A's anus or vagina with a part of B's body, or
   (d) penetration of A's mouth with B's penis,
   is liable, on conviction on indictment, to imprisonment for life.

31. Causing or inciting a person, with a mental disorder impeding choice, to engage in sexual activity

(1) A person (A) commits an offence if—
   (a) he intentionally causes or incites another person (B) to engage in an activity,
   (b) the activity is sexual,
   (c) B is unable to refuse because of or for a reason related to a mental disorder, and
   (d) A knows or could reasonably be expected to know that B has a mental disorder and that because of it or for a reason related to it B is likely to be unable to refuse.

(2) B is unable to refuse if—
   (a) he lacks the capacity to choose whether to agree to engaging in the activity caused or incited (whether because he lacks sufficient understanding of the nature or reasonably foreseeable consequences of the activity, or for any other reason), or
   (b) he is unable to communicate such a choice to A.

(3) A person guilty of an offence under this section, if the activity caused or incited involved—
   (a) penetration of B's anus or vagina,
   (b) penetration of B's mouth with a person's penis,
   (c) penetration of a person's anus or vagina with a part of B's body or by B with anything else, or
   (d) penetration of a person's mouth with B's penis,
   is liable, on conviction on indictment, to imprisonment for life.

32. Engaging in sexual activity in the presence of a person with a mental disorder impeding choice

(1) A person (A) commits an offence if—
   (a) he intentionally engages in an activity,
   (b) the activity is sexual,
   (c) for the purpose of obtaining sexual gratification, he engages in it—

    (i) when another person (B) is present or is in a place from which A can be observed, and

    (ii) knowing or believing that B is aware, or intending that B should be aware, that he is engaging in it,

 (d) B is unable to refuse because of or for a reason related to a mental disorder, and

 (e) A knows or could reasonably be expected to know that B has a mental disorder and that because of it or for a reason related to it B is likely to be unable to refuse.

 (2) B is unable to refuse if—

  (a) he lacks the capacity to choose whether to agree to being present (whether because he lacks sufficient understanding of the nature of the activity, or for any other reason), or

  (b) he is unable to communicate such a choice to A.

33. **Causing a person, with a mental disorder impeding choice, to watch a sexual act**

 (1) A person (A) commits an offence if—

  (a) for the purpose of obtaining sexual gratification, he intentionally causes another person (B) to watch a third person engaging in an activity, or to look at an image of any person engaging in an activity,

  (b) the activity is sexual,

  (c) B is unable to refuse because of or for a reason related to a mental disorder, and

  (d) A knows or could reasonably be expected to know that B has a mental disorder and that because of it or for a reason related to it B is likely to be unable to refuse.

 (2) B is unable to refuse if—

  (a) he lacks the capacity to choose whether to agree to watching or looking (whether because he lacks sufficient understanding of the nature of the activity, or for any other reason), or

  (b) he is unable to communicate such a choice to A.

34. **Inducement, threat or deception to procure sexual activity with a person with a mental disorder**

 (1) A person (A) commits an offence if—

  (a) with the agreement of another person (B) he intentionally touches that person,

  (b) the touching is sexual,

  (c) A obtains B's agreement by means of an inducement offered or given, a threat made or a deception practised by A for that purpose,

  (d) B has a mental disorder, and

  (e) A knows or could reasonably be expected to know that B has a mental disorder.

 (2) A person guilty of an offence under this section, if the touching involved—

  (a) penetration of B's anus or vagina with a part of A's body or anything else,

  (b) penetration of B's mouth with A's penis,

  (c) penetration of A's anus or vagina with a part of B's body, or

  (d) penetration of A's mouth with B's penis,

 is liable, on conviction on indictment, to imprisonment for life.

35. **Causing a person with a mental disorder to engage in or agree to engage in sexual activity by inducement, threat or deception**

 (1) A person (A) commits an offence if—

  (a) by means of an inducement offered or given, a threat made or a deception practised by him for this purpose, he intentionally causes another person (B) to engage in, or to agree to engage in, an activity,

  (b) the activity is sexual,

  (c) B has a mental disorder, and

  (d) A knows or could reasonably be expected to know that B has a mental disorder.

 (2) A person guilty of an offence under this section, if the activity caused or agreed to involved—

  (a) penetration of B's anus or vagina,

  (b) penetration of B's mouth with a person's penis,

(c)   penetration of a person's anus or vagina with a part of B's body or by B with anything else, or

(d)   penetration of a person's mouth with B's penis,

is liable, on conviction on indictment, to imprisonment for life.

36.   Engaging in sexual activity in the presence, procured by inducement, threat or deception, of a person with a mental disorder

(1)   A person (A) commits an offence if—

    (a)   he intentionally engages in an activity,

    (b)   the activity is sexual,

    (c)   for the purpose of obtaining sexual gratification, he engages in it—

        (i)   when another person (B) is present or is in a place from which A can be observed, and

        (ii)   knowing or believing that B is aware, or intending that B should be aware, that he is engaging in it,

    (d)   B agrees to be present or in the place referred to in paragraph (c)(i) because of an inducement offered or given, a threat made or a deception practised by A for the purpose of obtaining that agreement,

    (e)   B has a mental disorder, and

    (f)   A knows or could reasonably be expected to know that B has a mental disorder.

37.   Causing a person with a mental disorder to watch a sexual act by inducement, threat or deception

(1)   A person (A) commits an offence if—

    (a)   for the purpose of obtaining sexual gratification, he intentionally causes another person (B) to watch a third person engaging in an activity, or to look at an image of any person engaging in an activity,

    (b)   the activity is sexual,

    (c)   B agrees to watch or look because of an inducement offered or given, a threat made or a deception practised by A for the purpose of obtaining that agreement,

    (d)   B has a mental disorder, and

    (e)   A knows or could reasonably be expected to know that B has a mental disorder.

38.   Care workers: sexual activity with a person with a mental disorder

(1)   A person (A) commits an offence if—

    (a)   he intentionally touches another person (B),

    (b)   the touching is sexual,

    (c)   B has a mental disorder,

    (d)   A knows or could reasonably be expected to know that B has a mental disorder, and

    (e)   A is involved in B's care in a way that falls within section 42.

(2)   Where in proceedings for an offence under this section it is proved that the other person had a mental disorder, it is to be taken that the defendant knew or could reasonably have been expected to know that that person had a mental disorder unless sufficient evidence is adduced to raise an issue as to whether he knew or could reasonably have been expected to know it.

(3)   A person guilty of an offence under this section, if the touching involved—

    (a)   penetration of B's anus or vagina with a part of A's body or anything else,

    (b)   penetration of B's mouth with A's penis,

    (c)   penetration of A's anus or vagina with a part of B's body, or

    (d)   penetration of A's mouth with B's penis,

is liable, on conviction on indictment, to imprisonment for a term not exceeding 14 years.

39.   Care workers: causing or inciting sexual activity

(1)   A person (A) commits an offence if—

    (a)   he intentionally causes or incites another person (B) to engage in an activity,

    (b)   the activity is sexual,

     (c)   B has a mental disorder,

     (d)   A knows or could reasonably be expected to know that B has a mental disorder, and

     (e)   A is involved in B's care in a way that falls within section 42.

(2)   Where in proceedings for an offence under this section it is proved that the other person had a mental disorder, it is to be taken that the defendant knew or could reasonably have been expected to know that that person had a mental disorder unless sufficient evidence is adduced to raise an issue as to whether he knew or could reasonably have been expected to know it.

(3)   A person guilty of an offence under this section, if the activity caused or incited involved—

     (a)   penetration of B's anus or vagina,

     (b)   penetration of B's mouth with a person's penis,

     (c)   penetration of a person's anus or vagina with a part of B's body or by B with anything else, or

     (d)   penetration of a person's mouth with B's penis,

is liable, on conviction on indictment, to imprisonment for a term not exceeding 14 years.

40.   Care workers: sexual activity in the presence of a person with a mental disorder

(1)   A person (A) commits an offence if—

     (a)   he intentionally engages in an activity,

     (b)   the activity is sexual,

     (c)   for the purpose of obtaining sexual gratification, he engages in it—

         (i)   when another person (B) is present or is in a place from which A can be observed, and

         (ii)   knowing or believing that B is aware, or intending that B should be aware, that he is engaging in it,

     (d)   B has a mental disorder,

     (e)   A knows or could reasonably be expected to know that B has a mental disorder, and

     (f)   A is involved in B's care in a way that falls within section 42.

(2)   Where in proceedings for an offence under this section it is proved that the other person had a mental disorder, it is to be taken that the defendant knew or could reasonably have been expected to know that that person had a mental disorder unless sufficient evidence is adduced to raise an issue as to whether he knew or could reasonably have been expected to know it.

41.   Care workers: causing a person with a mental disorder to watch a sexual act

(1)   A person (A) commits an offence if—

     (a)   for the purpose of obtaining sexual gratification, he intentionally causes another person (B) to watch a third person engaging in an activity, or to look at an image of any person engaging in an activity,

     (b)   the activity is sexual,

     (c)   B has a mental disorder,

     (d)   A knows or could reasonably be expected to know that B has a mental disorder, and

     (e)   A is involved in B's care in a way that falls within section 42.

(2)   Where in proceedings for an offence under this section it is proved that the other person had a mental disorder, it is to be taken that the defendant knew or could reasonably have been expected to know that that person had a mental disorder unless sufficient evidence is adduced to raise an issue as to whether he knew or could reasonably have been expected to know it.

42.   Care workers: interpretation

(1)   For the purposes of sections 38 to 41, a person (A) is involved in the care of another person (B) in a way that falls within this section if any of subsections (2) to (4) applies.

(2)   This subsection applies if—

     (a)   B is accommodated and cared for in a care home, community home, voluntary home or children's home, and

      (b)   A has functions to perform in the home in the course of employment which have brought him or are likely to bring him into regular face to face contact with B.

(3)   This subsection applies if B is a patient for whom services are provided—
      (a)   by a National Health Service body or an independent medical agency, or
      (b)   in an independent clinic or an independent hospital,
   and A has functions to perform for the body or agency or in the clinic or hospital in the course of employment which have brought him or are likely to bring him into regular face to face contact with B.

(4)   This subsection applies if A—
      (a)   is, whether or not in the course of employment, a provider of care, assistance or services to B in connection with B's mental disorder, and
      (b)   as such, has had or is likely to have regular face to face contact with B.

(5)   In this section—
   'care home' means an establishment which is a care home for the purposes of the Care Standards Act 2000;
   'children's home' has the meaning given by section 1 of that Act;
   'community home' has the meaning given by section 53 of the Children Act 1989;
   'employment' means any employment, whether paid or unpaid and whether under a contract of service or apprenticeship, under a contract for services, or otherwise than under a contract;
   'independent clinic', 'independent hospital' and 'independent medical agency' have the meaning given by section 2 of the Care Standards Act 2000;
   'National Health Service body' means—
      (a)   a Health Authority,
      (b)   a National Health Service trust,
      (c)   a Primary Care Trust, or
      (d)   a Special Health Authority;
   'voluntary home' has the meaning given by section 60(3) of the Children Act 1989.

43.   **Sections 38 to 41: exception for spouses and civil partners**

(1)   Conduct by a person (A) which would otherwise be an offence under any of sections 38 to 41 against another person (B) is not an offence under that section if at the time—
      (a)   B is 16 or over, and
      (b)   A and B are lawfully married or civil partners of each other.

(2)   In proceedings for such an offence it is for the defendant to prove that A and B were at the time lawfully married or civil partners of each other.

44.   **Sections 38 to 41: sexual relationships which pre-date care relationships**

(1)   Conduct by a person (A) which would otherwise be an offence under any of sections 38 to 41 against another person (B) is not an offence under that section if, immediately before A became involved in B's care in a way that falls within section 42, a sexual relationship existed between A and B.

(2)   Subsection (1) does not apply if at that time sexual intercourse between A and B would have been unlawful.

(3)   In proceedings for an offence under any of sections 38 to 41 it is for the defendant to prove that such a relationship existed at that time.

47.   **Paying for sexual services of a child**

(1)   A person (A) commits an offence if—
      (a)   he intentionally obtains for himself the sexual services of another person (B),
      (b)   before obtaining those services, he has made or promised payment for those services to B or a third person, or knows that another person has made or promised such a payment, and
      (c)   either—
          (i)   B is under 18, and A does not reasonably believe that B is 18 or over, or
          (ii)   B is under 13.

(2) In this section, 'payment' means any financial advantage, including the discharge of an obligation to pay or the provision of goods or services (including sexual services) gratuitously or at a discount.

48. Causing or inciting child prostitution or pornography

(1) A person (A) commits an offence if—

(a) he intentionally causes or incites another person (B) to become a prostitute, or to be involved in pornography, in any part of the world, and

(b) either—

(i) B is under 18, and A does not reasonably believe that B is 18 or over, or

(ii) B is under 13.

49. Controlling a child prostitute or a child involved in pornography

(1) A person (A) commits an offence if—

(a) he intentionally controls any of the activities of another person (B) relating to B's prostitution or involvement in pornography in any part of the world, and

(b) either—

(i) B is under 18, and A does not reasonably believe that B is 18 or over, or

(ii) B is under 13.

50. Arranging or facilitating child prostitution or pornography

(1) A person (A) commits an offence if—

(a) he intentionally arranges or facilitates the prostitution or involvement in pornography in any part of the world of another person (B), and

(b) either—

(i) B is under 18, and A does not reasonably believe that B is 18 or over, or

(ii) B is under 13.

51. Sections 48 to 50: interpretation

(1) For the purposes of sections 48 to 50, a person is involved in pornography if an indecent image of that person is recorded; and similar expressions, and 'pornography', are to be interpreted accordingly.

(2) In those sections 'prostitute' means a person (A) who, on at least one occasion and whether or not compelled to do so, offers or provides sexual services to another person in return for payment or a promise of payment to A or a third person; and 'prostitution' is to be interpreted accordingly.

(3) In subsection (2), 'payment' means any financial advantage, including the discharge of an obligation to pay or the provision of goods or services (including sexual services) gratuitously or at a discount.

52. Causing or inciting prostitution for gain

(1) A person commits an offence if—

(a) he intentionally causes or incites another person to become a prostitute in any part of the world, and

(b) he does so for or in the expectation of gain for himself or a third person.

53. Controlling prostitution for gain

(1) A person commits an offence if—

(a) he intentionally controls any of the activities of another person relating to that person's prostitution in any part of the world, and

(b) he does so for or in the expectation of gain for himself or a third person.

54. Sections 52 and 53: interpretation

(1) In sections 52 and 53, 'gain' means—

(a) any financial advantage, including the discharge of an obligation to pay or the provision of goods or services (including sexual services) gratuitously or at a discount; or

    (b)   the goodwill of any person which is or appears likely, in time, to bring financial advantage.

(2)   In those sections 'prostitute' and 'prostitution' have the meaning given by section 51(2).

57.   **Trafficking into the UK for sexual exploitation**

(1)   A person commits an offence if he intentionally arranges or facilitates the arrival in the United Kingdom of another person (B) and either—

    (a)   he intends to do anything to or in respect of B, after B's arrival but in any part of the world, which if done will involve the commission of a relevant offence, or

    (b)   he believes that another person is likely to do something to or in respect of B, after B's arrival but in any part of the world, which if done will involve the commission of a relevant offence.

58.   **Trafficking within the UK for sexual exploitation**

(1)   A person commits an offence if he intentionally arranges or facilitates travel within the United Kingdom by another person (B) and either—

    (a)   he intends to do anything to or in respect of B, during or after the journey and in any part of the world, which if done will involve the commission of a relevant offence, or

    (b)   he believes that another person is likely to do something to or in respect of B, during or after the journey and in any part of the world, which if done will involve the commission of a relevant offence.

59.   **Trafficking out of the UK for sexual exploitation**

(1)   A person commits an offence if he intentionally arranges or facilitates the departure from the United Kingdom of another person (B) and either—

    (a)   he intends to do anything to or in respect of B, after B's departure but in any part of the world, which if done will involve the commission of a relevant offence, or

    (b)   he believes that another person is likely to do something to or in respect of B, after B's departure but in any part of the world, which if done will involve the commission of a relevant offence.

60.   **Sections 57 to 59: interpretation and jurisdiction**

(1)   In sections 57 to 59, 'relevant offence' means—

    (a)   an offence under this Part,

    (b)   an offence under section 1(1)(a) of the Protection of Children Act 1978, or

    (e)   anything done outside England and Wales which is not an offence within any of paragraphs (a) to (d) but would be if done in England and Wales.

(2)   Sections 57 to 59 apply to anything done—

    (a)   in the United Kingdom, or

    (b)   outside the United Kingdom, by a body incorporated under the law of a part of the United Kingdom or by an individual to whom subsection (3) applies.

(3)   This subsection applies to—

    (a)   a British citizen,

    (b)   a British overseas territories citizen,

    (c)   a British National (Overseas),

    (d)   a British Overseas citizen,

    (e)   a person who is a British subject under the British Nationality Act 1981,

    (f)   a British protected person within the meaning given by section 50(1) of that Act.

61.   **Administering a substance with intent**

(1)   A person commits an offence if he intentionally administers a substance to, or causes a substance to be taken by, another person (B)—

    (a)   knowing that B does not consent, and

    (b)   with the intention of stupefying or overpowering B, so as to enable any person to engage in a sexual activity that involves B.

62.   Committing an offence with intent to commit a sexual offence

(1)   A person commits an offence under this section if he commits any offence with the intention of committing a relevant sexual offence.

(2)   In this section, 'relevant sexual offence' means any offence under this Part (including an offence of aiding, abetting, counselling or procuring such an offence).

(3)   A person guilty of an offence under this section is liable on conviction on indictment, where the offence is committed by kidnapping or false imprisonment, to imprisonment for life.

63.   Trespass with intent to commit a sexual offence

(1)   A person commits an offence if—

     (a)   he is a trespasser on any premises,

     (b)   he intends to commit a relevant sexual offence on the premises, and

     (c)   he knows that, or is reckless as to whether, he is a trespasser.

(2)   In this section—

     'premises' includes a structure or part of a structure;

     'relevant sexual offence' has the same meaning as in section 62;

     'structure' includes a tent, vehicle or vessel or other temporary or movable structure.

64.   Sex with an adult relative: penetration

(1)   A person aged 16 or over (A) commits an offence if—

     (a)   he intentionally penetrates another person's vagina or anus with a part of his body or anything else, or penetrates another person's mouth with his penis,

     (b)   the penetration is sexual,

     (c)   the other person (B) is aged 18 or over,

     (d)   A is related to B in a way mentioned in subsection (2), and

     (e)   A knows or could reasonably be expected to know that he is related to B in that way.

(2)   The ways that A may be related to B are as parent, grandparent, child, grandchild, brother, sister, half-brother, half-sister, uncle, aunt, nephew or niece.

(3)   In subsection (2)—

     (a)   'uncle' means the brother of a person's parent, and 'aunt' has a corresponding meaning;

     (b)   'nephew' means the child of a person's brother or sister, and 'niece' has a corresponding meaning.

(4)   Where in proceedings for an offence under this section it is proved that the defendant was related to the other person in any of those ways, it is to be taken that the defendant knew or could reasonably have been expected to know that he was related in that way unless sufficient evidence is adduced to raise an issue as to whether he knew or could reasonably have been expected to know that he was.

65.   Sex with an adult relative: consenting to penetration

(1)   A person aged 16 or over (A) commits an offence if—

     (a)   another person (B) penetrates A's vagina or anus with a part of B's body or anything else, or penetrates A's mouth with B's penis,

     (b)   A consents to the penetration,

     (c)   the penetration is sexual,

     (d)   B is aged 18 or over,

     (e)   A is related to B in a way mentioned in subsection (2), and

     (f)   A knows or could reasonably be expected to know that he is related to B in that way.

(2)   The ways that A may be related to B are as parent, grandparent, child, grandchild, brother, sister, half-brother, half-sister, uncle, aunt, nephew or niece.

(3)   In subsection (2)—

     (a)   'uncle' means the brother of a person's parent, and 'aunt' has a corresponding meaning;

     (b)   'nephew' means the child of a person's brother or sister, and 'niece' has a corresponding meaning.

(4)   Where in proceedings for an offence under this section it is proved that the defendant was related to the other person in any of those ways, it is to be taken that the defendant knew or could reasonably have been expected to know that he was related in that way unless sufficient evidence is adduced to raise an issue as to whether he knew or could reasonably have been expected to know that he was.

66.   Exposure

(1)   A person commits an offence if—

(a)   he intentionally exposes his genitals, and

(b)   he intends that someone will see them and be caused alarm or distress.

67.   Voyeurism

(1)   A person commits an offence if—

(a)   for the purpose of obtaining sexual gratification, he observes another person doing a private act, and

(b)   he knows that the other person does not consent to being observed for his sexual gratification.

(2)   A person commits an offence if—

(a)   he operates equipment with the intention of enabling another person to observe, for the purpose of obtaining sexual gratification, a third person (B) doing a private act, and

(b)   he knows that B does not consent to his operating equipment with that intention.

(3)   A person commits an offence if—

(a)   he records another person (B) doing a private act,

(b)   he does so with the intention that he or a third person will, for the purpose of obtaining sexual gratification, look at an image of B doing the act, and

(c)   he knows that B does not consent to his recording the act with that intention.

(4)   A person commits an offence if he instals equipment, or constructs or adapts a structure or part of a structure, with the intention of enabling himself or another person to commit an offence under subsection (1).

68.   Voyeurism: interpretation

(1)   For the purposes of section 67, a person is doing a private act if the person is in a place which, in the circumstances, would reasonably be expected to provide privacy, and—

(a)   the person's genitals, buttocks or breasts are exposed or covered only with underwear,

(b)   the person is using a lavatory, or

(c)   the person is doing a sexual act that is not of a kind ordinarily done in public.

(2)   In section 67, 'structure' includes a tent, vehicle or vessel or other temporary or movable structure.

69.   Intercourse with an animal

(1)   A person commits an offence if—

(a)   he intentionally performs an act of penetration with his penis,

(b)   what is penetrated is the vagina or anus of a living animal, and

(c)   he knows that, or is reckless as to whether, that is what is penetrated.

(2)   A person (A) commits an offence if—

(a)   A intentionally causes, or allows, A's vagina or anus to be penetrated,

(b)   the penetration is by the penis of a living animal, and

(c)   A knows that, or is reckless as to whether, that is what A is being penetrated by.

70.   Sexual penetration of a corpse

(1)   A person commits an offence if—

(a)   he intentionally performs an act of penetration with a part of his body or anything else,

(b)   what is penetrated is a part of the body of a dead person,

(c)   he knows that, or is reckless as to whether, that is what is penetrated, and

(d)   the penetration is sexual.

71.   Sexual activity in a public lavatory

    (1)   A person commits an offence if—

        (a)   he is in a lavatory to which the public or a section of the public has or is permitted to have access, whether on payment or otherwise,

        (b)   he intentionally engages in an activity, and,

        (c)   the activity is sexual.

    (2)   For the purposes of this section, an activity is sexual if a reasonable person would, in all the circumstances but regardless of any person's purpose, consider it to be sexual.

72.   Offences outside the United Kingdom

    (1)   Subject to subsection (2), any act done by a person in a country or territory outside the United Kingdom which—

        (a)   constituted an offence under the law in force in that country or territory, and

        (b)   would constitute a sexual offence to which this section applies if it had been done in England and Wales or in Northern Ireland,

    constitutes that sexual offence under the law of that part of the United Kingdom.

    (2)   Proceedings by virtue of this section may be brought only against a person who was on 1st September 1997, or has since become, a British citizen or resident in the United Kingdom.

    (3)   An act punishable under the law in force in any country or territory constitutes an offence under that law for the purposes of this section, however it is described in that law.

    (7)   Schedule 2 lists the sexual offences to which this section applies.

73.   Exceptions to aiding, abetting and counselling

    (1)   A person is not guilty of aiding, abetting or counselling the commission against a child of an offence to which this section applies if he acts for the purpose of—

        (a)   protecting the child from sexually transmitted infection,

        (b)   protecting the physical safety of the child,

        (c)   preventing the child from becoming pregnant, or

        (d)   promoting the child's emotional well-being by the giving of advice,

    and not for the purpose of obtaining sexual gratification or for the purpose of causing or encouraging the activity constituting the offence or the child's participation in it.

    (2)   This section applies to—

        (a)   an offence under any of sections 5 to 7 (offences against children under 13);

        (b)   an offence under section 9 (sexual activity with a child);

        (c)   an offence under section 13 which would be an offence under section 9 if the offender were aged 18;

        (d)   an offence under any of sections 16, 25, 30, 34 and 38 (sexual activity) against a person under 16.

    (3)   This section does not affect any other enactment or any rule of law restricting the circumstances in which a person is guilty of aiding, abetting or counselling an offence under this Part.

74.   'Consent'

For the purposes of this Part, a person consents if he agrees by choice, and has the freedom and capacity to make that choice.

75.   Evidential presumptions about consent

    (1)   If in proceedings for an offence to which this section applies it is proved—

        (a)   that the defendant did the relevant act,

        (b)   that any of the circumstances specified in subsection (2) existed, and

        (c)   that the defendant knew that those circumstances existed,

    the complainant is to be taken not to have consented to the relevant act unless sufficient evidence is adduced to raise an issue as to whether he consented, and the defendant is to be taken not to have reasonably believed that the complainant consented unless sufficient evidence is adduced to raise an issue as to whether he reasonably believed it.

    (2)   The circumstances are that—

(a) any person was, at the time of the relevant act or immediately before it began, using violence against the complainant or causing the complainant to fear that immediate violence would be used against him;

(b) any person was, at the time of the relevant act or immediately before it began, causing the complainant to fear that violence was being used, or that immediate violence would be used, against another person;

(c) the complainant was, and the defendant was not, unlawfully detained at the time of the relevant act;

(d) the complainant was asleep or otherwise unconscious at the time of the relevant act;

(e) because of the complainant's physical disability, the complainant would not have been able at the time of the relevant act to communicate to the defendant whether the complainant consented;

(f) any person had administered to or caused to be taken by the complainant, without the complainant's consent, a substance which, having regard to when it was administered or taken, was capable of causing or enabling the complainant to be stupefied or overpowered at the time of the relevant act.

(3) In subsection (2)(a) and (b), the reference to the time immediately before the relevant act began is, in the case of an act which is one of a continuous series of sexual activities, a reference to the time immediately before the first sexual activity began.

76. Conclusive presumptions about consent

(1) If in proceedings for an offence to which this section applies it is proved that the defendant did the relevant act and that any of the circumstances specified in subsection (2) existed, it is to be conclusively presumed—

(a) that the complainant did not consent to the relevant act, and

(b) that the defendant did not believe that the complainant consented to the relevant act.

(2) The circumstances are that—

(a) the defendant intentionally deceived the complainant as to the nature or purpose of the relevant act;

(b) the defendant intentionally induced the complainant to consent to the relevant act by impersonating a person known personally to the complainant.

77. Sections 75 and 76: relevant acts

In relation to an offence to which sections 75 and 76 apply, references in those sections to the relevant act and to the complainant are to be read as follows—

Offence	*Relevant Act*
An offence under section 1 (rape).	The defendant intentionally penetrating, with his penis, the vagina, anus or mouth of another person ('the complainant').
An offence under section 2 (assault by penetration).	The defendant intentionally penetrating, with a part of his body or anything else, the vagina or anus of another person ('the complainant'), where the penetration is sexual.
An offence under section 3 (sexual assault).	The defendant intentionally touching another person ('the complainant'), where the touching is sexual.
An offence under section 4 (causing a person to engage in sexual activity without consent).	The defendant intentionally causing another person ('the complainant') to engage in an activity, where the activity is sexual.

78. 'Sexual'

For the purposes of this Part (except section 71), penetration, touching or any other activity is sexual if a reasonable person would consider that—

(a) whatever its circumstances or any person's purpose in relation to it, it is because of its nature sexual, or

(b)   because of its nature it may be sexual and because of its circumstances or the purpose of any person in relation to it (or both) it is sexual.

79.   **Part 1: general interpretation**

(1)   The following apply for the purposes of this Part.

(2)   Penetration is a continuing act from entry to withdrawal.

(3)   References to a part of the body include references to a part surgically constructed (in particular, through gender reassignment surgery).

(4)   'Image' means a moving or still image and includes an image produced by any means and, where the context permits, a three-dimensional image.

(5)   References to an image of a person include references to an image of an imaginary person.

(6)   'Mental disorder' has the meaning given by section 1 of the Mental Health Act 1983 (c 20).

(7)   References to observation (however expressed) are to observation whether direct or by looking at an image.

(8)   Touching includes touching—

     (a)   with any part of the body,

     (b)   with anything else,

     (c)   through anything,

   and in particular includes touching amounting to penetration.

(9)   'Vagina' includes vulva.

(10)   In relation to an animal, references to the vagina or anus include references to any similar part.

SCHEDULE 2

1.   In relation to England and Wales, the following are sexual offences to which section 72 applies—

     (a)   an offence under any of sections 5 to 15 (offences against children under 13 or under 16);

     (b)   an offence under any of sections 1 to 4, 16 to 41, 47 to 50 and 61 where the victim of the offence was under 16 at the time of the offence;

     (c)   an offence under section 62 or 63 where the intended offence was an offence against a person under 16;

     (d)   an offence under—

         (i)   section 1 of the Protection of Children Act 1978 (indecent photographs of children), or

         (ii)   section 160 of the Criminal Justice Act 1988 (possession of indecent photograph of child),

     in relation to a photograph or pseudo-photograph showing a child under 16.

SEXUAL OFFENCES (CONSPIRACY AND INCITEMENT) ACT 1996

2.   **Incitement to commit certain sexual acts outside the United Kingdom**

(1)   This section applies where—

     (a)   any act done by a person in England and Wales would amount to the offence of incitement to commit a listed sexual offence but for the fact that what he had in view would not be an offence triable in England and Wales,

     (b)   the whole or part of what he had in view was intended to take place in a country or territory outside the United Kingdom, and

     (c)   what he had in view would involve the commission of an offence under the law in force in that country or territory.

(2)   Where this section applies—

     (a)   what he had in view is to be treated as that listed sexual offence for the purposes of any charge of incitement brought in respect of that act, and

     (b)   any such charge is accordingly triable in England and Wales.

(3)   Any act of incitement by means of a message (however communicated) is to be treated as done in England and Wales if the message is sent or received in England and Wales.

3.   **Sections 1 and 2: supplementary**

(1)   Conduct punishable under the law in force in any country or territory is an offence under that law for the purposes of section 2, however it is described in that law.

(2)   Subject to subsection (3), a condition in section . . . 2(1)(c) is to be taken to be satisfied unless, not later than rules of court may provide, the defence serve on the prosecution a notice—

(a)   stating that, on the facts as alleged with respect to what the accused had in view, the condition is not in their opinion satisfied,

(b)   showing their grounds for that opinion, and

(c)   requiring the prosecution to show that it is satisfied.

(4)   The court, if it thinks fit, may permit the defence to require the prosecution to show that the condition is satisfied without the prior service of a notice under subsection (2).

(5)   In the Crown Court the question whether the condition is satisfied is to be decided by the judge alone.

(6)   In any proceedings in respect of any offence triable by virtue of section 2, it is immaterial to guilt whether or not the accused was a British citizen at the time of any act or other event proof of which is required for conviction of the offence.

(8)   References to an offence of incitement to commit a listed sexual offence include an offence triable in England and Wales as such an incitement by virtue of section 2 (without prejudice to subsection (2) of that section).

(9)   Subsection (8) applies to references in any enactment, instrument or document (except those in section 2 of this Act and in Part I of the Criminal Law Act 1977).

5.   **Interpretation**

In this Act 'listed sexual offence' has the meaning given by the Schedule.

SCHEDULE

LISTED SEXUAL OFFENCES

1.   (1)   In relation to England and Wales, the following are listed sexual offences:

(b)   an offence under any of sections 1 to 12, 14 and 15 to 26 of the Sexual Offences Act 2003.

(2)   Sub-paragraph (1)(b) does not apply where the victim of the offence has attained the age of sixteen years.

SUICIDE ACT 1961

1.   **Suicide to cease to be a crime**

The rule of law whereby it is a crime for a person to commit suicide is hereby abrogated.

2.   **Criminal liability for complicity in another's suicide**

(1)   A person who aids, abets, counsels or procures the suicide of another, or an attempt by another to commit suicide, shall be liable on conviction on indictment to imprisonment for a term not exceeding fourteen years.

(2)   If on the trial of an indictment for murder or manslaughter it is proved that the accused aided, abetted, counselled or procured the suicide of the person in question, the jury may find him guilty of that offence.

(4)   . . . no proceedings shall be instituted for an offence under this section except by or with the consent of the Director of Public Prosecutions.

TATTOOING OF MINORS ACT 1969

1.   **Prohibition of tattooing of minors**

It shall be an offence to tattoo a person under the age of eighteen except when the tattoo is performed for medical reasons by a duly qualified medical practitioner or by a person working under his direction, but it shall be a defence for a person charged to show that at the time the tattoo was performed he had reasonable cause to believe that the person tattooed was of or over the age of eighteen and did in fact so believe.

3.   **Definition**

For the purposes of this Act 'tattoo' shall mean the insertion into the skin of any colouring material designed to leave a permanent mark.

TERRORISM ACT 2000

PART I
INTRODUCTORY

1.   **Terrorism: interpretation**

(1)   In this Act 'terrorism' means the use or threat of action where—
        (a)   the action falls within subsection (2),
        (b)   the use or threat is designed to influence the government or an international governmental organisation or to intimidate the public or a section of the public, and
        (c)   the use or threat is made for the purpose of advancing a political, religious or ideological cause.

(2)   Action falls within this subsection if it—
        (a)   involves serious violence against a person,
        (b)   involves serious damage to property,
        (c)   endangers a person's life, other than that of the person committing the action,
        (d)   creates a serious risk to the health or safety of the public or a section of the public, or
        (e)   is designed seriously to interfere with or seriously to disrupt an electronic system.

(3)   The use or threat of action falling within subsection (2) which involves the use of firearms or explosives is terrorism whether or not subsection (1)(b) is satisfied.

(4)   In this section—
        (a)   'action' includes action outside the United Kingdom,
        (b)   a reference to any person or to property is a reference to any person, or to property, wherever situated,
        (c)   a reference to the public includes a reference to the public of a country other than the United Kingdom, and
        (d)   'the government' means the government of the United Kingdom, of a Part of the United Kingdom or of a country other than the United Kingdom.

(5)   In this Act a reference to action taken for the purposes of terrorism includes a reference to action taken for the benefit of a proscribed organisation.

PART II
PROSCRIBED ORGANISATIONS

3.   **Proscription**

(1)   For the purposes of this Act an organisation is proscribed if—
        (a)   it is listed in Schedule 2, or
        (b)   it operates under the same name as an organisation listed in that Schedule.

11.   **Membership**

(1)   A person commits an offence if he belongs or professes to belong to a proscribed organisation.

(2)   It is a defence for a person charged with an offence under subsection (1) to prove—
        (a)   that the organisation was not proscribed on the last (or only) occasion on which he became a member or began to profess to be a member, and
        (b)   that he has not taken part in the activities of the organisation at any time while it was proscribed.

(4)   In subsection (2) 'proscribed' means proscribed for the purposes of any of the following—
        (a)   this Act;

    (b)   the Northern Ireland (Emergency Provisions) Act 1996;
    (c)   the Northern Ireland (Emergency Provisions) Act 1991;
    (d)   the Prevention of Terrorism (Temporary Provisions) Act 1989;
    (e)   the Prevention of Terrorism (Temporary Provisions) Act 1984;
    (f)   the Northern Ireland (Emergency Provisions) Act 1978;
    (g)   the Prevention of Terrorism (Temporary Provisions) Act 1976;
    (h)   the Prevention of Terrorism (Temporary Provisions) Act 1974;
    (i)   the Northern Ireland (Emergency Provisions) Act 1973.

12.   Support

(1)   A person commits an offence if—
    (a)   he invites support for a proscribed organisation, and
    (b)   the support is not, or is not restricted to, the provision of money or other property (within the meaning of section 15).

(2)   A person commits an offence if he arranges, manages or assists in arranging or managing a meeting which he knows is—
    (a)   to support a proscribed organisation,
    (b)   to further the activities of a proscribed organisation, or
    (c)   to be addressed by a person who belongs or professes to belong to a proscribed organisation.

(3)   A person commits an offence if he addresses a meeting and the purpose of his address is to encourage support for a proscribed organisation or to further its activities.

(4)   Where a person is charged with an offence under subsection (2)(c) in respect of a private meeting it is a defence for him to prove that he had no reasonable cause to believe that the address mentioned in subsection (2)(c) would support a proscribed organisation or further its activities.

(5)   In subsections (2) to (4)—
    (a)   'meeting' means a meeting of three or more persons, whether or not the public are admitted, and
    (b)   a meeting is private if the public are not admitted.

13.   Uniform

(1)   A person in a public place commits an offence if he—
    (a)   wears an item of clothing, or
    (b)   wears, carries or displays an article,
in such a way or in such circumstances as to arouse reasonable suspicion that he is a member or supporter of a proscribed organisation.

PART III

TERRORIST PROPERTY

14.   Terrorist property

(1)   In this Act 'terrorist property' means—
    (a)   money or other property which is likely to be used for the purposes of terrorism (including any resources of a proscribed organisation),
    (b)   proceeds of the commission of acts of terrorism, and
    (c)   proceeds of acts carried out for the purposes of terrorism.

(2)   In subsection (1)—
    (a)   a reference to proceeds of an act includes a reference to any property which wholly or partly, and directly or indirectly, represents the proceeds of the act (including payments or other rewards in connection with its commission), and
    (b)   the reference to an organisation's resources includes a reference to any money or other property which is applied or made available, or is to be applied or made available, for use by the organisation.

15.   Fund-raising

(1)   A person commits an offence if he—

      (a)   invites another to provide money or other property, and
      (b)   intends that it should be used, or has reasonable cause to suspect that it may be used, for the purposes of terrorism.

(2)   A person commits an offence if he—
      (a)   receives money or other property, and
      (b)   intends that it should be used, or has reasonable cause to suspect that it may be used, for the purposes of terrorism.

(3)   A person commits an offence if he—
      (a)   provides money or other property, and
      (b)   knows or has reasonable cause to suspect that it will or may be used for the purposes of terrorism.

(4)   In this section a reference to the provision of money or other property is a reference to its being given, lent or otherwise made available, whether or not for consideration.

16.   Use and possession

(1)   A person commits an offence if he uses money or other property for the purposes of terrorism.

(2)   A person commits an offence if he—
      (a)   possesses money or other property, and
      (b)   intends that it should be used, or has reasonable cause to suspect that it may be used, for the purposes of terrorism.

17.   Funding arrangements

A person commits an offence if—
(a)   he enters into or becomes concerned in an arrangement as a result of which money or other property is made available or is to be made available to another, and
(b)   he knows or has reasonable cause to suspect that it will or may be used for the purposes of terrorism.

18.   Money laundering

(1)   A person commits an offence if he enters into or becomes concerned in an arrangement which facilitates the retention or control by or on behalf of another person of terrorist property—
      (a)   by concealment,
      (b)   by removal from the jurisdiction,
      (c)   by transfer to nominees, or
      (d)   in any other way.

(2)   It is a defence for a person charged with an offence under subsection (1) to prove that he did not know and had no reasonable cause to suspect that the arrangement related to terrorist property.

19.   Disclosure of information: duty

(1)   This section applies where a person—
      (a)   believes or suspects that another person has committed an offence under any of sections 15 to 18, and
      (b)   bases his belief or suspicion on information which comes to his attention in the course of a trade, profession, business or employment.

(1A) But this section does not apply if the information came to the person in the course of a business in the regulated sector.

(2)   The person commits an offence if he does not disclose to a constable as soon as is reasonably practicable—
      (a)   his belief or suspicion, and
      (b)   the information on which it is based.

(3)   It is a defence for a person charged with an offence under subsection (2) to prove that he had a reasonable excuse for not making the disclosure.

(4)   Where—

      (a)   a person is in employment,

      (b)   his employer has established a procedure for the making of disclosures of the matters specified in subsection (2), and

      (c)   he is charged with an offence under that subsection,

      it is a defence for him to prove that he disclosed the matters specified in that subsection in accordance with the procedure.

(5)   Subsection (2) does not require disclosure by a professional legal adviser of—

      (a)   information which he obtains in privileged circumstances, or

      (b)   a belief or suspicion based on information which he obtains in privileged circumstances.

(6)   For the purpose of subsection (5) information is obtained by an adviser in privileged circumstances if it comes to him, otherwise than with a view to furthering a criminal purpose—

      (a)   from a client or a client's representative, in connection with the provision of legal advice by the adviser to the client,

      (b)   from a person seeking legal advice from the adviser, or from the person's representative, or

      (c)   from any person, for the purpose of actual or contemplated legal proceedings.

(7)   For the purposes of subsection (1)(a) a person shall be treated as having committed an offence under one of sections 15 to 18 if—

      (a)   he has taken an action or been in possession of a thing, and

      (b)   he would have committed an offence under one of those sections if he had been in the United Kingdom at the time when he took the action or was in possession of the thing.

(7A) The reference to a business in the regulated sector must be construed in accordance with Schedule 3A.

(7B) The reference to a constable includes a reference to a member of the staff of the Serious Organised Crime Agency authorised for the purposes of this section by the Director General of that Agency.

21.   Cooperation with police

(1)   A person does not commit an offence under any of sections 15 to 18 if he is acting with the express consent of a constable.

(2)   Subject to subsections (3) and (4), a person does not commit an offence under any of sections 15 to 18 by involvement in a transaction or arrangement relating to money or other property if he discloses to a constable—

      (a)   his suspicion or belief that the money or other property is terrorist property, and

      (b)   the information on which his suspicion or belief is based.

(3)   Subsection (2) applies only where a person makes a disclosure—

      (a)   after he becomes concerned in the transaction concerned,

      (b)   on his own initiative, and

      (c)   as soon as is reasonably practicable.

(4)   Subsection (2) does not apply to a person if—

      (a)   a constable forbids him to continue his involvement in the transaction or arrangement to which the disclosure relates, and

      (b)   he continues his involvement.

(5)   It is a defence for a person charged with an offence under any of sections 15(2) and (3) and 16 to 18 to prove that—

      (a)   he intended to make a disclosure of the kind mentioned in subsections (2) and (3), and

      (b)   there is reasonable excuse for his failure to do so.

(6)   Where—

      (a)   a person is in employment, and

      (b)   his employer has established a procedure for the making of disclosures of the same kind as may be made to a constable under subsection (2),

      this section shall have effect in relation to that person as if any reference to disclosure to a constable included a reference to disclosure in accordance with the procedure.

(7)   A reference in this section to a transaction or arrangement relating to money or other property includes a reference to use or possession.

PART IV

TERRORIST INVESTIGATIONS

39.   Disclosure of information, etc.

(1)   Subsection (2) applies where a person knows or has reasonable cause to suspect that a constable is conducting or proposes to conduct a terrorist investigation.

(2)   The person commits an offence if he—

    (a)   discloses to another anything which is likely to prejudice the investigation, or

    (b)   interferes with material which is likely to be relevant to the investigation.

(3)   Subsection (4) applies where a person knows or has reasonable cause to suspect that a disclosure has been or will be made under any of sections 19 to 21 or 38B.

(4)   The person commits an offence if he—

    (a)   discloses to another anything which is likely to prejudice an investigation resulting from the disclosure under that section, or

    (b)   interferes with material which is likely to be relevant to an investigation resulting from the disclosure under that section.

(5)   It is a defence for a person charged with an offence under subsection (2) or (4) to prove—

    (a)   that he did not know and had no reasonable cause to suspect that the disclosure or interference was likely to affect a terrorist investigation, or

    (b)   that he had a reasonable excuse for the disclosure or interference.

(6)   Subsections (2) and (4) do not apply to a disclosure which is made by a professional legal adviser—

    (a)   to his client or to his client's representative in connection with the provision of legal advice by the adviser to the client and not with a view to furthering a criminal purpose, or

    (b)   to any person for the purpose of actual or contemplated legal proceedings and not with a view to furthering a criminal purpose.

(8)   For the purposes of this section—

    (a)   a reference to conducting a terrorist investigation includes a reference to taking part in the conduct of, or assisting, a terrorist investigation, and

    (b)   a person interferes with material if he falsifies it, conceals it, destroys it or disposes of it, or if he causes or permits another to do any of those things.

PART V

COUNTER-TERRORIST POWERS

48.   Authorisations

(1)   An authorisation under this section authorises any constable in uniform to prohibit or restrict the parking of vehicles on a road specified in the authorisation.

(2)   An authorisation may be given only if the person giving it considers it expedient for the prevention of acts of terrorism.

(3)   An authorisation may be given—

    (a)   where the road specified is outside Northern Ireland and is wholly or partly within a police area other than one mentioned in paragraphs (b) or (c), by a police officer for the area who is of at least the rank of assistant chief constable;

    (b)   where the road specified is wholly or partly in the metropolitan police district, by a police officer for the district who is of at least the rank of commander of the metropolitan police;

    (c)   where the road specified is wholly or partly in the City of London, by a police officer for the City who is of at least the rank of commander in the City of London police force;

    (d)   where the road specified is in Northern Ireland, by a member of the Police Service of Northern Ireland who is of at least the rank of assistant chief constable.

(4) If an authorisation is given orally, the person giving it shall confirm it in writing as soon as is reasonably practicable.

49. Exercise of power

(1) The power conferred by an authorisation under section 48 shall be exercised by placing a traffic sign on the road concerned.

51. Offences

(1) A person commits an offence if he parks a vehicle in contravention of a prohibition or restriction imposed by virtue of section 48.

(2) A person commits an offence if—

(a) he is the driver or other person in charge of a vehicle which has been permitted to remain at rest in contravention of any prohibition or restriction imposed by virtue of section 48, and

(b) he fails to move the vehicle when ordered to do so by a constable in uniform.

(3) It is a defence for a person charged with an offence under this section to prove that he had a reasonable excuse for the act or omission in question.

(4) Possession of a current disabled person's badge shall not itself constitute a reasonable excuse for the purposes of subsection (3).

52. Interpretation

In sections 48 to 51—

'disabled person's badge' means a badge issued, or having effect as if issued, under any regulations for the time being in force under section 21 of the Chronically Sick and Disabled Persons Act 1970;

'driver' means, in relation to a vehicle which has been left on any road, the person who was driving it when it was left there;

'parking' means leaving a vehicle or permitting it to remain at rest;

'traffic sign' has the meaning given in section 142(1) of the Road Traffic Regulation Act 1984;

'vehicle' has the same meaning as in section 99(5) of the Road Traffic Regulation Act 1984.

PART VI
MISCELLANEOUS

54. Weapons training

(1) A person commits an offence if he provides instruction or training in the making or use of—

(a) firearms,

(aa) radioactive material or weapons designed or adapted for the discharge of any radioactive material,

(b) explosives, or

(c) chemical, biological or nuclear weapons.

(2) A person commits an offence if he receives instruction or training in the making or use of—

(a) firearms,

(aa) radioactive material or weapons designed or adapted for the discharge of any radioactive material,

(b) explosives, or

(c) chemical, biological or nuclear weapons.

(3) A person commits an offence if he invites another to receive instruction or training and the receipt—

(a) would constitute an offence under subsection (2), or

(b) would constitute an offence under subsection (2) but for the fact that it is to take place outside the United Kingdom.

(4) For the purpose of subsections (1) and (3)—

(a) a reference to the provision of instruction includes a reference to making it available either generally or to one or more specific persons, and

(b) an invitation to receive instruction or training may be either general or addressed to one or more specific persons.

(5) It is a defence for a person charged with an offence under this section in relation to instruction or training to prove that his action or involvement was wholly for a purpose other than assisting, preparing for or participating in terrorism.

55. Weapons training: interpretation

In section 54—

'biological weapon' means a biological agent or toxin (within the meaning of the Biological Weapons Act 1974) in a form capable of use for hostile purposes or anything to which section 1(1)(b) of that Act applies,

'chemical weapon' has the meaning given by section 1 of the Chemical Weapons Act 1996, and

'radioactive material' means radioactive material capable of endangering life or causing harm to human health.

56. Directing terrorist organisation

(1) A person commits an offence if he directs, at any level, the activities of an organisation which is concerned in the commission of acts of terrorism.

57. Possession for terrorist purposes

(1) A person commits an offence if he possesses an article in circumstances which give rise to a reasonable suspicion that his possession is for a purpose connected with the commission, preparation or instigation of an act of terrorism.

(2) It is a defence for a person charged with an offence under this section to prove that his possession of the article was not for a purpose connected with the commission, preparation or instigation of an act of terrorism.

(3) In proceedings for an offence under this section, if it is proved that an article—

(a) was on any premises at the same time as the accused, or

(b) was on premises of which the accused was the occupier or which he habitually used otherwise than as a member of the public,

the court may assume that the accused possessed the article, unless he proves that he did not know of its presence on the premises or that he had no control over it.

58. Collection of information

(1) A person commits an offence if—

(a) he collects or makes a record of information of a kind likely to be useful to a person committing or preparing an act of terrorism, or

(b) he possesses a document or record containing information of that kind.

(2) In this section 'record' includes a photographic or electronic record.

(3) It is a defence for a person charged with an offence under this section to prove that he had a reasonable excuse for his action or possession.

59. England and Wales

(1) A person commits an offence if—

(a) he incites another person to commit an act of terrorism wholly or partly outside the United Kingdom, and

(b) the act would, if committed in England and Wales, constitute one of the offences listed in subsection (2).

(2) Those offences are—

(a) murder,

(b) an offence under section 18 of the Offences against the Person Act 1861 (wounding with intent),

(c) an offence under section 23 or 24 of that Act (poison),

(d) an offence under section 28 or 29 of that Act (explosions), and

(e) an offence under section 1(2) of the Criminal Damage Act 1971 (endangering life by damaging property).

(3) A person guilty of an offence under this section shall be liable to any penalty to which he would be liable on conviction of the offence listed in subsection (2) which corresponds to the act which he incites.

(4) For the purposes of subsection (1) it is immaterial whether or not the person incited is in the United Kingdom at the time of the incitement.

(5) Nothing in this section imposes criminal liability on any person acting on behalf of, or holding office under, the Crown.

62. Terrorist bombing: jurisdiction

(1) If—
   (a) a person does anything outside the United Kingdom as an act of terrorism or for the purposes of terrorism, and
   (b) his action would have constituted the commission of one of the offences listed in subsection (2) if it had been done in the United Kingdom,
   he shall be guilty of the offence.

(2) The offences referred to in subsection (1)(b) are—
   (a) an offence under section 2, 3 or 5 of the Explosive Substances Act 1883 (causing explosions, &c),
   (b) an offence under section 1 of the Biological Weapons Act 1974 (biological weapons), and
   (c) an offence under section 2 of the Chemical Weapons Act 1996 (chemical weapons).

PART VIII
GENERAL

118. Defences

(1) Subsection (2) applies where in accordance with a provision mentioned in subsection (5) it is a defence for a person charged with an offence to prove a particular matter.

(2) If the person adduces evidence which is sufficient to raise an issue with respect to the matter the court or jury shall assume that the defence is satisfied unless the prosecution proves beyond reasonable doubt that it is not.

(3) Subsection (4) applies where in accordance with a provision mentioned in subsection (5) a court—
   (a) may make an assumption in relation to a person charged with an offence unless a particular matter is proved, or
   (b) may accept a fact as sufficient evidence unless a particular matter is proved.

(4) If evidence is adduced which is sufficient to raise an issue with respect to the matter mentioned in subsection (3)(a) or (b) the court shall treat it as proved unless the prosecution disproves it beyond reasonable doubt.

(5) The provisions in respect of which subsections (2) and (4) apply are—
   (a) sections 12(4), 39(5)(a), 54, 57, 58, 77 and 103 of this Act.

121. Interpretation

In this Act—

'act' and 'action' include omission,

'article' includes substance and any other thing,

'British Transport Police Force' means the constables appointed under section 53 of the British Transport Commission Act 1949,

'customs officer' means an officer of Revenue and Customs,

'dwelling' means a building or part of a building used as a dwelling, and a vehicle which is habitually stationary and which is used as a dwelling,

'explosive' means—
   (a) an article or substance manufactured for the purpose of producing a practical effect by explosion,
   (b) materials for making an article or substance within paragraph (a),
   (c) anything used or intended to be used for causing or assisting in causing an explosion, and
   (d) a part of anything within paragraph (a) or (c),

'firearm' includes an air gun or air pistol,

'immigration officer' means a person appointed as an immigration officer under paragraph 1 of Schedule 2 to the Immigration Act 1971,

'the Islands' means the Channel Islands and the Isle of Man,

'organisation' includes any association or combination of persons,

'premises' includes any place and in particular includes—

(a)   a vehicle,

(b)   an offshore installation within the meaning given in section 44 of the Petroleum Act 1998, and

(c)   a tent or moveable structure,

'property' includes property wherever situated and whether real or personal, heritable or moveable, and things in action and other intangible or incorporeal property,

'public place' means a place to which members of the public have or are permitted to have access, whether or not for payment,

'road' has the same meaning as in the Road Traffic Act 1988 (in relation to England and Wales), and includes part of a road, and

'vehicle', except in sections 48 to 52 and Schedule 7, includes an aircraft, hovercraft, train or vessel.

TERRORISM ACT 2006

1.   **Encouragement of terrorism**

(1)   This section applies to a statement that is likely to be understood by some or all of the members of the public to whom it is published as a direct or indirect encouragement or other inducement to them to the commission, preparation or instigation of acts of terrorism or Convention offences.

(2)   A person commits an offence if—

(a)   he publishes a statement to which this section applies or causes another to publish such a statement; and

(b)   at the time he publishes it or causes it to be published, he—

(i)   intends members of the public to be directly or indirectly encouraged or otherwise induced by the statement to commit, prepare or instigate acts of terrorism or Convention offences; or

(ii)   is reckless as to whether members of the public will be directly or indirectly encouraged or otherwise induced by the statement to commit, prepare or instigate such acts or offences.

(3)   For the purposes of this section, the statements that are likely to be understood by members of the public as indirectly encouraging the commission or preparation of acts of terrorism or Convention offences include every statement which—

(a)   glorifies the commission or preparation (whether in the past, in the future or generally) of such acts or offences; and

(b)   is a statement from which those members of the public could reasonably be expected to infer that what is being glorified is being glorified as conduct that should be emulated by them in existing circumstances.

(4)   For the purposes of this section the questions how a statement is likely to be understood and what members of the public could reasonably be expected to infer from it must be determined having regard both—

(a)   to the contents of the statement as a whole; and

(b)   to the circumstances and manner of its publication.

(5)   It is irrelevant for the purposes of subsections (1) to (3)—

(a)   whether anything mentioned in those subsections relates to the commission, preparation or instigation of one or more particular acts of terrorism or Convention offences, of acts of terrorism or Convention offences of a particular description or of acts of terrorism or Convention offences generally; and,

(b)   whether any person is in fact encouraged or induced by the statement to commit, prepare or instigate any such act or offence.

(6)   In proceedings for an offence under this section against a person in whose case it is not proved that he intended the statement directly or indirectly to encourage or otherwise induce the commission, preparation or instigation of acts of terrorism or Convention offences, it is a defence for him to show—

(a)   that the statement neither expressed his views nor had his endorsement (whether by virtue of section 3 or otherwise); and

(b)   that it was clear, in all the circumstances of the statement's publication, that it did not express his views and (apart from the possibility of his having been given and failed to comply with a notice under subsection (3) of that section) did not have his endorsement.

(7)   A person guilty of an offence under this section shall be liable—

(a)   on conviction on indictment, to imprisonment for a term not exceeding 7 years or to a fine, or to both;

(b)   on summary conviction in England and Wales, to imprisonment for a term not exceeding 12 months or to a fine not exceeding the statutory maximum, or to both;

(c)   on summary conviction in Scotland or Northern Ireland, to imprisonment for a term not exceeding 6 months or to a fine not exceeding the statutory maximum, or to both.

(8)   In relation to an offence committed before the commencement of section 154(1) of the Criminal Justice Act 2003, the reference in subsection (7)(b) to 12 months is to be read as a reference to 6 months.

2.   Dissemination of terrorist publications

(1)   A person commits an offence if he engages in conduct falling within subsection (2) and, at the time he does so—

(a)   he intends an effect of his conduct to be a direct or indirect encouragement or other inducement to the commission, preparation or instigation of acts of terrorism;

(b)   he intends an effect of his conduct to be the provision of assistance in the commission or preparation of such acts; or

(c)   he is reckless as to whether his conduct has an effect mentioned in paragraph (a) or (b).

(2)   For the purposes of this section a person engages in conduct falling within this subsection if he—

(a)   distributes or circulates a terrorist publication;

(b)   gives, sells or lends such a publication;

(c)   offers such a publication for sale or loan;

(d)   provides a service to others that enables them to obtain, read, listen to or look at such a publication, or to acquire it by means of a gift, sale or loan;

(e)   transmits the contents of such a publication electronically; or

(f)   has such a publication in his possession with a view to its becoming the subject of conduct falling within any of paragraphs (a) to (e).

(3)   For the purposes of this section a publication is a terrorist publication, in relation to conduct falling within subsection (2), if matter contained in it is likely—

(a)   to be understood, by some or all of the persons to whom it is or may become available as a consequence of that conduct, as a direct or indirect encouragement or other inducement to them to the commission, preparation or instigation of acts of terrorism; or

(b)   to be useful in the commission or preparation of such acts and to be understood, by some or all of those persons, as contained in the publication, or made available to them, wholly or mainly for the purpose of being so useful to them.

(4)   For the purposes of this section matter that is likely to be understood by a person as indirectly encouraging the commission or preparation of acts of terrorism includes any matter which—

(a)   glorifies the commission or preparation (whether in the past, in the future or generally) of such acts; and

(b)   is matter from which that person could reasonably be expected to infer that what is being glorified is being glorified as conduct that should be emulated by him in existing circumstances.

(5)   For the purposes of this section the question whether a publication is a terrorist publication in relation to particular conduct must be determined—

(a)   as at the time of that conduct; and

(b)   having regard both to the contents of the publication as a whole and to the circumstances in which that conduct occurs.

(6)   In subsection (1) references to the effect of a person's conduct in relation to a terrorist publication include references to an effect of the publication on one or more persons to whom it is or may become available as a consequence of that conduct.

(7)   It is irrelevant for the purposes of this section whether anything mentioned in subsections (1) to (4) is in relation to the commission, preparation or instigation of one or more particular acts of terrorism, of acts of terrorism of a particular description or of acts of terrorism generally.

(8)   For the purposes of this section it is also irrelevant, in relation to matter contained in any article whether any person—

(a)   is in fact encouraged or induced by that matter to commit, prepare or instigate acts of terrorism; or

(b)   in fact makes use of it in the commission or preparation of such acts.

(9)   In proceedings for an offence under this section against a person in respect of conduct to which subsection (10) applies, it is a defence for him to show—

(a)   that the matter by reference to which the publication in question was a terrorist publication neither expressed his views nor had his endorsement (whether by virtue of section 3 or otherwise); and

(b)   that it was clear, in all the circumstances of the conduct, that that matter did not express his views and (apart from the possibility of his having been given and failed to comply with a notice under subsection (3) of that section) did not have his endorsement.

(10) This subsection applies to the conduct of a person to the extent that—

(a)   the publication to which his conduct related contained matter by reference to which it was a terrorist publication by virtue of subsection (3)(a); and

(b)   that person is not proved to have engaged in that conduct with the intention specified in subsection (1)(a).

(11) A person guilty of an offence under this section shall be liable—

(a)   on conviction on indictment, to imprisonment for a term not exceeding 7 years or to a fine, or to both;

(b)   on summary conviction in England and Wales, to imprisonment for a term not exceeding 12 months or to a fine not exceeding the statutory maximum, or to both;

(c)   on summary conviction in Scotland or Northern Ireland, to imprisonment for a term not exceeding 6 months or to a fine not exceeding the statutory maximum, or to both.

(12) In relation to an offence committed before the commencement of section 154(1) of the Criminal Justice Act 2003, the reference in subsection (11)(b) to 12 months is to be read as a reference to 6 months.

(13) In this section—

'lend' includes let on hire, and 'loan' is to be construed accordingly;

'publication' means an article or record of any description that contains any of the following, or any combination of them—

(a)   matter to be read;

(b)   matter to be listened to;

(c)   matter to be looked at or watched.

3.   Application of ss. 1 and 2 to internet activity etc.

(1)   This section applies for the purposes of sections 1 and 2 in relation to cases where—

(a) a statement is published or caused to be published in the course of, or in connection with, the provision or use of a service provided electronically; or

(b) conduct falling within section 2(2) was in the course of, or in connection with, the provision or use of such a service.

(2) The cases in which the statement, or the article or record to which the conduct relates, is to be regarded as having the endorsement of a person ('the relevant person') at any time include a case in which—

(a) a constable has given him a notice under subsection (3);

(b) that time falls more than 2 working days after the day on which the notice was given; and

(c) the relevant person has failed, without reasonable excuse, to comply with the notice.

(3) A notice under this subsection is a notice which—

(a) declares that, in the opinion of the constable giving it, the statement or the article or record is unlawfully terrorism-related;

(b) requires the relevant person to secure that the statement or the article or record, so far as it is so related, is not available to the public or is modified so as no longer to be so related;

(c) warns the relevant person that a failure to comply with the notice within 2 working days will result in the statement, or the article or record, being regarded as having his endorsement; and

(d) explains how, under subsection (4), he may become liable by virtue of the notice if the statement, or the article or record, becomes available to the public after he has complied with the notice.

(4) Where—

(a) a notice under subsection (3) has been given to the relevant person in respect of a statement, or an article or record, and he has complied with it, but

(b) he subsequently publishes or causes to be published a statement which is, or is for all practical purposes, the same or to the same effect as the statement to which the notice related, or to matter contained in the article or record to which it related, (a 'repeat statement');

the requirements of subsection (2)(a) to (c) shall be regarded as satisfied in the case of the repeat statement in relation to the times of its subsequent publication by the relevant person.

(5) In proceedings against a person for an offence under section 1 or 2 the requirements of subsection (2)(a) to (c) are not, in his case, to be regarded as satisfied in relation to any time by virtue of subsection (4) if he shows that he—

(a) has, before that time, taken every step he reasonably could to prevent a repeat statement from becoming available to the public and to ascertain whether it does; and

(b) was, at that time, a person to whom subsection (6) applied.

(6) This subsection applies to a person at any time when he—

(a) is not aware of the publication of the repeat statement; or

(b) having become aware of its publication, has taken every step that he reasonably could to secure that it either ceased to be available to the public or was modified as mentioned in subsection (3)(b).

(7) For the purposes of this section a statement or an article or record is unlawfully terrorism-related if it constitutes, or if matter contained in the article or record constitutes—

(a) something that is likely to be understood, by any one or more of the persons to whom it has or may become available, as a direct or indirect encouragement or other inducement to the commission, preparation or instigation of acts of terrorism or Convention offences; or

(b) information which—

(i) is likely to be useful to any one or more of those persons in the commission or preparation of such acts; and

(ii) is in a form or context in which it is likely to be understood by any one or more of those persons as being wholly or mainly for the purpose of being so useful.

(8) The reference in subsection (7) to something that is likely to be understood as an indirect encouragement to the commission or preparation of acts of terrorism or Convention offences includes anything which is likely to be understood as—

    (a) the glorification of the commission or preparation (whether in the past, in the future or generally) of such acts or such offences; and

    (b) a suggestion that what is being glorified is being glorified as conduct that should be emulated in existing circumstances.

(9) In this section 'working day' means any day other than—

    (a) a Saturday or a Sunday;

    (b) Christmas Day or Good Friday; or

    (c) a day which is a bank holiday under the Banking and Financial Dealings Act 1971 in any part of the United Kingdom.

4.   **Giving of notices under s. 3**

(1) Except in a case to which any of subsections (2) to (4) applies, a notice under section 3(3) may be given to a person only—

    (a) by delivering it to him in person; or

    (b) by sending it to him, by means of a postal service providing for delivery to be recorded, at his last known address.

(2) Such a notice may be given to a body corporate only—

    (a) by delivering it to the secretary of that body in person; or

    (b) by sending it to the appropriate person, by means of a postal service providing for delivery to be recorded, at the address of the registered or principal office of the body.

(3) Such a notice may be given to a firm only—

    (a) by delivering it to a partner of the firm in person;

    (b) by so delivering it to a person having the control or management of the partnership business; or

    (c) by sending it to the appropriate person, by means of a postal service providing for delivery to be recorded, at the address of the principal office of the partnership.

(4) Such a notice may be given to an unincorporated body or association only—

    (a) by delivering it to a member of its governing body in person; or

    (b) by sending it to the appropriate person, by means of a postal service providing for delivery to be recorded, at the address of the principal office of the body or association.

(5) In the case of—

    (a) a company registered outside the United Kingdom,

    (b) a firm carrying on business outside the United Kingdom, or

    (c) an unincorporated body or association with offices outside the United Kingdom,

the references in this section to its principal office include references to its principal office within the United Kingdom (if any).

(6) In this section 'the appropriate person' means—

    (a) in the case of a body corporate, the body itself or its secretary;

    (b) in the case of a firm, the firm itself or a partner of the firm or a person having the control or management of the partnership business; and

    (c) in the case of an unincorporated body or association, the body or association itself or a member of its governing body.

(7) For the purposes of section 3 the time at which a notice under subsection (3) of that section is to be regarded as given is—

    (a) where it is delivered to a person, the time at which it is so delivered; and

    (b) where it is sent by a postal service providing for delivery to be recorded, the time recorded as the time of its delivery.

(8) In this section 'secretary', in relation to a body corporate, means the secretary or other equivalent officer of the body.

Preparation of terrorist acts and terrorist training

5.   Preparation of terrorist acts

(1)   A person commits an offence if, with the intention of—

(a)   committing acts of terrorism, or

(b)   assisting another to commit such acts,

he engages in any conduct in preparation for giving effect to his intention.

(2)   It is irrelevant for the purposes of subsection (1) whether the intention and preparations relate to one or more particular acts of terrorism, acts of terrorism of a particular description or acts of terrorism generally.

(3)   A person guilty of an offence under this section shall be liable, on conviction on indictment, to imprisonment for life.

6.   Training for terrorism

(1)   A person commits an offence if—

(a)   he provides instruction or training in any of the skills mentioned in subsection (3); and

(b)   at the time he provides the instruction or training, he knows that a person receiving it intends to use the skills in which he is being instructed or trained—

(i)   for or in connection with the commission or preparation of acts of terrorism or Convention offences; or

(ii)   for assisting the commission or preparation by others of such acts or offences.

(2)   A person commits an offence if—

(a)   he receives instruction or training in any of the skills mentioned in subsection (3); and

(b)   at the time of the instruction or training, he intends to use the skills in which he is being instructed or trained—

(i)   for or in connection with the commission or preparation of acts of terrorism or Convention offences; or

(ii)   for assisting the commission or preparation by others of such acts or offences.

(3)   The skills are—

(a)   the making, handling or use of a noxious substance, or of substances of a description of such substances;

(b)   the use of any method or technique for doing anything else that is capable of being done for the purposes of terrorism, in connection with the commission or preparation of an act of terrorism or Convention offence or in connection with assisting the commission or preparation by another of such an act or offence; and

(c)   the design or adaptation for the purposes of terrorism, or in connection with the commission or preparation of an act of terrorism or Convention offence, of any method or technique for doing anything.

(4)   It is irrelevant for the purposes of subsections (1) and (2)—

(a)   whether any instruction or training that is provided is provided to one or more particular persons or generally;

(b)   whether the acts or offences in relation to which a person intends to use skills in which he is instructed or trained consist of one or more particular acts of terrorism or Convention offences, acts of terrorism or Convention offences of a particular description or acts of terrorism or Convention offences generally; and

(c)   whether assistance that a person intends to provide to others is intended to be provided to one or more particular persons or to one or more persons whose identities are not yet known.

(5)   A person guilty of an offence under this section shall be liable—

(a)   on conviction on indictment, to imprisonment for a term not exceeding 10 years or to a fine, or to both;

(b)   on summary conviction in England and Wales, to imprisonment for a term not exceeding 12 months or to a fine not exceeding the statutory maximum, or to both;

(c)   on summary conviction in Scotland or Northern Ireland, to imprisonment for a term not exceeding 6 months or to a fine not exceeding the statutory maximum, or to both.

(6) In relation to an offence committed before the commencement of section 154(1) of the Criminal Justice Act 2003, the reference in subsection (5)(b) to 12 months is to be read as a reference to 6 months.

(7) In this section—

'noxious substance' means—

    (a) a dangerous substance within the meaning of Part 7 of the Anti-terrorism, Crime and Security Act 2001; or

    (b) any other substance which is hazardous or noxious or which may be or become hazardous or noxious only in certain circumstances;

'substance' includes any natural or artificial substance (whatever its origin or method of production and whether in solid or liquid form or in the form of a gas or vapour) and any mixture of substances.

8. Attendance at a place used for terrorist training

(1) A person commits an offence if—

    (a) he attends at any place, whether in the United Kingdom or elsewhere;

    (b) while he is at that place, instruction or training of the type mentioned in section 6(1) of this Act or section 54(1) of the Terrorism Act 2000 (weapons training) is provided there;

    (c) that instruction or training is provided there wholly or partly for purposes connected with the commission or preparation of acts of terrorism or Convention offences; and

    (d) the requirements of subsection (2) are satisfied in relation to that person.

(2) The requirements of this subsection are satisfied in relation to a person if—

    (a) he knows or believes that instruction or training is being provided there wholly or partly for purposes connected with the commission or preparation of acts of terrorism or Convention offences; or

    (b) a person attending at that place throughout the period of that person's attendance could not reasonably have failed to understand that instruction or training was being provided there wholly or partly for such purposes.

(3) It is immaterial for the purposes of this section—

    (a) whether the person concerned receives the instruction or training himself; and

    (b) whether the instruction or training is provided for purposes connected with one or more particular acts of terrorism or Convention offences, acts of terrorism or Convention offences of a particular description or acts of terrorism or Convention offences generally.

(4) A person guilty of an offence under this section shall be liable—

    (a) on conviction on indictment, to imprisonment for a term not exceeding 10 years or to a fine, or to both;

    (b) on summary conviction in England and Wales, to imprisonment for a term not exceeding 12 months or to a fine not exceeding the statutory maximum, or to both;

    (c) on summary conviction in Scotland or Northern Ireland, to imprisonment for a term not exceeding 6 months or to a fine not exceeding the statutory maximum, or to both.

(5) In relation to an offence committed before the commencement of section 154(1) of the Criminal Justice Act 2003, the reference in subsection (4)(b) to 12 months is to be read as a reference to 6 months.

(6) References in this section to instruction or training being provided include references to its being made available.

Offences involving radioactive devices and materials and nuclear facilities and sites

9. Making and possession of devices or materials

(1) A person commits an offence if—

    (a) he makes or has in his possession a radioactive device, or

    (b) he has in his possession radioactive material,

with the intention of using the device or material in the course of or in connection with the commission or preparation of an act of terrorism or for the purposes of terrorism, or of making it available to be so used.

(2) It is irrelevant for the purposes of subsection (1) whether the act of terrorism to which an intention relates is a particular act of terrorism, an act of terrorism of a particular description or an act of terrorism generally.

(3) A person guilty of an offence under this section shall be liable, on conviction on indictment, to imprisonment for life.

(4) In this section—

'radioactive device' means—

(a) a nuclear weapon or other nuclear explosive device;

(b) a radioactive material dispersal device;

(c) a radiation-emitting device;

'radioactive material' means nuclear material or any other radioactive substance which—

(a) contains nuclides that undergo spontaneous disintegration in a process accompanied by the emission of one or more types of ionising radiation, such as alpha radiation, beta radiation, neutron particles or gamma rays; and

(b) is capable, owing to its radiological or fissile properties, of—

(i) causing serious bodily injury to a person;

(ii) causing serious damage to property;

(iii) endangering a person's life; or

(iv) creating a serious risk to the health or safety of the public.

(5) In subsection (4)—

'device' includes any of the following, whether or not fixed to land, namely, machinery, equipment, appliances, tanks, containers, pipes and conduits;

'nuclear material' has the same meaning as in the Nuclear Material (Offences) Act 1983 (see section 6 of that Act).

10. Misuse of devices or material and misuse and damage of facilities

(1) A person commits an offence if he uses—

(a) a radioactive device, or

(b) radioactive material,

in the course of or in connection with the commission of an act of terrorism or for the purposes of terrorism.

(2) A person commits an offence if, in the course of or in connection with the commission of an act of terrorism or for the purposes of terrorism, he uses or damages a nuclear facility in a manner which—

(a) causes a release of radioactive material; or

(b) creates or increases a risk that such material will be released.

(3) A person guilty of an offence under this section shall be liable, on conviction on indictment, to imprisonment for life.

(4) In this section—

'nuclear facility' means—

(a) a nuclear reactor, including a reactor installed in or on any transportation device for use as an energy source in order to propel it or for any other purpose; or

(b) a plant or conveyance being used for the production, storage, processing or transport of radioactive material;

'radioactive device' and 'radioactive material' have the same meanings as in section 9.

(5) In subsection (4)—

'nuclear reactor' has the same meaning as in the Nuclear Installations Act 1965 (see section 26 of that Act);

'transportation device' means any vehicle or any space object (within the meaning of the Outer Space Act 1986).

11.   Terrorist threats relating to devices, materials or facilities

(1)   A person commits an offence if, in the course of or in connection with the commission of an act of terrorism or for the purposes of terrorism—

(a)   he makes a demand—

(i)   for the supply to himself or to another of a radioactive device or of radioactive material;

(ii)   for a nuclear facility to be made available to himself or to another; or

(iii)   for access to such a facility to be given to himself or to another;

(b)   he supports the demand with a threat that he or another will take action if the demand is not met; and

(c)   the circumstances and manner of the threat are such that it is reasonable for the person to whom it is made to assume that there is real risk that the threat will be carried out if the demand is not met.

(2)   A person also commits an offence if—

(a)   he makes a threat falling within subsection (3) in the course of or in connection with the commission of an act of terrorism or for the purposes of terrorism; and

(b)   the circumstances and manner of the threat are such that it is reasonable for the person to whom it is made to assume that there is real risk that the threat will be carried out, or would be carried out if demands made in association with the threat are not met.

(3)   A threat falls within this subsection if it is—

(a)   a threat to use radioactive material;

(b)   a threat to use a radioactive device; or

(c)   a threat to use or damage a nuclear facility in a manner that releases radioactive material or creates or increases a risk that such material will be released.

(4)   A person guilty of an offence under this section shall be liable, on conviction on indictment, to imprisonment for life.

(5)   In this section—

'nuclear facility' has the same meaning as in section 10;

'radioactive device' and 'radioactive material' have the same meanings as in section 9.

THEFT ACT 1968

1.   Basic definition of theft

(1)   A person is guilty of theft if he dishonestly appropriates property belonging to another with the intention of permanently depriving the other of it; and 'thief' and 'steal' shall be construed accordingly.

(2)   It is immaterial whether the appropriation is made with a view to gain, or is made for the thief's own benefit.

(3)   The five following sections of this Act shall have effect as regards the interpretation and operation of this section (and, except as otherwise provided by this Act, shall apply only for purposes of this section).

2.   'Dishonestly'

(1)   A person's appropriation of property belonging to another is not to be regarded as dishonest—

(a)   if he appropriates the property in the belief that he has in law the right to deprive the other of it, on behalf of himself or of a third person; or

(b)   if he appropriates the property in the belief that he would have the other's consent if the other knew of the appropriation and the circumstances of it; or

(c)   (except where the property came to him as trustee or personal representative) if he appropriates the property in the belief that the person to whom the property belongs cannot be discovered by taking reasonable steps.

(2)   A person's appropriation of property belonging to another may be dishonest notwithstanding that he is willing to pay for the property.

3.   **'Appropriates'**

(1)   Any assumption by a person of the rights of an owner amounts to an appropriation, and this includes, where he has come by the property (innocently or not) without stealing it, any later assumption of a right to it by keeping or dealing with it as owner.

(2)   Where property or a right or interest in property is or purports to be transferred for value to a person acting in good faith, no later assumption by him of rights which he believed himself to be acquiring shall, by reason of any defect in the transferor's title, amount to theft of the property.

4.   **'Property'**

(1)   'Property' includes money and all other property, real or personal, including things in action and other intangible property.

(2)   A person cannot steal land, or things forming part of land and severed from it by him or by his directions, except in the following cases, that is to say—

(a)   when he is a trustee or personal representative, or is authorised by power of attorney, or as liquidator of a company, or otherwise, to sell or dispose of land belonging to another, and he appropriates the land or anything forming part of it by dealing with it in breach of the confidence reposed in him; or

(b)   when he is not in possession of the land and appropriates anything forming part of the land by severing it or causing it to be severed, or after it has been severed; or

(c)   when, being in possession of the land under a tenancy, he appropriates the whole or part of any fixture or structure let to be used with the land.

For purposes of this subsection 'land' does not include incorporeal hereditaments; 'tenancy' means a tenancy for years or any less period and includes an agreement for such a tenancy, but a person who after the end of a tenancy remains in possession as statutory tenant or otherwise is to be treated as having possession under the tenancy, and 'let' shall be construed accordingly.

(3)   A person who picks mushrooms growing wild on any land, or who picks flowers, fruit or foliage from a plant wild on any land, does not (although not in possession of the land) steal what he picks, unless he does it for reward or for sale or other commercial purpose.

For purposes of this subsection 'mushroom' includes any fungus, and 'plant' includes any shrub or tree.

(4)   Wild creatures, tamed or untamed, shall be regarded as property; but a person cannot steal a wild creature not tamed nor ordinarily kept in captivity, or the carcase of any such creature, unless either it has been reduced into possession by or on behalf of another person and possession of it has not since been lost or abandoned, or another person is in course of reducing it into possession.

5.   **'Belonging to another'**

(1)   Property shall be regarded as belonging to any person having possession or control of it, or having in it any proprietary right or interest (not being an equitable interest arising only from an agreement to transfer or grant an interest).

(2)   Where property is subject to a trust, the persons to whom it belongs shall be regarded as including any person having a right to enforce the trust, and an intention to defeat the trust shall be regarded accordingly as an intention to deprive of the property any person having that right.

(3)   Where a person receives property from or on account of another, and is under an obligation to the other to retain and deal with that property or its proceeds in a particular way, the property or proceeds shall be regarded (as against him) as belonging to the other.

(4)   Where a person gets property by another's mistake, and is under an obligation to make restoration (in whole or in part) of the property or its proceeds or of the value thereof, then to the extent of that obligation the property or proceeds shall be regarded (as against him) as belonging to the person entitled to restoration, and an intention not to make restoration shall be regarded accordingly as an intention to deprive that person of the property or proceeds.

(5)   Property of a corporation sole shall be regarded as belonging to the corporation
      notwithstanding a vacancy in the corporation.

6.   'With the intention of permanently depriving the other of it'

(1)   A person appropriating property belonging to another without meaning the other
      permanently to lose the thing itself is nevertheless to be regarded as having the intention of
      permanently depriving the other of it if his intention is to treat the thing as his own to
      dispose of regardless of the other's rights; and a borrowing or lending of it may amount to so
      treating it if, but only if, the borrowing or lending is for a period and in circumstances
      making it equivalent to an outright taking or disposal.

(2)   Without prejudice to the generality of subsection (1) above, where a person, having
      possession or control (lawfully or not) of property belonging to another, parts with the
      property under a condition as to its return which he may not be able to perform, this (if done
      for purposes of his own and without the other's authority) amounts to treating the property
      as his own to dispose of regardless of the other's rights.

7.   Theft

A person guilty of theft shall on conviction on indictment be liable to imprisonment for a term not
exceeding seven years.

8.   Robbery

(1)   A person is guilty of robbery if he steals, and immediately before or at the time of doing so,
      and in order to do so, he uses force on any person or puts or seeks to put any person in fear
      of being then and there subjected to force.

(2)   A person guilty of robbery, or of an assault with intent to rob, shall on conviction on
      indictment be liable to imprisonment for life.

9.   Burglary

(1)   A person is guilty of burglary if—
      (a)   he enters any building or part of a building as a trespasser and with intent to commit
            any such offence as is mentioned in subsection (2) below; or
      (b)   having entered any building or part of a building as a trespasser he steals or attempts to
            steal anything in the building or that part of it or inflicts or attempts to inflict on any
            person therein any grievous bodily harm.

(2)   The offences referred to in subsection (1)(a) above are offences of stealing anything in the
      building or part of a building in question, of inflicting on any person therein any grievous
      bodily harm therein, and of doing unlawful damage to the building or anything therein.

(3)   A person guilty of burglary shall on conviction on indictment be liable to imprisonment for
      a term not exceeding—
      (a)   where the offence was committed in respect of a building or part of a building which is
            a dwelling, fourteen years;
      (b)   in any other case, ten years.

(4)   References in subsections (1) and (2) above to a building, and the reference in subsection (3)
      above to a building which is a dwelling, shall apply also to an inhabited vehicle or vessel,
      and shall apply to any such vehicle or vessel at times when the person having a habitation in
      it is not there as well as at times when he is.

10.   Aggravated burglary

(1)   A person is guilty of aggravated burglary if he commits any burglary and at the time has
      with him any firearm or imitation firearm, any weapon of offence, or any explosive; and for
      this purpose—
      (a)   'firearm' includes an airgun or air pistol, and 'imitation firearm' means anything
            which has the appearance of being a firearm, whether capable of being discharged or
            not; and
      (b)   'weapon of offence' means any article made or adapted for use for causing injury to or
            incapacitating a person, or intended by the person having it with him for such use; and

(c)   'explosive' means any article manufactured for the purpose of producing a practical effect by explosion, or intended by the person having it with him for that purpose.

(2)   A person guilty of aggravated burglary shall on conviction on indictment be liable to imprisonment for life.

11.   Removal of articles from places open to the public

(1)   Subject to subsections (2) and (3) below, where the public have access to a building in order to view the building or part of it, or a collection or part of a collection housed in it, any person who without lawful authority removes from the building or its grounds the whole or part of any article displayed or kept for display to the public in the building or that part of it or in its grounds shall be guilty of an offence.

For this purpose 'collection' includes a collection got together for a temporary purpose, but references in this section to a collection do not apply to a collection made or exhibited for the purpose of effecting sales or other commercial dealings.

(2)   It is immaterial for purposes of subsection (1) above, that the public's access to a building is limited to a particular period or particular occasion; but where anything removed from a building or its grounds is there otherwise than as forming part of, or being on loan for exhibition with, a collection intended for permanent exhibition to the public, the person removing it does not thereby commit an offence under this section unless he removes it on a day when the public have access to the building as mentioned in subsection (1) above.

(3)   A person does not commit an offence under this section if he believes that he has lawful authority for the removal of the thing in question or that he would have it if the person entitled to give it knew of the removal and the circumstances of it.

12.   Taking motor vehicle or other conveyance without authority

(1)   Subject to subsections (5) and (6) below, a person shall be guilty of an offence if, without having the consent of the owner or other lawful authority, he takes any conveyance for his own or another's use or, knowing that any conveyance has been taken without such authority, drives it or allows himself to be carried in or on it.

(2)   A person guilty of an offence under subsection (1) above shall be liable on summary conviction to a fine not exceeding level 5 on the standard scale, to imprisonment for a term not exceeding six months, or to both.

(4)   If on the trial of an indictment for theft the jury are not satisfied that the accused committed theft, but it is proved that the accused committed an offence under subsection (1) above, the jury may find him guilty of the offence under subsection (1) and if he is found guilty of it, he shall be liable as he would have been liable under subsection (2) above on summary conviction.

(5)   Subsection (1) above shall not apply in relation to pedal cycles; but, subject to subsection (6) below, a person who, without having the consent of the owner or other lawful authority, takes a pedal cycle for his own or another's use, or rides a pedal cycle knowing it to have been taken without such authority, shall on summary conviction be liable to a fine not exceeding level 3 on the standard scale.

(6)   A person does not commit an offence under this section by anything done in the belief that he has lawful authority to do it or that he would have the owner's consent if the owner knew of his doing it and the circumstances of it.

(7)   For purposes of this section—

(a)   'conveyance' means any conveyance constructed or adapted for the carriage of a person or persons whether by land, water or air, except that it does not include a conveyance constructed or adapted for use only under the control of a person not carried in or on it, and 'drive' shall be construed accordingly; and

(b)   'owner', in relation to a conveyance which is the subject of a hiring agreement or hire-purchase agreement, means the person in possession of the conveyance under that agreement.

12A.   Aggravated vehicle-taking

(1)   Subject to subsection (3) below, a person is guilty of aggravated taking of a vehicle if—

      (a)   he commits an offence under section 12(1) above (in this section referred to as a 'basic offence') in relation to a mechanically propelled vehicle; and

      (b)   it is proved that, at any time after the vehicle was unlawfully taken (whether by him or another) and before it was recovered, the vehicle was driven, or injury or damage was caused, in one or more of the circumstances set out in paragraphs (a) to (d) of subsection (2) below.

(2)   The circumstances referred to in subsection (1)(b) above are—

      (a)   that the vehicle was driven dangerously on a road or other public place;

      (b)   that, owing to the driving of the vehicle, an accident occurred by which injury was caused to any person;

      (c)   that, owing to the driving of the vehicle, an accident occurred by which damage was caused to any property, other than the vehicle;

      (d)   that damage was caused to the vehicle.

(3)   A person is not guilty of an offence under this section if he proves that, as regards any such proven driving, injury or damage as is referred to in subsection (1)(b) above, either—

      (a)   the driving, accident or damage referred to in subsection (2) above occurred before he committed the basic offence; or

      (b)   he was neither in nor on nor in the immediate vicinity of the vehicle when that driving, accident or damage occurred.

(4)   A person guilty of an offence under this section shall be liable on conviction on indictment to imprisonment for a term not exceeding two years or, if it is proved that, in circumstances falling within subsection (2)(b) above, the accident caused the death of the person concerned, fourteen years.

(5)   If a person who is charged with an offence under this section is found not guilty of that offence but it is proved that he committed a basic offence, he may be convicted of the basic offence.

(7)   For the purposes of this section a vehicle is driven dangerously if—

      (a)   it is driven in a way which falls far below what would be expected of a competent and careful driver; and

      (b)   it would be obvious to a competent and careful driver that driving the vehicle in that way would be dangerous.

(8)   For the purposes of this section a vehicle is recovered when it is restored to its owner or to other lawful possession or custody; and in this subsection 'owner' has the same meaning as in section 12 above.

13.   Abstracting of electricity

A person who dishonestly uses without due authority, or dishonestly causes to be wasted or diverted, any electricity shall on conviction on indictment be liable to imprisonment for a term not exceeding five years.

15.   Obtaining property by deception

(1)   A person who by any deception dishonestly obtains property belonging to another, with the intention of permanently depriving the other of it, shall on conviction on indictment be liable to imprisonment for a term not exceeding ten years.

(2)   For purposes of this section a person is to be treated as obtaining property if he obtains ownership, possession or control of it, and 'obtain' includes obtaining for another or enabling another to obtain or to retain.

(3)   Section 6 above shall apply for purposes of this section, with the necessary adaptation of the reference to appropriating, as it applies for purposes of section 1.

(4)   For purposes of this section 'deception' means any deception (whether deliberate or reckless) by words or conduct as to fact or as to law, including a deception as to the present intentions of the person using the deception or any other person.

15A.   Obtaining a money transfer by deception

(1)   A person is guilty of an offence if by any deception he dishonestly obtains a money transfer for himself or another.

(2) A money transfer occurs when—

    (a) a debit is made to one account,

    (b) a credit is made to another, and

    (c) the credit results from the debit or the debit results from the credit.

(3) References to a credit and to a debit are to a credit of an amount of money and to a debit of an amount of money.

(4) It is immaterial (in particular)—

    (a) whether the amount credited is the same as the amount debited;

    (b) whether the money transfer is effected on presentment of a cheque or by another method;

    (c) whether any delay occurs in the process by which the money transfer is effected;

    (d) whether any intermediate credits or debits are made in the course of the money transfer;

    (e) whether either of the accounts is overdrawn before or after the money transfer is effected.

(5) A person guilty of an offence under this section shall be liable on conviction on indictment to imprisonment for a term not exceeding ten years.

15B. Section 15A: supplementary

(1) The following provisions have effect for the interpretation of section 15A of this Act.

(2) 'Deception' has the same meaning as in section 15 of this Act.

(3) 'Account' means an account kept with—

    (a) a bank; or

    (b) a person carrying on a business which falls within subsection (4) below.

(4) A business falls within this subsection if—

    (a) in the course of the business money received by way of deposit is lent to others; or

    (b) any other activity of the business is financed, wholly or to any material extent, out of the capital of or the interest on money received by way of deposit;

(4A) References in subsection (4) to a deposit must be read with—

    (a) section 22 of the Financial Services and Markets Act 2000;

    (b) any relevant order under that section; and

    (c) Schedule 2 to that Act,

but any restriction on the meaning of deposit which arises from the identity of the person making it is to be disregarded.

(5) For the purposes of subsection (4) above—

    (a) all the activities which a person carries on by way of business shall be regarded as a single business carried on by him; and

    (b) 'money' includes money expressed in a currency other than sterling or in the European currency unit (as defined in Council Regulation No 3320/94/EC or any Community instrument replacing it).

16. Obtaining pecuniary advantage by deception

(1) A person who by any deception dishonestly obtains for himself or another any pecuniary advantage shall on conviction on indictment be liable to imprisonment for a term not exceeding five years.

(2) The cases in which a pecuniary advantage within the meaning of this section is to be regarded as obtained for a person are cases where—

    (b) he is allowed to borrow by way of overdraft, or to take out any policy of insurance or annuity contract, or obtains an improvement of the terms on which he is allowed to do so; or

    (c) he is given the opportunity to earn remuneration or greater remuneration in an office or employment, or to win money by betting.

(3) For purposes of this section 'deception' has the same meaning as in section 15 of this Act.

17.   False accounting

> (1)   Where a person dishonestly, with a view to gain for himself or another or with intent to cause loss to another,—
>
> > (a)   destroys, defaces, conceals or falsifies any account or any record or document made or required for any accounting purpose; or
> >
> > (b)   in furnishing information for any purpose produces or makes use of any account, or any such record or document as aforesaid, which to his knowledge is or may be misleading, false or deceptive in a material particular;
>
> he shall, on conviction on indictment, be liable to imprisonment for a term not exceeding seven years.
>
> (2)   For purposes of this section a person who makes or concurs in making in an account or other document an entry which is or may be misleading, false or deceptive in a material particular, or who omits or concurs in omitting a material particular from an account or other document, is to be treated as falsifying the account or document.

18.   Liability of company officers for certain offences by company

> (1)   Where an offence committed by a body corporate under section 15, 16 or 17 of this Act is proved to have been committed with the consent or connivance of any director, manager, secretary or other similar officer of the body corporate, or any person who was purporting to act in any such capacity, he as well as the body corporate shall be guilty of that offence, and shall be liable to be proceeded against and punished accordingly.
>
> (2)   Where the affairs of a body corporate are managed by its members, this section shall apply in relation to the acts and defaults of a member in connection with his functions of management as if he were a director of the body corporate.

19.   False statements by company directors, etc.

> (1)   Where an officer of a body corporate or unincorporated association (or person purporting to act as such), with intent to deceive members or creditors of the body corporate or association about its affairs, publishes or concurs in publishing a written statement or account which to his knowledge is or may be misleading, false or deceptive in a material particular, he shall on conviction on indictment be liable to imprisonment for a term not exceeding seven years.
>
> (2)   For purposes of this section a person who has entered into a security for the benefit of a body corporate or association is to be treated as a creditor of it.
>
> (3)   Where the affairs of a body corporate or association are managed by its members, this section shall apply to any statement which a member publishes or concurs in publishing in connection with his functions of management as if he were an officer of the body corporate or association.

20.   Suppression, etc. of documents

> (1)   A person who dishonestly, with a view to gain for himself or another or with intent to cause loss to another, destroys, defaces or conceals any valuable security, any will or other testamentary document or any original document of or belonging to, or filed or deposited in, any court of justice or any government department shall on conviction on indictment be liable to imprisonment for a term not exceeding seven years.
>
> (2)   A person who dishonestly, with a view to gain for himself or another or with intent to cause loss to another, by any deception procures the execution of a valuable security shall on conviction on indictment be liable to imprisonment for a term not exceeding seven years; and this subsection shall apply in relation to the making, acceptance, indorsement, alteration, cancellation or destruction in whole or in part of a valuable security, and in relation to the signing or sealing of any paper or other material in order that it may be made or converted into, or used or dealt with as, a valuable security, as if that were the execution of a valuable security.
>
> (3)   For purposes of this section 'deception' has the same meaning as in section 15 of this Act, and 'valuable security' means any document creating, transferring, surrendering or releasing any right to, in or over property, or authorising the payment of money or delivery of any

property, or evidencing the creation, transfer, surrender or release of any such right, or the payment of money or delivery of any property, or the satisfaction of any obligation.

21.   Blackmail

(1)   A person is guilty of blackmail if, with a view to gain for himself or another or with intent to cause loss to another, he makes any unwarranted demand with menaces; and for this purpose a demand with menaces is unwarranted unless the person making it does so in the belief—

(a)   that he has reasonable grounds for making the demand; and

(b)   that the use of the menaces is a proper means of reinforcing the demand.

(2)   The nature of the act or omission demanded is immaterial, and it is also immaterial whether the menaces relate to action to be taken by the person making the demand.

(3)   A person guilty of blackmail shall on conviction on indictment be liable to imprisonment for a term not exceeding fourteen years.

22.   Handling stolen goods

(1)   A person handles stolen goods if (otherwise than in the course of the stealing) knowing or believing them to be stolen goods he dishonestly receives the goods, or dishonestly undertakes or assists in their retention, removal, disposal or realisation by or for the benefit of another person, or if he arranges to do so.

(2)   A person guilty of handling stolen goods shall on conviction on indictment be liable to imprisonment for a term not exceeding fourteen years.

23.   Advertising rewards for return of goods stolen or lost

Where any public advertisement of a reward for the return of any goods which have been stolen or lost uses any words to the effect that no questions will be asked, or that the person producing the goods will be safe from apprehension or inquiry, or that money paid for the purchase of the goods or advanced by way of loan on them will be repaid, the person advertising the reward and any person who prints or publishes the advertisement shall on summary conviction be liable to a fine not exceeding level 3 on the standard scale.

24.   Scope of offences relating to stolen goods

(1)   The provisions of this Act relating to goods which have been stolen shall apply whether the stealing occurred in England or Wales or elsewhere, and whether it occurred before or after the commencement of this Act, provided that the stealing (if not an offence under this Act) amounted to an offence where and at the time when the foods were stolen; and references to stolen goods shall be construed accordingly.

(2)   For purposes of those provisions references to stolen goods shall include, in addition to the goods originally stolen and parts of them (whether in their original state or not),—

(a)   any other goods which directly or indirectly represent or have at any time represented the stolen goods in the hands of the thief as being the proceeds of any disposal or realisation of the whole or part of the goods stolen or of goods so representing the stolen goods; and

(b)   any other goods which directly or indirectly represent or have at any time represented the stolen goods in the hands of a handler of the stolen goods or any part of them as being the proceeds of any disposal or realisation of the whole or part of the stolen goods handled by him or of goods so representing them.

(3)   But no goods shall be regarded as having continued to be stolen goods after they have been restored to the person from whom they were stolen or to other lawful possession or custody, or after that person and any other person claiming through him have otherwise ceased as regards those goods to have any right to restitution in respect of the theft.

(4)   For purposes of the provisions of this Act relating to goods which have been stolen (including subsections (1) to (3) above) goods obtained in England or Wales or elsewhere either by blackmail or in the circumstances described in section 15(1) of this Act shall be regarded as stolen; and 'steal', 'theft' and 'thief' shall be construed accordingly.

24A.   Dishonestly retaining a wrongful credit

(1)   A person is guilty of an offence if—

(a)   a wrongful credit has been made to an account kept by him or in respect of which he has any right or interest;

(b)   he knows or believes that the credit is wrongful; and

(c)   he dishonestly fails to take such steps as are reasonable in the circumstances to secure that the credit is cancelled.

(2)   References to a credit are to a credit of an amount of money.

(3)   A credit to an account is wrongful if it is the credit side of a money transfer obtained contrary to section 15A of this Act.

(4)   A credit to an account is also wrongful to the extent that it derives from—

(a)   theft;

(b)   an offence under section 15A of this Act;

(c)   blackmail; or

(d)   stolen goods.

(5)   In determining whether a credit to an account is wrongful, it is immaterial (in particular) whether the account is overdrawn before or after the credit is made.

(6)   A person guilty of an offence under this section shall be liable on conviction on indictment to imprisonment for a term not exceeding ten years.

(7)   Subsection (8) below applies for purposes of provisions of this Act relating to stolen goods (including subsection (4) above).

(8)   References to stolen goods include money which is dishonestly withdrawn from an account to which a wrongful credit has been made, but only to the extent that the money derives from the credit.

(9)   In this section 'account' and 'money' shall be construed in accordance with section 15B of this Act.

25.   Going equipped for stealing, etc.

(1)   A person shall be guilty of an offence if, when not at his place of abode, he has with him any article for use in the course of or in connection with any burglary, theft or cheat.

(2)   A person guilty of an offence under this section shall on conviction on indictment be liable to imprisonment for a term not exceeding three years.

(3)   Where a person is charged with an offence under this section, proof that he had with him any article made or adapted for use in committing a burglary, theft or cheat shall be evidence that he had it with him for such use.

(4)   . . .

(5)   For purposes of this section an offence under section 12(1) of this Act of taking a conveyance shall be treated as theft, and 'cheat' means an offence under section 15 of this Act.

27.   Evidence and procedure on charge of theft or handling stolen goods

(3)   Where a person is being proceeded against for handling stolen goods (but not for any offence other than handling stolen goods), then at any stage of the proceedings, if evidence has been given of his having or arranging to have in his possession the goods the subject of the charge, or of his undertaking or assisting in, or arranging to undertake or assist in, their retention, removal, disposal or realisation, the following evidence shall be admissible for the purpose of proving that he knew or believed the goods to be stolen goods:—

(a)   evidence that he has had in his possession, or has undertaken or assisted in the retention, removal, disposal or realisation of, stolen goods from any theft taking place not earlier than twelve months before the offence charged; and

(b)   (provided that seven days' notice in writing has been given to him of the intention to prove the conviction) evidence that he has within the five years preceding the date of the offence charged been convicted of theft or of handling stolen goods.

32.   Effect on existing law and construction of references to offences

(1)   The following offences are hereby abolished for all purposes not relating to offences committed before the commencement of this Act, that is to say—

(a)   any offence at common law of larceny, robbery, burglary, receiving stolen property, obtaining property by threats, extortion by colour of office or franchise, false accounting by public officers, concealment of treasure trove and, except as regards offences relating to the public revenue, cheating.

34.   Interpretation

(1)   Sections 4(1) and 5(1) of this Act shall apply generally for purposes of this Act as they apply for purposes of section 1.

(2)   For purposes of this Act—

(a)   'gain' and 'loss' are to be construed as extending only to gain or loss in money or other property, but as extending to any such gain or loss whether temporary or permanent; and—

(i)   'gain' includes a gain by keeping what one has, as well as a gain by getting what one has not; and

(ii)   'loss' includes a loss by not getting what one might get, as well as a loss by parting with what one has;

(b)   'goods', except in so far as the context otherwise requires, includes money and every other description of property except land, and includes things severed from the land by stealing.

SCHEDULE 1
OFFENCES OF TAKING, ETC., FISH

2.   Taking or destroying fish

(1)   Subject to subparagraph (2) below, a person who unlawfully takes or destroys, or attempts to take or destroy, any fish in water which is private property or in which there is any private right of fishery shall on summary conviction be liable to imprisonment for a term not exceeding three months or to a fine not exceeding level 3 on the standard scale or to both.

(2)   Subparagraph (1) above shall not apply to taking or destroying fish by angling in the daytime (that is to say, in the period beginning one hour before sunrise and ending one hour after sunset); but a person who by angling in the daytime unlawfully takes or destroys, or attempts to take or destroy, any fish in water which is private property or in which there is any private right of fishery shall on summary conviction be liable to a fine not exceeding level 1 on the standard scale.

THEFT ACT 1978

1.   Obtaining services by deception

(1)   A person who by any deception dishonestly obtains services from another shall be guilty of an offence.

(2)   It is an obtaining of services where the other is induced to confer a benefit by doing some act, or causing or permitting some act to be done, on the understanding that the benefit has been or will be paid for.

(3)   Without prejudice to the generality of subsection (2) above, it is an obtaining of services where the other is induced to make a loan, or to cause or permit a loan to be made, on the understanding that any payment (whether by way of interest or otherwise) will be or has been made in respect of the loan.

2.   Evasion of liability by deception

(1)   Subject to subsection (2) below, where a person by any deception—

(a)   dishonestly secures the remission of the whole or part of any existing liability to make a payment, whether his own liability or another's; or

(b)   with intent to make permanent default in whole or in part on any existing liability to make a payment, or with intent to let another do so, dishonestly induces the creditor or any person claiming payment on behalf of the creditor to wait for payment (whether or not the due date for payment is deferred) or to forgo payment; or

     (c)   dishonestly obtains any exemption from or abatement of liability to make a payment; he shall be guilty of an offence.

(2)   For purposes of this section 'liability' means legally enforceable liability; and subsection (1) shall not apply in relation to a liability that has not been accepted or established to pay compensation for a wrongful act or omission.

(3)   For purposes of subsection (1)(b) a person induced to take in payment a cheque or other security for money by way of conditional satisfaction of a pre-existing liability is to be treated not as being paid but as being induced to wait for payment.

(4)   For purposes of subsection (1)(c) 'obtains' includes obtaining for another or enabling another to obtain.

3.   Making off without payment

(1)   Subject to subsection (3) below, a person who, knowing that payment on the spot for any goods supplied or service done is required or expected from him, dishonestly makes off without having paid as required or expected and with intent to avoid payment of the amount due shall be guilty of an offence.

(2)   For purposes of this section 'payment on the spot' includes payment at the time of collecting goods on which work has been done or in respect of which service has been provided.

(3)   Subsection (1) above shall not apply where the supply of the goods or the doing of the service is contrary to law, or where the service done is such that payment is not legally enforceable.

(4)   . . .

4.   Punishments

(1)   Offences under this Act shall be punishable either on conviction on indictment or on summary conviction.

(2)   A person convicted on indictment shall be liable—

    (a)   for an offence under section 1 or section 2 of this Act, to imprisonment for a term not exceeding five years; and

    (b)   for an offence under section 3 of this Act, to imprisonment for a term not exceeding two years.

(3)   A person convicted summarily of any offence under this Act shall be liable—

    (a)   to imprisonment for a term not exceeding six months; or

    (b)   to a fine not exceeding the prescribed sum for the purposes of section 32 of the Magistrates' Courts Act 1980 (punishment on summary conviction of offences triable either way: £1,000 or other sum substituted by order under that Act),

   or to both.

5.   Supplementary

(1)   For purposes of sections 1 and 2 above 'deception' has the same meaning as in section 15 of the Theft Act 1968, that is to say, it means any deception (whether deliberate or reckless) by words or conduct as to fact or as to law, including a deception as to the present intentions of the person using the deception or any other person; and section 18 of that Act (liability of company officers for offences by the company) shall apply in relation to sections 1 and 2 above as it applies in relation to section 15 of that Act.

(2)   Sections 30(1) (husband and wife), 31(1) (effect on civil proceedings) and 34 (interpretation) of the Theft Act 1968, so far as they are applicable in relation to this Act, shall apply as they apply in relation to that Act.

TRIAL OF LUNATICS ACT 1883

2.   Special verdict where accused found guilty, but insane at date of act or omission charged, and orders thereupon

(1)   Where in any indictment or information any act or omission is charged against any person as an offence, and it is given in evidence on the trial of such person for that offence that he was

insane, so as not to be responsible, according to law, for his actions at the time when the act was done or omission made, then, if it appears to the jury before whom such person is tried that he did the act or made the omission charged, but was insane as aforesaid at the time when he did or made the same, the jury shall return a special verdict that the accused is not guilty by reason of insanity.

WATER RESOURCES ACT 1991

85. Offences of polluting controlled waters

(1) A person contravenes this section if he causes or knowingly permits any poisonous, noxious or polluting matter or any solid waste matter to enter any controlled waters.

(3) A person contravenes this section if he causes or knowingly permits any trade effluent or sewage effluent to be discharged—

    (a) into any controlled waters; or

    (b) from land in England and Wales, through a pipe, into the sea outside the seaward limits of controlled waters.

(5) A person contravenes this section if he causes or knowingly permits any matter whatever to enter any inland freshwaters so as to tend (either directly or in combination with other matter which he or another person causes or permits to enter those waters) to impede the proper flow of the waters in a manner leading, or likely to lead, to a substantial aggravation of—

    (a) pollution due to other causes; or

    (b) the consequences of such pollution.

(6) Subject to the following provisions of this Chapter, a person who contravenes this section or the conditions of any consent given under this Chapter for the purposes of this section shall be guilty of an offence and liable—

    (a) on summary conviction, to imprisonment for a term not exceeding three months or to a fine not exceeding £20,000 or to both;

    (b) on conviction on indictment, to imprisonment for a term not exceeding two years or to a fine or to both.

89. Other defences to principal offences

(1) A person shall not be guilty of an offence under section 85 above in respect of the entry of any matter into any waters or any discharge if—

    (a) the entry is caused or permitted, or the discharge is made, in an emergency in order to avoid danger to life or health;

    (b) that person takes all such steps as are reasonably practicable in the circumstances for minimising the extent of the entry or discharge and of its polluting effects; and

    (c) particulars of the entry or discharge are furnished to the Agency as soon as reasonably practicable after the entry occurs.

(2) A person shall not be guilty of an offence under section 85 above by reason of his causing or permitting any discharge of trade or sewage effluent from a vessel.

(3) A person shall not be guilty of an offence under section 85 above by reason only of his permitting water from an abandoned mine or an abandoned part of a mine to enter controlled waters.

(4) A person shall not, otherwise than in respect of the entry of any poisonous, noxious or polluting matter into any controlled waters, be guilty of an offence under section 85 above by reason of his depositing the solid refuse of a mine or quarry on any land so that it falls or is carried into inland freshwaters if—

    (a) he deposits the refuse on the land with the consent of the Agency;

    (b) no other site for the deposit is reasonably practicable; and

    (c) he takes all reasonably practicable steps to prevent the refuse from entering those inland freshwaters.

WIRELESS TELEGRAPHY ACT 1949

1.   Licensing of wireless telegraphy

(1)   No person shall establish or use any station for wireless telegraphy or instal or use any apparatus for wireless telegraphy except under the authority of a licence in that behalf granted under this section by OFCOM and any person who establishes or uses any station for wireless telegraphy or instals or uses any apparatus for wireless telegraphy except under and in accordance with such a licence shall be guilty of an offence under this Act:

Provided that OFCOM may by regulations exempt from the provisions of this subsection the establishment, installation or use of stations for wireless telegraphy or wireless telegraphy apparatus of such classes or descriptions as may be specified in the regulations, either absolutely or subject to such terms, provisions and limitations as may be so specified.

(5)   Where a wireless telegraphy licence has expired or has been revoked, it shall be the duty of the person to whom the licence was issued, and of every other person in whose possession or under whose control the licence may be, to cause the licence to be surrendered to OFCOM if required by them to do so, and any person who without reasonable excuse fails or refuses to comply with the provisions of this subsection shall be guilty of an offence under this Act:

Provided that this subsection shall not apply to a licence relating solely to apparatus not designed or adapted for emission (as opposed to reception).

1A.   Offence of keeping wireless telegraphy station or apparatus available for unauthorised use

Any person who has any station for wireless telegraphy or apparatus for wireless telegraphy in his possession or under his control and either—

(a)   intends to use it in contravention of section 1 of this Act; or

(b)   knows, or has reasonable cause to believe, that another person intends to use it in contravention of that section,

shall be guilty of an offence.

1B.   Offence of allowing premises to be used for purpose of unlawful broadcasting

(1)   A person who is in charge of any premises which are used for making an unlawful broadcast, or for sending signals for the operation or control of any apparatus used for the purpose of making an unlawful broadcast from any other place, shall be guilty of an offence if—

(a)   he knowingly causes or permits the premises to be so used; or

(b)   having reasonable cause to believe that the premises are being so used, he fails to take such steps as are reasonable in the circumstances of the case to prevent the premises from being so used.

(2)   For the purposes of this section a person is in charge of any premises if he—

(a)   is the owner or occupier of the premises; or

(b)   has, or acts or assists in, the management or control of the premises.

(3)   For the purposes of this section a broadcast is unlawful if—

(a)   it is made by means of the use of any station for wireless telegraphy or apparatus for wireless telegraphy in contravention of section 1 of this Act; or

(b)   the making of the broadcast contravenes any provision of the Marine, &c., Broadcasting (Offences) Act 1967.

(4)   In this section—

'broadcast' has the same meaning as in the Marine, &c., Broadcasting (Offences) Act 1967;

'premises' includes any place and, in particular, includes—

(a)   any vehicle, vessel or aircraft; and

(b)   any structure or other object (whether movable or otherwise and whether on land or otherwise).

19.   Interpretation

(1)   In this Act, except where the context otherwise requires, the expression 'wireless telegraphy' means the emitting or receiving, over paths which are not provided by any material substance constructed or arranged for that purpose, of electro-magnetic energy of a frequency not exceeding three million megacycles a second, being energy which either—

(a)   serves for the conveying of messages, sound or visual images (whether the messages, sound or images are actually received by any person or not), or for the actuation or control of machinery or apparatus; or

(b)   is used in connection with the determination of position, bearing, or distance, or for the gaining of information as to the presence, absence, position or motion of any object or of any objects of any class,

and references to stations for wireless telegraphy and apparatus for wireless telegraphy or wireless telegraphy apparatus shall be construed as references to stations and apparatus for the emitting or receiving as aforesaid of such electro-magnetic energy as aforesaid.

INDEX